INDIA'S PAKISTAN POLICY

This book critically examines the role of think tanks as foreign policy actors. It looks at the origins and development of foreign policy think tanks in India and their changing relevance and position as agents within the policy-making process.

The book uses a comparative framework and explores the research discourse of prominent Indian think tanks, particularly on the India–Pakistan dispute, and offers unique insights and perspectives on their research design and methodology. It draws attention to the policy discourse of think tanks during the Composite Dialogue peace process between India and Pakistan and the subsequent support from the government which further expanded their role. One of the first books to offer empirical analyses into the role of these organisations in India, this book highlights the relevance of and the crucial role that these institutions have played as non-state policy actors.

Insightful and topical, this book will be of interest to researchers focused on international relations, foreign policy analysis and South Asian politics. It would also be a good resource for students interested in a theoretical understanding of foreign policy institutions in general and Indian foreign policy in particular.

Stuti Bhatnagar is an adjunct fellow associated with the School of Social Sciences at the University of Adelaide and the University of New South Wales, Australia. With a PhD in politics and international relations from the University of Adelaide, she specialises in Indian foreign policy, especially the role and rising influence of think tanks in India. Additional research interests include the examination of political dynamics that drive India–Pakistan relations and India's changing foreign policy interests.

INDIA'S PAKISTAN POLICY

How Think Tanks Are Shaping Foreign Relations

Stuti Bhatnagar

LONDON AND NEW YORK

First published 2021
by Routledge
2 Park Square, Milton Park, Abingdon, Oxon OX14 4RN

and by Routledge
52 Vanderbilt Avenue, New York, NY 10017

Routledge is an imprint of the Taylor & Francis Group, an informa business

© 2021 Stuti Bhatnagar

The right of Stuti Bhatnagar to be identified as author of this work has been asserted by her in accordance with sections 77 and 78 of the Copyright, Designs and Patents Act 1988.

All rights reserved. No part of this book may be reprinted or reproduced or utilised in any form or by any electronic, mechanical, or other means, now known or hereafter invented, including photocopying and recording, or in any information storage or retrieval system, without permission in writing from the publishers.

Trademark notice: Product or corporate names may be trademarks or registered trademarks, and are used only for identification and explanation without intent to infringe.

British Library Cataloguing-in-Publication Data
A catalogue record for this book is available from the British Library

Library of Congress Cataloging-in-Publication Data
A catalog record for this book has been requested

ISBN: 978-0-367-33475-8 (hbk)
ISBN: 978-0-367-33476-5 (pbk)
ISBN: 978-0-429-32004-0 (ebk)

Typeset in Bembo
by Apex CoVantage, LLC

CONTENTS

Acknowledgements   *vi*
List of abbreviations   *vii*

1   Introduction   1

2   Think tanks and foreign policy – a Discursive Institutionalist–Gramscian approach   16

3   Think tanks and Indian foreign policy – an overview   34

4   Government think tanks – promoting security-centred government narratives on Pakistan   62

5   Non-government policy think tanks   84

6   Peacebuilding think tanks   112

7   Foreign policy think tanks – challenging or building consensus on India's Pakistan policy?   135

Bibliography   *148*
Index   *164*

ACKNOWLEDGEMENTS

This book has its origins in a doctoral thesis written at the University of Adelaide. I would like to thank friends and colleagues at the School of Social Sciences at Adelaide for their support. My supervisors Dr. Priya Chacko and Prof. Timothy Doyle offered invaluable advice, input, assistance and encouragement. Their support made the process fulfilling. I also want to take this opportunity to thank Prof. Kanishka Jayasuriya (now at University of Murdoch) for taking time out to guide me on interview strategies and research design.

Additionally, I am grateful for the support that I have received from the staff and students at the Department of Politics and International Studies and the School of Social Sciences at the University of Adelaide. They have given me ample opportunities to gain experience, engage in intelligent conversation, and learn what it is to be part of the broader academic community. The thesis and the research visit to India would not have been possible without a travelling fellowship that enabled me to gather the resources and insights that added to the strength of my arguments.

I must also extend my heartfelt gratitude to my family and friends, especially to my husband Ashish and my daughter Aarzoo, who have endured my busy schedule and mood swings associated with PhD research and its subsequent revision for this book. Thanks also to my sister Madhur and my parents for all their encouragement despite the distance and to Zahid for all the guidance. I am also grateful for all the friends I have made these past few years in Australia, making the research and writing experience more enjoyable. I am grateful for you all, every single day.

This project began with a hope for peace between the people of India and Pakistan, and I hope the knowledge I have gained will help me further in this journey.

ABBREVIATIONS

AFSPA	Armed Forces Special Powers Act
AGPL	Actual Ground Position Line
AJK	Azad Jammu and Kashmir
APAO	Alternative Policy Advisory Organisations
APHC	All Parties Hurriyat Conference
ASEAN	Association of South East Asian Nations
BJP	Bharatiya Janata Party
BRICS	Brazil, Russia, India, China, South Africa
CAPS	Centre for Air Power Studies
CBM	Confidence-Building Measures
CD	Composite Dialogue
CDR	Centre for Dialogue and Reconciliation
CFR	Council on Foreign Relations
CLAWS	Centre for Land Warfare Studies
COSATT	Consortium of South Asian Think Tanks
CPR	Centre for Policy Research
CRPF	Central Reserve Police Force
CSA	Centre for Security Analysis
CT	Conflict Transformation
DGMO	Director General of Military Operations
DI	Discursive Institutionalism
DND	Draft Nuclear Doctrine
DPG	Delhi Policy Group
DRDO	Defence Research and Development Organisation
ECCP	Economic Cross-Cultural Programme
FCRA	Foreign Contribution (Regulation) Act
FNS	Friedrich Naumann Stiftung

GOI	Government of India
HM	Hizbul Mujahideen
IAF	Indian Air Force
IBSA	India Brazil South Africa
ICRIER	Indian Council for Research on International Economic Relations
ICSSR	Indian Council for Social Science Research
ICWA	Indian Council of World Affairs
IDRC	International Development Research Centre
IDSA	Institute for Defence Studies and Analyses
IF	India Foundation
IFS	Indian Foreign Service
IISS	International Institute for Strategic Studies
IPCS	Institute of Peace and Conflict Studies
IPRI	Islamabad Peace Research Institute
ISI	Inter-Services Intelligence
IWT	Indus Waters Treaty
JATM	Joint Anti-Terror Mechanism
JEM	Jaish-e-Mohammed
JNU	Jawaharlal Nehru University
JUD	Jamaat-ud-Dawa
KRC	Kargil Review Committee
LET	Lashkar-e-Taiba
LoC	Line of Control
LSR	Lady Shri Ram
MEA	Ministry of External Affairs
MFN	Most Favoured Nation
MoD	Ministry of Defence
NDA	National Democratic Alliance
NGO	Non-Governmental Organisation
NMF	National Maritime Foundation
NRRM	Nuclear Risk Reduction Measures
NSA	National Security Advisor
NSAB	National Security Advisory Board
NSC	National Security Council
NSCS	National Security Council Secretariat
NTI	Nuclear Threat Initiative
NTS	Non-Traditional Security
ORF	Observer Research Foundation
PAI	Pakistan-Afghanistan-India
PAK	Pakistan-Administered Kashmir
PIPFPD	Pakistan India Peoples' Forum for Peace and Democracy
PMO	Prime Minister's Office
POK	Pakistan-Occupied Kashmir
RAW	Research and Analysis Wing

RCSS	Regional Centre for Strategic Studies
RIS	Research and Information System for Developing Countries
RSS	Rashtriya Swayamsevak Sangh
SAARC	South Asian Association for Regional Cooperation
TNW	Tactical Nuclear Weapons
UPA	United Progressive Alliance
USI	United Service Institution of India
VIF	Vivekananda International Foundation
WHAM	Winning Hearts and Minds
WISCOMP	Women in Security, Conflict Management and Peace

1
INTRODUCTION

India in the present day has made forays into forming international linkages, developing partnerships with superpowers and playing an active role as a leader of the Global South, forming new associations with other emerging world powers such as Brazil, China and South Africa (BRICS, IBSA). On the path of forging a high-profile power status, it has demonstrated high growth and advanced military capabilities and remains a firm adherent to the multilateral United Nations system. India has also taken a keen interest in global issues such as climate change, global trade negotiations and nuclear disarmament and remains a key proponent for regional cooperation. While international factors are significant, India's foreign policy behaviour is also conditioned by its domestic political imperatives, namely its political leadership and its institutions.[1] However, more often than not, the study of Indian foreign policy has remained limited to a study of its bilateral and regional relationships rather than a nuanced understanding of foreign policy institutions and foreign policy actors. What is missing is a comprehensive exploration of the policy process, the actors and institutions involved, and the path that the policy process takes, to create policy narratives and policy frameworks.

While the relevance and central position of the Ministry of External Affairs (MEA) in making policy is often clearly articulated in the literature, there exists in India an informal network of think tanks that engage with its foreign policy and strategic doctrines. Based on recent statistics, with 509 operational think tanks, India is placed second in the list of countries with the largest think tanks, and Indian think tanks have figured in the top 50 in the global think tank rankings for several years now.[2] With organisational capacity deriving from retired diplomats, bureaucrats, retired military personnel and academics, think tanks in India are also notable for a growing body of intellectual elites – adding to the public debate on policy issues. However, the role and relevance of think tanks, the importance of these intellectuals and their specific engagements with policy processes is unclear. This in essence is the central research problem that this book addresses. While Indian think tanks are sometimes identified as civil society actors and while their research contributions are being recognised, there is limited engagement with the specific role that they play in policy making, particularly on issues of foreign policy.[3] This book aims to fill in this gap in the literature by critically examining the role think tanks play in foreign policy and developing a novel framework with which to analyse this relationship.

India's unique political context, its various institutional structures and their material and intellectual capacities have had a direct impact on the growth and position of think tanks within the policy landscape. Yet, while there exist considerable analyses with respect to American and European think tanks and their influence on some notable foreign policy decisions, in Asia and in South Asia, think tanks have only begun to be recognised as viable players. Addressing this gap in the literature, this book examines their growth and development in India and highlights their growing relevance to policy making. It also highlights the specific structural constraints and the relative position of Indian think tanks within the policy structures. In doing so, a distinctive approach referred to as the Discursive Institutionalist–Gramscian (DI-Gramscian) framework is advanced to analyse the role of think tanks in foreign policy making.

In critically examining the position of think tanks in policy making, this volume concentrates particularly on their role in one of India's most important foreign policy concerns, its relationship with Pakistan. India's relations with Pakistan have been characterised by disputes on several issues, such as the political status of Kashmir and the contested borders. This was complicated further by four wars fought in 1948, 1965, 1971 and most recently in 1998 in Kargil. Other disputes revolve around the sharing of river waters, contending nuclear doctrines, Pakistan's support to separatist groups in Kashmir as well as its alleged complicity in acts of terrorism in India. The India–Pakistan conflictual relationship has left its mark on regional integration efforts in South Asia and is also often reflected in international alliances and partnerships with the two South Asian neighbours. As a key security concern for India, therefore, the dynamics of the relationship with Pakistan has created both official and unofficial interest. Engagement with India's strategy towards Pakistan has been at the forefront of research agendas in most security policy think tanks. Yet, a critical examination into think tank discourse on India's Pakistan policy is missing. Further, the existing literature has not considered the unique contribution of think tanks in formulating a discourse on peacebuilding that makes way for an emboldened and more substantive foreign policy towards Pakistan. A critical examination of India's Pakistan policy therefore presents a good test case for the analysis of the role of think tanks in general, and an examination of the nature of their policy ideas in challenging or supporting existing policy frameworks in particular. The examination of a specific foreign policy issue also presents an opportunity to investigate the place of Indian think tanks within the policy-making institutional set-up in India – a subject that has not been studied so far.

This chapter presents an overview of the overarching arguments presented in this volume. It begins with explaining the relevance of the India–Pakistan dispute to think tank development and their engagement with policy agendas on Pakistan, particularly during the structured Composite Dialogue (CD) initiated in 2004. Responding to inadequacies in the literature, the subsequent sections highlight the particular research contribution of this volume and the development of the DI-Gramscian model as the most adequate theoretical explanation of think tank behaviour in India. The chapter details the research design and methodology used to account for the think tank role in India, using comparative categories of prominent Indian think tanks and their research programmes on India–Pakistan relations.

Think tanks and India's Pakistan policy

As a key security and foreign policy subject, focus on India–Pakistan relations has been of considerable interest to Indian think tanks. In India, as the evidence shows, most foreign and security policy think tanks have had an active research and advocacy component centred on policy towards Pakistan. However, it is unclear how think tanks – both government and non-government – have framed the discourse on India's relations with Pakistan and if their linkages with the government of India (GOI) help or challenge the introduction of new ideas on India's Pakistan policy.

To begin to understand think tank discourse on Pakistan, it is first essential to present the broad characteristics of the India–Pakistan relationship. Some of the general features of India's Pakistan policy have been its emphasis on bilateralism as a principle for conflict resolution; the need to protect the sanctity of geographical borders in Kashmir, Siachen and Sir Creek; a focus on developments in Pakistan-administered Kashmir (PAK)[4] as counter to Pakistani policies in Indian Kashmir; competing with Pakistan's influence in the region; and the continuing emphasis on terrorism as a major hurdle in the bilateral relationship. All other issues of concern between the two neighbours are in turn seen through these broad contours of policy, based primarily on national security concerns. While there exist some examples of successful dialogue – as seen in the Indus Waters Treaty (IWT) or the formal agreement on exchange of information regarding nuclear power research facilities and a commitment not to attack each other's nuclear installations – efforts to sustain a structured dialogue process have not been successful. There have been, however, sporadic attempts to engage in multi-track diplomacy through bilateral dialogues (Track One), back-channel talks and civil society dialogues, represented in the various Track II and Track III forums.

Representing a significant change, the CD was the longest sustained and institutionalised effort at peace between India and Pakistan, which was formalised in 2004 and continued until 2014 with some periods of disruption. The roots of the India–Pakistan CD date back to May 1997, when at Male, then Indian Prime Minister Inder Kumar Gujral and his Pakistani counterpart Nawaz Sharif mooted the idea of a structured dialogue.[5] The idea was first proposed in 1997, but several years passed before the CD could begin formally. The CD framework comprised discussions on eight key issues that inform India–Pakistan relations, namely, Peace and Security; Kashmir; Sir Creek; Siachen; Terrorism; Wullar Barrage/Tulbul Navigation channel (that is essentially a debate on the IWT); Drug Trafficking; and the Promotion of Friendly Exchanges in various fields. The dialogue structure was based on an incremental approach, attempting a simultaneous consideration of all key issues. It represented a departure from previously held positions and articulated a policy moving away from an excessive focus on Kashmir to one that attempted parallel progress on all issues.[6]

The CD created new spaces for out-of-the-box thinking on India–Pakistan relations and generated an atmosphere conducive for think tanks and research organisations to engage with policy making. The dialogue process at this time also attempted to expand the stakeholders, "involving for the first time, the people of India and Pakistan with an orientation to work at all different levels of state and civil society."[7] This ran concurrent with a more liberal funding structure that enabled foreign funding and a further involvement of think tanks. However, even though there are examples of think tank interface with the formal dialogue through their research and active participation in multi-track initiatives, their specific policy discourse has not been examined. It remains unclear if think tanks at this point broadened/strengthened the government agenda or challenged dominant narratives during this period, offering new policy ideas relevant to specific aspects of the relationship. Think tank policy ideas and their specific involvement in the dialogue process will thus be detailed in this book with special emphasis on policy discourse that was developed on the specific basket of issues identified within the CD framework.

Central argument

While think tanks in India have developed to become a noticeable part of the Indian policy-making scenario, and some analysis and commentary has reasoned that think tanks should play a larger role in Indian foreign policy, research on their specific positions within policy structures and their engagement with important foreign policy choices is missing.[8] Questions such as who makes India's foreign policy; what constitutes the policy-making establishment; who are the actors and agents responsible for formulating the foreign policy in India; and how far each is influential remain unanswered and underexplored. Dominant scholarship has been limited to American and European case studies and has not taken into account the role of Indian think tanks. A dominant theme in the global literature has been the bridging role of think tanks as organisations engaged in research and advocacy on public policy, acting as a bridge between knowledge and power in modern democracies.[9] While the limited literature on Indian think tanks has identified this bridging role, their discourse is seen to be lacking in policy relevance.[10] Further, scholarship on Indian think tanks fails to critically examine the symbiotic and interdependent relationship and the existence of a "knowledge/power nexus" manifested in the collaboration between think tanks and formal structures of policymaking.[11] Often considered as secondary actors, state-centric foreign policy making in India is emphasised that significantly curtails the foreign policy role of think tanks. Through an examination of think tank position within the policy process, this volume builds on the understanding of think tanks as policy actors/agents/idea brokers and information filters. It responds to inadequacies in the literature and critically examines the policy discourse of Indian think tanks and their specific part in promoting and challenging policy narratives set by the state.

The book develops a DI-Gramscian framework that analyses think tank interactive processes and identifies their position in India as ideational actors. It explores their role in building consensus on the Indian government's Pakistan policy and their possible potential to challenge dominant narratives and introduce alternative policy ideas. Through an examination of their roles in policymaking, creating a discourse on Pakistan and contributing to public opinion, the DI-Gramscian framework enables a look at "both the specific and the general influence on foreign policy . . . as catalysts and crystallizers of policy thought."[12] This approach also provides an analysis of the intellectual elite at Indian think tanks and their specific social and political backgrounds that have had an impact on their foreign policy ideas as well as their ability to enable absorption of their ideas into policy frames. While discursive institutionalism (DI) is found useful for processual analysis, the recourse to Gramsci provides a theory of state-society relations that enables an examination that goes beyond elites and ideas. Gramsci's emphasis on the state's role in building consensus through collaboration with private organisations to mobilise and advance its own causes and to legitimise and promote its own interests is particularly relevant. While Gramsci's understanding was based on domestic politics, its application to the study of think tanks is a new idea.[13] The elites for their part, particularly the body of intellectual elites that form think tank institutional opinions, symbolise Gramsci's concept of 'state spirit'. Private non-state actors including think tanks therefore become relevant for some decisions and are used for generating public opinion in others. Together, the DI-Gramscian approach helps to understand how think tanks have tried to strike a balance between developing independent research agendas while benefiting from continued government patronage and support. The application of this framework to India's Pakistan policy highlights significant patterns in think tank behaviour and their developing role in foreign policy decision making.

The central argument of this book is that the institutionalisation and government patronage to think tanks in India has enabled the Indian government to build consensus on policy directions on Pakistan. This is aided by similarities in think tank membership and the close collaboration between think tank intellectual elites and policy elites manifested in policy discourse and the think tank contribution to public opinion. While think tanks provide an academic understanding of policy debates, their policy discourse has perpetuated government thinking on Pakistan, and alternative perspectives have often been sidelined. The infusion of foreign funding and relative independence from the government, however, has also enabled some think tanks to challenge government positions on Pakistan and introduce new and innovative policy ideas. Nonetheless, proximity to the government has had a direct link with the ability of a think tank to introduce policy ideas and retain relevance as non-state policy actors. This argument is supported by a closer look at the institutional structures and material capacities that have had an impact on the place of think tanks in the policy sphere and their ability to influence specific foreign policy decisions. With regard to policy paradigms on Pakistan, therefore, policy direction has been provided by the state and has been subsequently adopted, refined and articulated by think tank research and analysis, making these foreign policy think tanks active participants within the policy process.

In addition to policy influence and the capacity to introduce new ideas, this book also considers the question of institutional embeddedness and the institutional relevance of think tanks themselves, particularly when so many of them look to the government for financial support. The synthesis of the DI-Gramscian perspective enables a better understanding of the material interests and the elite character of think tanks, particularly visible in India where they represent the intellectual elite composed of retired diplomats, bureaucrats and senior members of Indian academia and civil society. The DI-Gramscian approach also provides an insight into research manoeuvring by think tanks to please funding bodies and government elites. Therefore, rather than portraying think tanks benignly, this study provides a more critical examination of the nature of interactions between policy elites and intellectual elites.

Through case-study analysis, the volume highlights that research agendas at government think tanks are provided guidance and direction by policy elites in the government, and while each of these think tanks has followed its own distinct research direction, policy ideas on Pakistan have often overlapped. Similar membership patterns and similarities of opinion represented by intellectual elites have favoured dominant ideas on national security, often undermining deviation from government policy direction. Further, the creation of these think tanks and the support to the body of intellectual elites is an attempt by the GOI to institutionalise consensus on policy directions, particularly on security. In comparison, non-government think tanks are not dependent on government funding alone and have therefore developed a broader understanding of Indo-Pak issues and offered some new policy ideas. Yet, the involvement of their intellectual elites in government committees and specific projects funded by the government aimed at providing policy expertise in areas where the bureaucracy lacks capacity have fostered linkages with government viewpoints on Pakistan. Further, similarities in the nature of this elite have also impacted the nature of their policy discourse on Pakistan.

Approach and methods

As mentioned earlier, this study develops a DI-Gramscian framework, which is a synthesis of Gramsci's concept of the 'integral state' and the Discursive Institutionalist conception of the socially constructed nature of institutions. Recognising the inadequacies in the literature to account for the role of Indian think tanks, the use of DI enables an enquiry of the different levels and different types of policy ideas as well as the interactive processes by which ideas are translated into policy. Such an approach is particularly useful when causal links between actors involved in policy construction and policy change are difficult to ascertain. This is of particular relevance to the Indian policy-making scenario as the path to policy construction is unclear, made further complicated by the interactions (both institutional and non-official) between think tanks and the permanent bureaucratic structures.

Examining policy making in India through the formal institutional settings described by DI supports the argument that there exists space for outside expertise – for actors such as think tanks to impact the policy process. However, think tank impact is selective, based on issues and rather than being directly involved in the adoption and implementation of policy, they contribute instead to the innovation and diffusion of policy ideas.[14] The focus of this book is therefore not so much on direct policy impact but on bringing to light the interactive aspects and the specific strategies that think tanks have used to have an impact and establish themselves as significant civil society actors.

Other works on think tanks – including James McGann's impact assessment based on resource, demand and impact indicators – focus on the think tank role in issue articulation, policy formulation and policy implementation.[15] In addition, think tank impact has been considered through their advisory role to the government. Parmar, in his extensive analysis of American think tanks, particularly in the early years for instance, focused on a comparative analysis of each organisation's membership, the social background of the leadership and the worldviews and institutional line that each think tank adopts and an examination of their role in particular foreign policy decisions.[16] This book relies on Parmar's methods of analysis, using the India–Pakistan relationship as a test case both for think tank influence as well as for an examination of think tank position and hierarchy in the policy landscape in India. Through an extensive discourse analysis of foreign policy think tanks in India, in particular their discourse on relations with Pakistan during the CD process, the interactive processes in practice are highlighted.

Using DI, the emphasis on the interactive dimension of discourse – both the coordinative and communicative functions – is adopted to understand the processes through which think tanks in India seek to have policy influence. In addition, the synthesis of DI and the Gramscian framework allows for an examination of the relationship between think tanks and the foreign policy bureaucracy, highlighting the symbiotic relationship between knowledge and policy.[17] Using the DI-Gramscian approach, the role of Indian think tanks both in contributing policy inputs on Pakistan in addition to their crucial role in mobilising public opinion on government policy on Pakistan is examined – looking at "both the specific and the general influence on foreign policy."[18] The emphasis is on a critical examination of think tank discourse on India's Pakistan policy – either endorsing or challenging government narratives.

The relevance and position of think tanks within the policy process and their ability to assume importance during what Ladi describes as "critical junctures" is also an important aspect here. Critical junctures "refer to particular historical moments that have lasting consequences and can provoke changes in policy."[19] The positive atmosphere created by the CD and its structure represented such a "critical juncture" wherein avenues for policy change in India's relations with Pakistan were available and active civil society engagement was encouraged. The discourse developed by think tanks during this period is thus a significant focus of this study.

For DI scholars, the main explanatory task is that of demonstrating the causal influence of ideas and discourse. DI thus uses tools provided by process tracing to identify the intervening causal process – between an independent variable (foreign policy) and the outcome of the dependent variable (think tanks).[20] The idea is to create a narrative of events to analyse the level of influence of think tanks that may explain "how specific actors carried certain ideas into the policy-making fray and used them effectively."[21] These actors are often academics and other intellectuals (including think tanks) whose claim to knowledge and expertise enables their voice to be heard above others.[22] Zimmerman also employed process tracing as a methodology to investigate think tank endorsement of the Non-Traditional Security (NTS) agenda in South East Asia and determined the "causal process between the actions of think tanks, the promotion of the NTS agenda and changes in the institutional structures in the region."[23] Applying this methodology to an examination of Indian think tanks' role in the framing of India's Pakistan policy is, however, problematic as policy processes in India are unclear and the dominance of government narratives makes process tracing inadequate in explaining the particular influence of think tanks. The focus on process tracing also insufficiently analyses the composition of the intellectual elite at Indian think tanks and their specific socio-economic and political backgrounds that have had an impact on their foreign policy ideas as well as their ability to communicate these ideas into policy frames.

Other limitations of the DI approach identified particularly during the research process include an over-reliance on ideas and the under-estimation of material constraints. This was the rationale for the introduction of a Gramscian framework to consider the power of the state and the material/structural limitations of non-state institutions such as think tanks. Such a framework was found more suited to examine Indian think tanks, their role in policy making and to account for an analysis into state-society relations. The approach places emphasis on elites – their intellectual backgrounds, membership patterns and collaboration with the state – highlighting the Indian state's potential in building hegemony on its policy directions towards Pakistan. The methodology and design of this project has thus developed throughout the course of the research process and field research in India that brought to light the specific environment in which think tanks operate. The understanding of think tank policy narratives on Pakistan and insights into their role in policy making has involved a detailed discourse analysis of policy ideas from think tanks, tracing their interaction with policy processes and determining how they sought to introduce these ideas into the policy frameworks on India's Pakistan policy.

Beginning with DI's emphasis on the interactive dimension of discourse, both the coordinative and communicative functions of think tanks were analysed to understand the processes through which think tanks in India sought policy influence.[24] Further, an examination of the role of the intellectual elite at Indian think tanks was conducted to uncover their contribution to think tank policy relevance and proximity to policy elites. As a relatively new phenomenon, think tanks in India are still dependent on government funding and patronage, very often a function of the think tank intellectuals. To incorporate this dimension, different categories of think tanks based on funding and membership patterns were chosen as the most useful way to examine their role in foreign policy.

Examination of these differing categories allowed for an enquiry into the material and structural capabilities of think tanks as well as their role in influencing India's Pakistan policy. Case study analysis enabled a "detailed consideration of contexual factors," particularly when variables such as "democracy, power, political culture, state strength and so on are notoriously difficult to measure."[25] Particularly relevant to this project, case studies also helped in the empirical identification of "new variables and hypotheses through the study of deviant or outlier cases and in the course of field work – such as archival research and interviews with participants, area experts and historians."[26] The insights from the fieldwork conducted in India brought to light the specific significance of think tank intellectual elite and their informal yet substantial ties with policy elites.

The adopted categories therefore delineate think tanks on the basis of their funding patterns and their relative proximity to the government of India. They highlight the processes that think tanks are involved in as well as specific policy recommendations on Pakistan as represented in their research outputs. The first category is of government think tanks that are directly funded by the GOI and include the Institute for Defence Studies and Analyses (IDSA), the Indian Council of World Affairs (ICWA), the Centre for Land Warfare Studies (CLAWS), the National Maritime Foundation (NMF) and the Centre for Air Power Studies (CAPS). Secondly, non-government think tanks that have secured private funding but continue to have significant linkages with the government were analysed. Think tanks in this category include the Observer Research Foundation

(ORF), the Centre for Policy Research (CPR), the Vivekananda International Foundation (VIF) and the India Foundation (IF). The third and final category also includes non-government think tanks but focuses the analysis on smaller institutions that significantly lack resources and government patronage. These are the Institute of Peace and Conflict Studies (IPCS), the Delhi Policy Group (DPG), the Women in Security, Conflict Management and Peace (WISCOMP) and the Centre for Dialogue and Reconciliation (CDR). The use of these categories in this research has incorporated the synthesis of the DI-Gramscian approach and has allowed for a critical examination of specific constraints – structural and ideological – that have impacted the way a particular think tank has been situated in the Indian policy-making scene.

Policy inputs from think tanks were analysed through their research publications – policy briefs, project reports, conference proceedings – secondary data on the evolving India–Pakistan policy debates, as well as writings of think tank elite in popular media. Research outputs on crucial issues of significance between India and Pakistan were examined to investigate the involvement of think tanks in the formulation (coordinative discourse) and the communication of policy deliberations and achievements (communicative discourse). Within the broader narrative of India's Pakistan policy, a particular focus was on the period of the Composite Dialogue from 2004 and its attention to eight key issues of concern. This period also reflected a proliferation of foreign policy think tanks in India and a change in conceptions of security, with an increased emphasis on human security as well as active government engagement with the civil society and intellectual elites.

Think tank engagement with policy issues in India, however, is often not institutionalised and operates at an informal level, leaving their specific involvement in the policy processes undocumented. This gap was mitigated to the best extent possible through semi-structured interviews. The interview material provided insights from the personal observations of experts on some of the undocumented aspects as well as an insider perspective into think tank positions. For this purpose, 30 interviews were conducted with senior researchers in leadership positions who could provide insights into organisational goals and decision making. Added attention was given to include researchers who were actively involved in projects related to India's Pakistan policy. The interview process was very beneficial, as "interviewing is often the most productive approach when influence over the outcome of interest was restricted to a few select decision-makers, creating a bottleneck of political power that increases the importance of agency in the story."[27] It was also useful to establish structural causes as it helped to "establish whether a political actor felt under pressure from forces beyond his or her control, and what those forces were, particularly when there are multiple independent variables in the theoretical mix."[28]

The list of think tanks is restricted to those in the national capital of Delhi as most foreign policy think tanks are situated there, and it is where India's foreign policy bureaucracy is based. While several influential think tanks operate outside the national capital, they came to the scene when the CD process was waning, and there was a significant decline in think tank interest in Pakistan in response to both government policy direction as well as general public opinion. To incorporate the government and policymaker perspectives, some interviews, although limited, were also organised with current and former bureaucrats. The interviews were also used as an opportunity to gather think tank research materials not available in the public domain.

Challenges

While case study analysis illustrated how think tanks in India analysed and introduced policy ideas on Pakistan, there were challenges in examining this role. The insights gained from the interviews were able to alleviate some of these, but a significant challenge was the nature of the issue itself. The volatility and complex nature of India–Pakistan relations has affected think tank involvement and was also reflected in some of the interview responses that offered a very general perspective rather than a detailed account of think tank involvement. Further, an aspect of think tank–government interaction in India is the exchange of classified policy briefs that were not made available for analysis. Some think tanks also maintained ambiguity on their funding information as well as specific project funding towards projects on Pakistan. Additionally, viewpoints from within think tanks were also likely to be biased in favour of their role and organisational influence. While there were attempts to include more government actors to present a more balanced picture, appointments were provided only for junior-level bureaucrats or retired diplomats and bureaucrats, whose insights while helpful were dated.

An additional dimension of note in Indian think tanks is the lack of diversity in think tank membership patterns that also resonates with the Gramscian framework. With the predominant presence of former bureaucrats, defence officials, diplomats and academicians from a narrow socio-economic base, think tanks form a part of the power bloc in India. This was also an aspect that enables the hegemony of intellectual ideas that are not far from government thinking. Also visible was a gendered dynamic, because the majority of interviewees were men, with a very small sample of women-led think tanks or women researchers. This has also changed the way ideas were represented in think tank discourse, with only limited attention to foreign policy ideas that focused on the different impact that the India–Pakistan conflict has had on men and women. While there is some attention in this book to think tanks that actively articulate women's voices (WISCOMP, CDR, DPG), they represent a minority perspective.

Since May 2014, there have been significant changes in India's relations with Pakistan under new political leadership in India and in Pakistan. In addition, under the Narendra Modi government, the institutional position of think tanks, their funding structures and their ability to engage with policy processes has changed. There is also an emergence of new US-styled think tanks including the Gateway House: Indian Council on Global Relations, Brookings and Carnegie India, which are funded primarily by corporate interests in India and are changing the relative position of think tanks. The changing think tank discourse on Pakistan since 2014 has been elaborated on in the concluding chapter that also underscores the changing relationship of think tanks with the Modi administration.

Book outline

A DI-Gramscian framework forms the core of enquiry in this research, highlighting the collaboration of policy elites and intellectual elites in making policy on Pakistan. Chapter 1 therefore begins with a review of literature on think tanks, moving into a detailed analysis of the Indian policy-making landscape. DI provides the tools to establish processes of interaction between think tanks and policy, and the focus on Gramsci indicates the state's collaborative influence. Think tanks are characterised on the basis of funding and affiliation, highlighting membership patterns and composition of intellectual elites at government and non-government think tanks; their role as policy actors through an examination of their discourse on Pakistan; and their role in policy promotion and contribution to public opinion.

Chapter 2 sheds light on the theoretical arguments that best explain the behaviour and impact of think tanks in the literature. In understanding the role of non-state actors, including think tanks within the policy process, this chapter highlights the literature on the role of ideas and discourses, and identifies the various policy processes in which think tanks are involved. The interactive processes of policy construction as emphasised by the DI approach are detailed and the framework is applied to think tanks both in terms of their potential in creating discursive spaces and their contribution as discursive and ideational actors. Further, the chapter introduces the DI-Gramscian approach to examine the symbiotic relationship between the policy elite and the intellectual elite within think tanks.

After introducing the broader theoretical and conceptual literature on think tanks, Chapter 3 presents an overview of Indian think tanks. This chapter considers the trajectory of the foreign policy planning process in India and investigates the engagement with civil society and grassroots actors. It elaborates on the structure of policy making in India, the origins and development of think tanks and their changing relevance and position. The second part of this chapter discusses India's foreign policy discourse towards Pakistan, focusing particularly on the structured dialogue process initiated by the CD in 2004. It also highlights how the period of the CD expanded the space for think tanks in India, particularly those dealing with foreign and security policy.

The next three chapters focus on the specific think tank categories. Demarcated on the basis of affiliation and support from the Indian government, the focus of the analysis is on organisational membership, leadership and worldviews as well as the specific role in policymaking and public opinion mobilisation with regards to relations with Pakistan.

Chapter 4 focuses on government think tanks, namely the Institute for Defence Studies and Analyses (IDSA), the Indian Council of World Affairs (ICWA), the Centre for Air Power Studies (CAPS), the Centre for Land Warfare Studies (CLAWS) and the National Maritime Foundation (NMF). The chapter focuses on membership, funding arrangements, specific research agendas and policy ideas for relations with Pakistan that emerge from these think tanks. Using a DI-Gramscian framework, the relevance of the intellectual elite is highlighted through a focus on partnerships and networks, indicating inroads into formal policy making. The critical examination of policy discourses provides evidence that the emphasis of policy ideas at government think tanks has been to highlight dominant viewpoints of each of the defence forces from where these think tanks receive patronage. While they may differ on operational details, they have reflected the interests of India's defence and foreign policy community towards Pakistan, through discourses emphasising national security concerns.

Both Chapters 5 and 6 analyse non-government think tanks, but while the former examines some of the bigger and better resourced institutes with broad research agendas, the latter's focus is on think tanks with a specific emphasis on peacebuilding. Chapter 5 examines four important think tanks in this category, namely the Observer Research Foundation (ORF), the Centre for Policy Research (CPR), the Vivekananda International Foundation (VIF) and the India Foundation (IF). With diversified funding, the ability of these think tanks to challenge government policy narratives on Pakistan was enhanced, reflected in a broader and more academically informed policy discourse. However, the Indian government's control over funding legislation and the close involvement of think tank elite in government policy initiatives has restricted the research independence of these think tanks. This was demonstrated in changes in policy directions as the CD process faltered and was prompted by the continuing need to balance proximity to policy elites and retain institutional relevance.

The second part of the analysis on non-government think tanks in Chapter 6 concentrates on institutions with research agendas specifically focused on peacebuilding and reconciliation, namely the Institute of Peace and Conflict Studies (IPCS), the Delhi Policy Group (DPG), the Women in Security, Conflict Management and Peace (WISCOMP) and the Centre for Dialogue and Reconciliation (CDR). It examines how relative freedom from government funding brought about by India's liberalisation process and the specific focus on peacebuilding impacted upon the nature of policy discourse emerging from these think tanks. Further removed from government patronage, these think tanks were able to expand narratives on India's Pakistan policy, articulating the specific concerns of the civil society, notably women and youth perspectives. Yet, their relatively weaker linkages with formal policy elites and a distinct membership style also restricted their ability to influence policy changes on Pakistan.

The study concludes in Chapter 7 with a discussion on specific patterns that emerge in think tank membership, the nature of intellectual elites and the level of interaction and communication with policy elites. Through a summary of material conditions that enabled or restricted think tank involvement in the policy processes, the chapter argues that although policy directions and foreign policy agendas were primarily the domain of the government and top leadership in India, Indian think tanks were crucial actors used for the promotion of ideas in support of dominant state narratives and filling in knowledge gaps in new policy areas, particularly with regards to the discourse on India's Pakistan policy. Hence, think tanks were used to build consent for government policy and had little space to challenge dominant ideas. Taking cognisance of the changing nature of India's foreign policy following the election of Narendra Modi as Prime Minister in 2014, the chapter also presents a brief analysis of contemporary India–Pakistan relations and a summary of the changed nature of interactions between think tanks in India and the new Modi dispensation and the change in think tank attitudes towards India's Pakistan policy in the contemporary period.

Notes

1 Harsh V. Pant, "A Rising India's Search for a Foreign Policy", *Orbis*, 53:2, 2009a, p. 251.
2 The Think Tanks and Civil Societies Program (TTCSP) of the Lauder Institute at the University of Pennsylvania conducts research on the role policy institutes play in governments and civil societies around the world every year. These statistics are based on their most recent report titled, James G. McGann, "2018 Global Go to Think Tank Index Report", *TTCSP Global Go To Think Tank Index Reports*, 16, 2019, https://repository.upenn.edu/cgi/viewcontent.cgi?article=1017&context=think_tanks
3 Muthiah Alagappa, "Galvanising International Studies", *Pragati: The Indian National Interest Review*, 30, September 2009, pp. 11–16.
4 To accurately reflect think tank policy discourse, I have retained their categorisation of the disputed territory in Kashmir, thus, when think tank publications use the term Pakistan-Occupied Kashmir (POK), I have retained the term. My personal preference, however, is the use of the term Pakistan-Administered Kashmir (PAK) in keeping with more objective analysis.
5 Sajjad Padder, "The Composite Dialogue between India and Pakistan: Structure, Process and Agency", *Heidelberg Papers in South Asian and Comparative Politics*, Working Paper, 65, February 2012, p. 2.
6 Ashutosh Misra, "An Audit of the India-Pakistan Peace Process", *Australian Journal of International Affairs*, 61:4, 2007, p. 506.
7 As stated by National Security Advisor (NSA) Shiv Shankar Menon during a Conference in New Delhi. For a detailed report, see Stuti Bhatnagar, Deepti Mahajan and Manjrika Sewak, *Collaborative Explorations: Fifth Annual Conflict Transformation Workshop Report* (New Delhi: WISCOMP, 2007).
8 While Daniel Markey has argued that think tanks have the potential to be a part of India's "foreign policy software," Alagappa identifies them as an integral part of India's IR architecture but is critical of their role in providing policy alternatives. For more, see Muthiah Alagappa, "Galvanising International Studies", *Pragati: The Indian National Interest Review*, 30, September 2009, pp. 11–16; Daniel Markey, "Developing India's Foreign Policy 'Software'", *Asia Policy*, 8, July 2009, pp. 73–96.
9 Matthew Taylor, "Think Tanks, Public Policy and Academia", *Public Money & Management*, 31:1, 2011, pp. 10–11; Donald E. Abelson, "Old World, New World: The Evolution and Influence of Foreign Affairs Think-Tanks", *International Affairs*, 90:1, 2014, pp. 125–142; Stella Ladi, *International Encyclopedia of Political Science* (Thousand Oaks: Sage, 2011); Andjelkovic Branka, "A Limited Dialogue: Think Tanks and the Policy

Making Process in Serbia", in UNDP (ed.) *Thinking the Unthinkable* (Bratislava: UNDP Regional Bureau for Europe and the Commonwealth of Independent States, 2003).
10 This insight also emerged from many of the interviews, particularly with former policymakers. For more, see Sanjaya Baru, "Can Indian Think Tanks and Research Institutes Cope with the Rising Demand for Foreign and Security Policy Research", *ISAS Working Paper* (National University of Singapore), 67, June 16, 2009; Dhruv Jaishankar, "Can India's Think Tanks Be Truly Effective?", *The Huffington Post India*, April 15, 2016, www.huffingtonpost.in/dhruva-jaishankar/can-indias-think-tanks-be_b_9688434.html
11 Diane Stone, "Recycling Bins, Garbage Cans or Think Tanks? Three Myths Regarding Policy Analysis Institutes", *Public Administration*, 85:2, 2007, p. 276.
12 Inderjeet Parmar, *Think Tanks and Power in Foreign Policy* (New York: Palgrave MacMillan, 2004), p. 119.
13 It has been used by Inderjeet Parmar in his comparative analysis of the Council on Foreign Relations (CFR) and Chatham House in Inderjeet Parmar, *Think Tanks and Power in Foreign Policy* (New York: Palgrave MacMillan, 2004).
14 Diane Stone, *Capturing the Political Imagination: Think Tanks and the Policy Process* (London: Frank Cass, 1996), p. 4.
15 James McGann, *2012 Global Go to Think Tanks Report and Policy Advice* (Philadelphia: University of Pennsylvania, 2013), p. 29.
16 Inderjeet Parmar, *Think Tanks and Power in Foreign Policy* (New York: Palgrave MacMillan, 2004).
17 Diane Stone, "Recycling Bins, Garbage Cans or Think Tanks? Three Myths Regarding Policy Analysis Institutes", *Public Administration*, 85:2, 2007, p. 274.
18 Inderjeet Parmar, *Think Tanks and Power in Foreign Policy* (New York: Palgrave MacMillan, 2004), p. 119.
19 Stella Ladi, "Think Tanks, Discursive Institutionalism and Policy Change", in Georgios Papanagnou (ed.) *Social Science and Policy Challenges: Democracy, Values and Capacities* (Paris: UNESCO, 2011), p. 208.
20 Alexander L. George and Andrew Bennett, *Case Studies and Theory Development in the Social Sciences* (Cambridge, MA: Belfer Center for Science and International Affairs, 2005), p. 206.
21 John L. Campbell, "Ideas, Politics and Public Policy", *Annual Review of Sociology*, 28, 2002, p. 29.
22 ibid.
23 Erin Zimmerman, *Think Tanks and Non-Traditional Security: Governance Entrepreneurs in Asia* (Basingstoke: Palgrave MacMillan, 2016), p. 62.
24 Developing the Discursive Institutionalist approach, Vivien Schmidt's writings have elaborated on the specific types of ideas and interactive discursive processes that contribute to policy change. For more, see Vivien Schmidt, "Discursive Institutionalism: The Explanatory Power of Ideas and Discourse", *Annual Review of Political Science*, 11, 2008, pp. 303–326.
25 Alexander L. George and Andrew Bennett, *Case Studies and Theory Development in the Social Sciences* (Cambridge, MA: Belfer Center for Science and International Affairs, 2005), p. 19.
26 ibid., p. 20.
27 Brian C. Rathbun, "Interviewing and Qualitative Field Methods: Pragmatism and Practicalities", in Janet M. Box-Steffensmeier, Henry E. Brady and David Collier (eds.) *The Oxford Handbook of Political Methodology* (Oxford: Oxford University Press, 2008), p. 686.
28 ibid.

2
THINK TANKS AND FOREIGN POLICY

A Discursive Institutionalist–Gramscian approach

The growth and development of think tanks in India is a part of a global phenomenon of think tanks playing an increasingly important role in policy making. While later chapters highlight specifically the role of Indian think tanks in the policy process, this chapter sheds light on the theoretical and methodological arguments that best explain the behaviour and impact of think tanks in the literature. The conceptual analysis of think tanks has moved from their dismissal as viable actors to a grudging acceptance of their role. Further, the literature on ideational structures and more recently institutionalism has adopted a more nuanced understanding of think tanks, their role and their influence in shaping foreign policy choices. Identifying think tanks as non-state actors and highlighting their interaction with state structures through their position in the policy sphere this book advances a Discursive Institutionalist–Gramscian framework (DI-Gramscian). The approach seeks to understand processes/interactions through which think tanks attempt to create discursive spaces to contribute as policy actors in India. Institutionalists have argued that think tanks as policy agents are involved in framing and agenda-setting as well as the articulation of foreign policy for the purpose of creating public opinion. The power of discourse as highlighted by the DI approach, in particular the emphasis on the interactive processes of policy construction, is helpful, as causal relationships between think tank research and tangible policy decisions are difficult to find. Such an approach is particularly relevant to a restrictive bureaucratic structure as is prevalent in India. There has also been a proliferation of foreign and security policy think tanks in India in recent years, therefore making it imperative to examine the role that these expanding institutions play in India's foreign policy making.

While DI helps in identifying processes that think tanks are involved in, it lacks in the explanation of material interest calculations and the bureaucratic bargaining of think tanks, particularly visible in the case of Indian think tanks.

Therefore, to overcome the inadequacies of the DI approach, I combine Gramsci's understanding of the role of the elite and introduce the DI-Gramscian framework as a synthesis of the two perspectives. The need for such a fusion is also a result of the research process and the specific context within which Indian think tanks articulate policy discourse on Pakistan. The DI-Gramscian approach thus enables a more suitable understanding of think tank behaviour in India with its emphasis on the role of the intellectual elite and its collaborative relationship with the state. It is better able to substantiate the think tank role within the policy landscape in India, represented in the symbiotic relationship between foreign policy elite and think tank intellectuals. This chapter considers the theoretical approaches that have accounted for think tank influence in policy and in identifying think tanks as important policy actors. It presents the work of scholars of ideas and institutions and their critique that has led to the development of the DI-Gramscian perspective in this study.

Definitions and typologies

The literature on think tanks has grappled significantly with issues of definition and typologies.[1] Think tanks are identified as actors, agents or simply research institutes narrowly focused on academic research. A generally accepted definition describes think tanks as organisations that are distinct from the government and whose objective is to provide advice on a diverse range of policy issues through the use of specialised knowledge and the activation of networks.[2] Often referred to as civil society organisations or policy research institutes, they are different from philanthropic organisations and are both non-governmental organisations (NGOs) and international non-governmental organisations. The bridging role of think tanks has been a dominant theme in the literature, with think tanks often characterised as organisations that engage in research and advocacy on matters of public policy and act as a bridge between knowledge actors and those at the centre of policy construction.[3]

There does exist, however, criticism of this dual characterisation of think tanks. Highlighting the symbiotic and interdependent relationship between knowledge and policy, Stone concludes that "think tanks are not bridges but a manifestation of the knowledge/power nexus."[4] The limitations of the traditional definitions are also complicated by the expansion of think tank networks, each operating within their own unique cultural, political and historical environments, also emphasised by Inderjeet Parmar.[5] The over-emphasis of predominantly Anglo-American definitions is inadequate to account for the specific political context in which think tanks develop or the proliferation of think tanks in political contexts outside of Europe and the US. This book therefore attempts to define and contextualise think tanks in India operating within their distinct political and bureaucratic settings.

There are no specific definitions adopted for think tanks in Asia, but the attention of this book is on institutions that have been focused on research-based policy planning and advocacy in India, particularly on foreign policy.[6] Think tanks and policy research institutions in this research closely resemble what Weaver and Stares call Alternative Policy Advisory Organisations (APAOs) – organisations outside of government departments which serve as institutionalised sources of policy expertise for government policymakers.[7] Thus, think tanks go beyond the lobbying groups and formal governmental sub-committees that are constituted to design a specialised policy initiative. Yet, the proximity to policymakers and their specific position in the society also indicates their relative significance to the policy landscape – an aspect that is better understood through a theoretical examination of think tanks.

Theorising the role of think tanks

The theoretical understanding of think tanks has essentially emerged through an analysis of their place within policy circles, their engagement with formal state structures and the power of their ideas to influence policy and ultimately to create a structural change in policy frameworks. Theoretical explanations offered so far have analysed think tanks through their position vis-à-vis the formal state policy apparatus. While realists dismiss think tanks as irrelevant, liberal formulations place state interest and authority above those of think tanks, described as secondary actors.[8] Similarly, depicting think tanks as a closed network of corporate, financial and political elites, for some theorists they are "instruments deployed in the service of a ruling class political agenda with the sole purpose of assisting top down policymaking."[9] Dependent on funding and political support by policy elites, think tanks are recognised as instruments that gather information and develop policy alternatives but remain limited by the issues of concern highlighted by the elites themselves. Indian think tanks such as the Institute for Defence Studies and Analysis, the Indian Council of World Affairs and the armed forces think tanks, based on such a statist and elitist point of view, would be subservient to agendas defined by the government, particularly when completely reliant on government funding.

Pluralist explanations of think tanks, particularly within debates on the nature and distribution of political influence in the United States during the 1960s and 1970s, have identified think tanks as one kind of organisation among many that compete to shape public policy, thus discounting the power of the ruling state. For pluralists, as Parmar argues, think tanks like Chatham House and Council on Foreign Relations (CFR) would be expected to be "independent of the state and self-interested."[10] Such institutes thus would be able to "exert significant influence over a relatively weak state/governmental system of policy formation."[11] The recent proliferation of think tanks in India, particularly those with independent financial resources, has also led some towards the pluralist point of view.[12] The growing potential of think tanks has also led to arguments that think tanks have the potential to be a part of India's "foreign policy software" and a viable institution of foreign policy in the future.[13]

The Marxist perspective, as highlighted by Parmar, is also likely to be dominated by ruling class interests.[14] Indian think tanks, often seen as "retirement posts" for the bureaucratic and military elite in India, carrying official baggage and lacking new innovative policy ideas on foreign policy, could be characterised in this way.[15] Such a viewpoint, however, tends to undermine the power of the state. The Indian state represented by the political leadership and an influential foreign policy establishment are actively involved in policy making. This aspect is observed more prominently with respect to a securitised and sensitive subject such as India's relations with Pakistan.

Broadly therefore, the analysis on think tanks has moved from their relative position within the power hierarchies into the realm of knowledge and ideas and normative understandings that began to be emphasised by the constructivists and the neo-Gramscians. The focus also shifted to the role of "research communities" and the recognition of think tanks as ideational actors – crucial for the generation of ideas and their subsequent adoption into formal policy frameworks.[16] The influence of ideas on politics and the particular role of think tanks has been the considerable focus of researchers who debate the role of ideas in policy, the particular role of think tanks as "interpretive communities" and their significance to the regional cooperation mechanisms in place within the Association of Southeast Asian Nations (ASEAN).[17]

Furthermore, a focus on discourse and the discursive processes has particular significance to the Indian scenario, as think tanks hold relatively little political authority and work on the periphery of the political process, making it difficult to establish causal influence. Also relevant to the Indian case is the role of the elite that inform and guide think tank policy formulations. The proliferation of think tanks in India, their significant research outputs and the growing number of intellectual elites proficient in policy analysis makes it worthwhile to study the policy discourse emerging from Indian think tanks.

Think tanks and the role of ideas in policy

Several theoretical approaches have sought to explain the impact of ideas on policy.[18] It is also a common theme running within the more recent literature on think tanks. Specifically, there is a consensus that the primary role of think tanks is to establish a dynamic between ideas and policy making through policy-relevant enquiry. This is complemented by strategic practices to develop advisory ties to the government, industry or the public.[19] If think tanks are to be understood as ideational actors, then the effect that defining, framing and institutionalising ideas within policy making and the interactive processes and institutional constraints that emerge out of this interaction also become important. The specific argument in support of the relevance of ideas is that

> by specifying what kinds of ideas serve what functions, how ideas of different types interact with one another, how ideas change over time, and how

ideas shape and are shaped by actors' choices, social scientists can provide greater analytic purchase on the question of exactly how ideas matter.[20]

While ideas are often identified as one concept, Mehta recognises three different levels of ideas that are relevant to the understanding of the policy process, an understanding also used by the DI framework that will be elaborated on later in this chapter.[21] Ideas can be limited to policies or more complex formulations that include programmatic changes and shifts in philosophies. As policy solutions, ideas provide guidelines for solving given political problems and thus become a vehicle for political action and policy making. In the Indian case, this would include policy ideas by Indian think tanks on dealing with particular conflicts/disputes with Pakistan as identified by the Indian government, for instance on Kashmir, or the resolution of the Siachen dispute. Policy changes may also stem from new programmatic ideas that are defined as precise ideas that facilitate policy making among elites by specifying how to solve particular policy problems. These are broader than individual policies and have the ability to provide "focal points around which policy makers can most easily build political coalitions."[22] Public philosophies are the final tier and exist at a more fundamental level than either policy or programmatic ideas. These are the most difficult to change. Campbell too argues that "paradigm shifts occur when policy makers suddenly find themselves faced with unusual political economic problems for which the current paradigm offers no clear-cut solutions."[23]

The big question in addition to the nature of ideas themselves is thus to examine why some ideas become the policies, programs and philosophies while others do not.[24] Within the study of ideas is also situated the ability of think tanks to act as idea brokers and information filters for governments and institutions, which is especially relevant in the light of new security concerns and complex policy problems.[25] New conceptions of security and additional foreign policy concerns have corresponded with the proliferation and expansion of public policy research institutes, thus putting think tanks in a good position to act as ideational agents.[26] Think tanks are increasingly also being seen as an extension of the governmental bureaucracy that lacks resources, and thus possess the capability to invent new ideas.[27] In India too, as will be highlighted in Chapter 3, the formal bureaucracy faces new challenges – due to new conceptions of security and India's changing global position – which the current institutional policy structure is unable to meet. Owing to their assumed independent nature and disconnect from formal structures, this adds to the think tank potential to introduce new ideas and new narratives to foreign policy. This statement will, however, be problematised in later sections of this chapter and in other parts of the book through a detailed analysis of think tank programmes and discourse.

Think tanks are often identified as organisations that promote and offer a way for policy ideas to gain supporters and to contribute to policy debates. In addition to their policy inputs directly to the government, several other ways in which think tanks seek to impact policy making include conferences, formal and informal interactions with the policymakers, and through their participation in several multi-track initiatives. The dissemination of policy ideas through the vast range of research publications and the close interaction with the media is also an important tool that think tanks use to influence policy making. In addition, some think tanks are also invited by the government to organise trainings for government officials. Think tanks also create networks and "horizontal linkages" with other think tanks, particularly evident from analysis of think tanks in China, though instances of this phenomenon are rare in India.[28] The creation of think tank networks and a neutral and unofficial political space can nonetheless be an important avenue for the introduction of new ideas with more autonomy. In addition to ideational networks, the question of institutional embeddedness is also important. Thus, the ways in which think tanks are linked to the state helps determine which ideas affect policy making.[29]

The think tank role thus extends to problem framing, agenda setting and formation of ideational networks aimed at introducing the different levels of policy ideas. Arguing in favour of the role of think tanks in creating non-traditional security frames in South East Asia, Zimmerman for instance contends that

> the implication is that once a frame has gained a certain level of acceptance, policy actors must engage with the ideas it contains and that by framing information in a certain context, think tanks are able to privilege the desired understanding of an issue.[30]

Once a frame has been established, think tanks are then engaged in pushing ideas into the political agenda. The network-building potential of think tanks is also examined in the literature in the form of advocacy coalitions, creation of epistemic communities and also the personal networks of think tank personnel.[31] Recognising human agency in policy making, Peter Haas further examines the role that networks of knowledge-based experts – epistemic communities – "play in articulating the cause and effect relationships of complex problems, helping states identify their interests, framing the issues for collective debate, proposing specific policies and identifying salient points for negotiation."[32]

The ability of think tanks to establish networks and in particular the potential to exploit the networks of think tank personnel are very important factors in the case of India, as many former bureaucrats and policy experts are now a part of the think tank machinery with established links with formal structures of policy making. This ability will be explored through an analysis of think tank research discourse in later chapters of this volume.

Discursive institutionalism (DI)

While attention has been devoted to the influence of ideas on policy, the processes through which ideas are conveyed, accepted and revised and actors that carry these ideas into the policy process are questions that still remain. This brings the analysis to the concept of discourse and the particular question of agency. Theoretical traditions including the realist, statist, elitist and even the orthodox Marxists discussed earlier have considered the role of the "state" as central in the construction of policy and often dismiss private think tanks with little or no influence. The pluralists, however, relegate the state as a passive force and over-emphasise the independence of think tanks. In contrast, the framework provided by the institutionalists developed in response to approaches that over-emphasise agency without structure take account of institutions. DI introduces the element of discourse and its relationship and interaction with institutions, notably seen in the work of Schmidt. Identifying discourse as a "more versatile and overarching concept than ideas," Schmidt argues that DI enables an analysis of the different levels and different types of ideas as well as the interactive processes by which ideas are translated into policies.[33]

In introducing the element of discourse and the relationship between structure and agency, DI

> sets ideas and discourse in an institutional context and addresses explicitly the representation of ideas (how agents say what they are thinking of doing) and the discursive interactions through which actors generate and communicate ideas (to whom they say it) within given institutional contexts (where and when they say it).[34]

Moving beyond the content of ideas, the attention is therefore on the interactive processes – an approach that is particularly useful when causal links between actors involved in policy construction and policy changes are difficult to ascertain. According to Schmidt, the discursive interactions may involve policy actors in "coordinative discourse" or "communicative discourse":[35]

> the coordinative discourse consists of individuals and groups at the centre of policy construction (civil servants, elected officials, experts and others), the communicative discourse consists of individuals and groups involved in the presentation, deliberation and legitimation of political ideas to the general public (leaders, social activists, think tanks)[36]

The discursive process for DI is often a top-down process where discourse is developed by policy elites and communicated to the general public by political elites.[37] However, the role of civil society and social and political activists could also reverse the process of interaction. Schmidt also accounts for the lack of interaction between the coordinative and communicative discourses when policy ideas remain out of public view in closed debates or if political elites choose to legitimate their policy ideas using arguments other than those used in the coordinative discourse.[38]

The emphasis here is also on the specific institutional setting, of timing and the right audience – important elements needed for the discourse to be successful.

A distinction is also made on differing governing structures in "simple polities" where governance is channelled through a single authority with little consultation with outside experts, as in Britain and France. In this case the communicative discourse tends to be more elaborate than the coordinative discourse. In "compound" polities, however, with multiple centres of power, such as the federal democracies of Germany and the United States, the coordinative discourse with several policy actors tends to be stronger.[39] A strong bureaucratic society such as India would fit well into the "simple" polity classification, particularly when foreign policy formulation is controlled by top leadership and the foreign policy bureaucracy. However, as this volume highlights, despite government control, the effect of non-state institutions including think tanks, the media and academia in foreign policy formation and articulation cannot be dismissed. To investigate the relevant success of a discourse, DI uses the methods of process tracing, the analysis of speeches and debates of political elites that lead to political action, opinion polls and surveys to measure the impact of the communicative discourse, and interviews and network analysis to gauge the significance of the coordinative discourse.

Discursive Institutionalism and think tanks

In developing the DI framework, Schmidt identifies a "discursive sphere" within which "practitioners can discuss, deliberate, argue and contest one another's ideas about ideas and discourse from epistemological, ontological and methodological vantage points."[40] In making the connection between ideas and collective action, the importance of agents who articulate and communicate ideas through discourse, discussion, deliberation, negotiation and contestation is also foregrounded.

Using DI to conceptualise the role of South East Asian think tanks, Zimmerman broadens the concept to what she calls "discursive spaces," highlighting that "to enhance their discursive ability, think tanks have created unique discursive spaces where they can control the discursive process."[41] Her research identifies these spaces alongside formal governing processes but free from the strict political limitations imposed on governmental venues. This, it is argued, "provides the opportunity for state and non-state actors alike to discuss delicate security matters in a more flexible environment for instance in think tank organised dialogues, meetings, conferences and networks characterising the Track 2 processes."[42] DI is therefore for this analysis found well suited to studying think tanks because it can analyse their position both within and outside existing governing structures and is able to clarify how by operating in the 'middle' of formal and informal process, think tanks can wield political influence.[43]

Ladi and Medvetz have also analysed think tanks as crucial agents of policy making explained through the institutionalist tradition. While Ladi conceptualises think tanks as carriers in the coordinative and communicative discourse spheres with special emphasis on their role during "critical junctures," Medvetz credits the institutionalist tradition for explaining think tank involvement during different stages of the policy process.[44] While Zimmerman, Ladi and Medvetz analyse think tanks and think tank networks as leading to policy and institutional changes, Hope and Raudla outline how DI can be reconceptualised to understand policy stasis in simple and compound polities using Estonian fiscal policy and the federal climate change policy in the US as comparative case studies.[45]

DI has only recently been applied to the study of think tanks, and it has not been used to analyse think tank influence on Indian foreign policy.[46] Work on the institutionalist perspective in India has been limited to research on economic policy and issues of governance.[47] Studies on foreign policy in India often overlook the political processes that translate ideas into policy change, and thus a focus on DI will be useful here. The next chapter will explore critically the coordinative and communicative processes in the creation of discourse in the Indian context, providing important insights into the discursive practices involved in the formulation of India's foreign policy. It will further highlight the relevance of think tanks to these discursive practices, particularly with regards to India's relationship with Pakistan.

In examining policy making in India, particularly in the institutional setting, there is arguably space for outside expertise and for think tanks in particular to impact the policy process. While informal networks of think tanks, as evidenced from back-channel and track two diplomatic efforts often initiated by think tanks, are visible, ideas introduced remain unimplemented and think tank influence often remains unrepresented.[48] When the dialogue process between India and Pakistan peaked between 2004 and 2008, think tanks appeared to enjoy considerable leverage in making policy recommendations. The relevance and position of think tanks within the policy process and their ability to assume importance during what Ladi describes as "critical junctures" is an important aspect here. Critical junctures, as described by Ladi, "refer to particular historical moments that have lasting consequences and can provoke changes in policy."[49] The positive atmosphere of the CD can be perceived as one such "critical juncture" wherein avenues for policy change in India's relations with Pakistan were available and active civil society engagement was encouraged.

Although removed from the formal structures of foreign policy making and significantly different in their influence and resourcefulness, particularly when compared to American think tanks, Indian policy research institutes are now visible players. Yet, rather than establishing causal linkages, which are difficult to find, the arguments in this book emphasise the ways in which think tanks attempt to become policy actors. Therefore, the aim is "to illustrate what it is that think tanks did that could have been policy relevant and to make statements about congruence between policy output and policy."[50] With an understanding of think tanks as agents in the political process, this study assesses their ability and impact on foreign policy discourse and the generation of new ideas and alternative policy frameworks, if any. In addition to policy influence and the capacity to introduce new ideas, the question of institutional embeddedness and the institutional relevance of think tanks themselves needs to be considered, particularly when so many of them look to the government for financial support.

The representation of think tanks through the DI perspective is, however, not free from critique. It often disregards material interests and the elite character of institutions such as think tanks. This is particularly visible in India where think tanks represent the intellectual elite. The over-simplification of the ideational role of think tanks based on the DI perspective also misses out on the research manoeuvring that think tanks often resort to in order to please funding bodies and government elites, leading quite often to a benign portrayal. The following section therefore turns to some of the major critiques of DI and introduces the DI-Gramscian viewpoint to overcome some of these challenges.

Limits and challenges of DI

While DI offers a middle ground between discourse and institutional analysis and is useful in analysing think tank participation in the policy process, there has been significant criticism of the approach. The major strands of critique have been its over-emphasis on ideas and the missing or under-explored emphasis on the material interests of policy actors, in this case think tanks.[51] Stephen Bell, for instance, has highlighted the under-explored potential of the ideational approaches in addressing questions regarding the power of business interests, arguing that "while constructivists concede that agency is important for enacting ideas and norms, there has only been limited understanding of how to operationalise this interaction."[52] On similar grounds, Medvetz argues that in looking at the interactive processes of discourse, DI remains restricted to the official political domain alone. He makes the argument that the impact of think tanks extends well beyond the political sphere into other social settings and particularly what he calls the "business activist" movement that has played a leading role in the promotion of pre-market ideology since the 1960s.[53] Also identified as a problem is the missing emphasis on interests and the notion that actors in politics have interests that they fulfil through political processes. It is argued that while causal linkages between ideas and policy are difficult to identify, the linkages between interests and policy are more readily demonstrable.[54] On its part, the literature on DI responds to these concerns and argues that "one cannot distinguish interests from ideas" and ideas are often used to justify interests.[55] For discursive institutionalists, however, "ideas and values infuse and influence perceptions of position and often give power to actors even when they might lack the power of position as in the case of social movements who set the agenda for reform in policy."[56]

At another level, DI is criticised for being overly deterministic or idealistic with regard to the role of ideas and discourse and not accounting for processes of change that are unconscious, such as "critical junctures."[57] While DI places emphasis on agency, the particular aspect of time is also relevant, and historical moments that can often have lasting consequences must be taken into consideration. For Ladi, critical junctures offer opportunities to think tanks to "increase their visibility as carriers of new discourse and can facilitate change."[58]

The limitations of the DI literature become clear in the Indian context, too. The actor-centred approach fails to differentiate the effects of ideas themselves from the effects of the actors who bear them. There is also evidence that the status of actors bearing new ideas affects the odds that policymakers will adopt their ideas.[59] This is particularly relevant to the Indian scenario where the authority to introduce political ideas lies with the political elite, and therefore the connections between think tanks and the political elite warrant consideration.

Zimmerman has underscored the control of political spaces by think tanks in South East Asia and their specific expertise on NTS that has enabled them to become primary actors pushing NTS ideas into political agendas.[60] Think tanks, according to this conceptualisation, are "idea brokers" with noticeable "ideational authority" on non-traditional security issues.[61] Yet in India, the policy elite is represented by the formal bureaucracy and the topmost foreign policy leadership. Also, the "intricate regional network of think tanks" that Zimmerman identifies in the South East Asian countries does not exist in India. Think tanks in India instead continue to be rather an informal network of intellectual elites. The nature of the issue under consideration is also pertinent. The nature of India–Pakistan relations and its inherent volatility and political sensitivity, coupled with a focus on traditional security concerns, impacts the ability of think tanks to exert influence. Zimmerman also argues that because of their close but informal relationships with the governments, think tanks in South East Asia have a distinct advantage when it comes to institutional change in Asia; however, proximity to the government has not provided such a "space" to Indian think tanks, and they are seemingly less ideologically driven as those in South East Asia or China.

The aspect of institutional context in which and through which ideas are communicated via discourse has also been given attention by Schmidt. DI articulates that agents operate within institutions that shape the opportunities available to them; at the same time, agents are able to alter institutions through the use of discourse. It is at this point of discourse (interaction) between agents and institutions where ideas are transferred and institutional change starts. The research on Indian think tanks, however, deviates from this point. The interaction between agents and institutions can also consolidate traditional institutions and curtail institutional change, in turn impacting the ability of think tanks to exercise influence. While there is truth in Zimmerman's argument that think tanks are more agile and flexible in responding to emerging policy challenges than governmental bureaucracies, this gives them the opportunity to supply the conceptual language and paradigms for emerging security problems facing Asia.[62] In India, however, particularly with respect to foreign and security policy, while think tanks represent a significant forum for policy debates, policy paradigms are instead established by the state and refined by think tank research and analysis.

The relationship between the state and independent agents such as think tanks therefore warrants further examination.

Using a Discursive Institutionalist–Gramscian framework

While DI is useful for processual analysis, it does not adequately explain the processes through which think tanks can embed themselves into existing policy institutions to have wider influence on policy change. DI scholars have moved the debate into recognising the ideational and agency role of think tanks through their interactive participation in the policy process. They too, however, overemphasise ideational influence and leave gaps in the explanation of material conditions in which these non-state actors operate, a challenge that will be addressed through the focus on a DI-Gramscian analysis.

The question of institutional embeddedness is addressed somewhat by the literature on bureaucratic politics and the emphasis on bargaining and a distinction between "embedded institutions," which over time can spread ideas but are more likely to get ideologically absorbed into the stronger bureaucratic frameworks or "insulation" that can reduce the institution's influence over foreign policy.[63] Stone and Higgott also argue that think tanks indulge in "research brokerage" and tend to "adapt scholarship to forms palatable for decision makers – more so when funding comes from the government."[64]

Perhaps more relevant to this study is the Gramscian perspective that appreciates the interdependence of ideas and material conditions.[65] Gramsci provides a theory for state-society relations that goes beyond elites and ideas. In examining the role of intellectuals in society, Gramsci broke down "the superstructure into two great 'floors', which he described as 'civil society' and 'political society'."[66] The interactions between these elements for Gramsci incorporated "active political strategies that would forge these historic blocs."[67] According to Gramsci,

> the ruling class exerts its power over society on both of these "floors" of action, but by very different methods. Civil society is the marketplace of ideas, where intellectuals enter as "salesmen" of contending cultures. The intellectuals succeed in creating hegemony to the extent that they extend the world view of the rulers to the ruled, and thereby secure the "free" consent of the masses to the law and order of the land. To the extent that the intellectuals fail to create hegemony, the ruling class falls back on the state's coercive apparatus which disciplines those who do not "consent," and which is "constructed" for all society in anticipation of moments of crisis of command . . . when spontaneous consensus declines.[68]

The impact of Gramsci's ideas is that there exist constant negotiations between the civil society and the state. The value of agency in the political struggle and the concept of the intellectual is therefore important.[69] Gramscian analysis is also able to combine a "constructivist" understanding of the role of ideas with a clear acknowledgement of the importance of their material structure.[70] The emphasis on the "organic intellectuals" playing a central role in hegemonic projects where specific sets of ideas are funded, generated and disseminated by foundations, think tanks, publishing houses and NGOs is of particular relevance to this book. For Gramsci, the role of organic intellectuals "in directing the ideas and aspirations of the class to which they organically belong" is crucial.[71] At think tanks, these intellectuals are the knowledge elites who, owing to their cooperative engagement with the state and their ability to shape policy ideas, identify intricately with, and subsequently promote the interests of, the state.

This approach is employed by Inderjeet Parmar in his discussion of American and British think tanks. While Parmar and others have referred to the existence of a formal foreign policy establishment, in the Indian context where think tanks are a relatively new phenomena, Raja Mohan for instance concludes that it is difficult to discern the existence of such a permanent establishment.[72] What exists instead is an informal network that is led by a small but shifting group of experts within and outside the government. Raja Mohan also talks about the "existence of tiny, informal and consequential networks spanning the full spectrum of the Indian elite opinion and acting as the vanguard of India's new foreign policy."[73] While he insists that this informal network has an impact on vocabulary and concepts of mainstream foreign policy discourse within the nation, the arguments presented in this book contend that the "state" introduces the vocabulary subsequently promoted by this informal network.

The Gramscian approach emphasises the power of the state and the private forces – especially intellectuals. Parmar argues that a strong state is required to mobilise strong groups – such as the intellectuals and experts at Chatham House – to legitimise its own foreign policy reform programmes. The Gramscian view also resorts to a traditional focus on the domestic sources of power and political behaviour. This is of particular relevance to the India–Pakistan case, where much impetus for policy decisions derives from domestic politics rather than changes in global patterns. This volume bridges the perspective of the Gramscians with the DI focus on institutions to account for the think tank position in Indian policy structures. The DI-Gramscian framework analyses think tank interactive processes and identifies the position of think tanks in India as ideational actors. It enables a critical examination of the role of think tanks in building consensus on the Indian government's Pakistan policy and their potential in challenging dominant narratives and in introducing alternative policy ideas. Through an examination of think tanks' discourse on Pakistan and the crucial role they play in contributing to public opinion, the DI-Gramscian framework enables a look at "both the specific and the general influence on foreign policy . . . as catalysts and crystallizers of policy thought."[74] Indian think tanks are also closely associated with various committees and institutions affiliated to the state. If they identify with the broader interests of the state and Gramsci's 'state spirit' is a question this volume addresses. Also in cases where think tanks work "independently," the DI-Gramscian model permits an enquiry into think tank programmes, developed and conducted in close consultation with the state and benefitting from specific government-sanctioned project funding.

Conclusion

In understanding the role of think tanks within the policy process, this chapter has highlighted the emphasis in the literature on the role of ideas and discourses and the DI focus on policy processes in which think tanks are involved. While DI offers a good methodological tool to investigate the involvement of think tanks, the arguments in this chapter also brought into focus the Gramscian model that offers the best explanation of state-society policy interactions. In addition to policy influence and the capacity to introduce new ideas, Gramsci enables a closer look at institutional embeddedness and the institutional relevance of think tanks, particularly when many are still reliant on the government for financial support. The synthesis of the DI-Gramscian perspective is therefore better suited to examine the material interests and the elite character of think tanks, particularly visible in India where they represent the intellectual elite. The DI-Gramscian perspective also provides an insight into research manoeuvring by think tanks to retain relevance for funding bodies and government elites. Thus, rather than portraying think tanks benignly, this approach enables a more critical examination of the nature of interactions between policy elites and intellectual elites.

The role of intellectuals in the making of policy and the importance of 'collective intellectual' narratives is particularly important in the discourse towards Pakistan. I argue that the state in India generates popular and elite consensus in conjunction with the actions of private ruling class forces.[75] As Parmar argues, the broad policy ideas emerging from Chatham House and CFR were similar to that of the official discourse, however, they differed on "tactics, details, timing and emphases, rather than fundamentals . . . converting Chatham House into an arm of official foreign policy within an agenda largely determined by the state."[76] The agency role of Indian think tanks is also restricted by funding, the inability to form advocacy coalitions and viable horizontal networks around issue areas, and the lack of considerable presence outside Delhi. Think tanks in India represent privileged knowledge – led by political and socio-economic elites. They could therefore be described as "recycling bins" operating at two levels: making/translating academic research into policy-relevant ideas and also recycling the experience of practitioners.[77] The latter practice is particularly evident wherein the bulk of organisational capacity derives from retired diplomats, bureaucrats and retired military personnel. The strength of the DI-Gramscian framework is that it enables a critical examination of the specific ideas and particular interactions of think tanks, while also explaining their position within formal structures of policy making. Stone argues that "the constant restatement of policy message via different formats and products . . . broadcasts and amplifies policy research" – a role that Indian think tanks are actively involved with, especially through their discourse on Pakistan.[78] Think tanks also blur the boundaries between knowledge and policy. Having said that, it is also important to understand the private interests of think tanks themselves and their efforts to maintain their relevance and institutional strength – an aspect that will be highlighted through a DI-Gramscian analysis of think tanks in India.

Notes

1 Stella Ladi, *International Encyclopedia of Political Science* (Thousand Oaks: Sage, 2011); R. Kent Weaver and Paul B. Stares, *Guidance for Governance: An Overview* (Tokyo: Japan Center for International Exchange, 2001), pp. 71–88; Tom Medvetz, *Think Tanks as an Emergent Field* (New York: Social Science Research Council, October 2008).
2 Stella Ladi, *International Encyclopedia of Political Science* (Thousand Oaks: Sage, 2011), p. 3.
3 Andjelkovic Branka, "A Limited Dialogue: Think Tanks and the Policy Making Process in Serbia", in UNDP (ed.) *Thinking the Unthinkable* (Bratislava: UNDP Regional Bureau for Europe and the Commonwealth of Independent States, 2003).
4 ibid., p. 26.
5 Inderjeet Parmar, "Institutes of International Affairs: Their Roles in Foreign Policy-Making, Opinion Mobilization and Unofficial Diplomacy", in Diane Stone and Andrew Denham (eds.) *Think Tank Traditions: Policy Research and the Politics of Ideas* (Manchester: Manchester University Press, 2004).
6 Some classifications used to define think tanks in India include: Myron Weiner, "Social Science Research and Public Policy in India", *Economic and Political Weekly*, 14:37, September 1979, pp. 1579–1587; Jayati Srivastava, *Think Tanks in South Asia: Analysing the Knowledge-Power Interface* (London: Overseas Development Institute, 2011). While Srivastava defines think tanks more broadly as a heterogeneous group of organisations, engaged primarily in research-based policy advocacy, Weiner classifies them into four kinds: 1) research institutions under the jurisdiction of central or state government departments; 2) government-funded but legally autonomous organisations; 3) educational institutions and 4) private consultancy firms that conduct research under contract.
7 R. Kent Weaver and Paul B. Stares, *Guidance for Governance: An Overview* (Tokyo: Japan Center for International Exchange, 2001), pp. 71–88.
8 Diane Stone, "The ASEAN-ISIS Network: Interpretive Communities, Informal Diplomacy and Discourses of Region", *Minerva*, 49, 2011, pp. 242, 243.
9 Thomas Medvetz, *Think Tanks in America* (Chicago: University of Chicago Press, 2012); Thomas R. Dye, *Top Down Policymaking* (New York and London: Chatham House, 2001).
10 Inderjeet Parmar, *Think Tanks and Power in Foreign Policy* (New York: Palgrave MacMillan, 2004), p. 12.
11 ibid., p. 13.
12 Muthiah Alagappa, "Galvanising International Studies", *Pragati: The Indian National Interest Review*, 30, September 2009, pp. 11–16.
13 Daniel Markey, "Developing India's Foreign Policy 'Software'", *Asia Policy*, 8, July 2009, pp. 73–96.
14 Inderjeet Parmar, *Think Tanks and Power in Foreign Policy* (New York: Palgrave MacMillan, 2004), p. 16.
15 Dhruv Jaishankar, "Can India's Think Tanks Be Truly Effective?", *The Huffington Post India*, April 15, 2016, www.huffingtonpost.in/dhruva-jaishankar/can-indias-think-tanks-be_b_9688434.html; Mohan Guruswamy, "Think Tanks Help the Nation's Intellectual Churn", *Rediff*, August 19, 2014, www.rediff.com/news/column/think-tanks-help-the-nations-intellectual-churn/20140819.htm

16 Diane Stone, "The ASEAN-ISIS Network: Interpretive Communities, Informal Diplomacy and Discourses of Region", *Minerva*, 49, 2011, pp. 242, 243.
17 Amitav Acharya, "How Ideas Spread: Whose Norms Matter? Norm Localization and Institutional Change in Asian Regionalism", *International Organization*, 58, 2004, pp. 239–275.
18 Daniel Beland and Robert Henry Cox (eds.), *Ideas and Politics in Social Science Research* (New York: Oxford University Press, 2011); Andreas Gofas and Colin Hay (eds.), *The Role of Ideas in Political Analysis* (London and New York: Routledge, 2010); John L. Campbell, "Ideas, Politics and Public Policy", *Annual Review of Sociology*, 28, 2002, pp. 21–38.
19 Diane Stone, *Capturing the Political Imagination: Think Tanks and the Policy Process* (London: Frank Cass, 1996).
20 Jal Mehta, "The Varied Roles of Ideas in Politics: From 'Whether' to 'How'", in Daniel Beland and Robert Henry Cox (eds.) *Ideas and Politics in Social Science Research* (New York: Oxford University Press, 2011), p. 25.
21 ibid., p. 27.
22 John L. Campbell, "Ideas, Politics and Public Policy", *Annual Review of Sociology*, 28, 2002, p. 29.
23 ibid., p. 23.
24 Vivien A. Schmidt, "Discursive Institutionalism: The Explanatory Power of Ideas and Discourse", *Annual Review of Political Science*, 11, 2008, p. 307.
25 James McGann and Richard Sabatini, *Global Think Tanks: Policy Networks and Governance Global Institutions* (Abingdon, Oxon and New York: Routledge, 2011), p. 1.
26 ibid.
27 John J. Hamre, "The Constructive Role of Think Tanks in the Twenty-First Century", *Asia-Pacific Review*, 15:2, 2008, p. 2.
28 Bonnie S. Glaser and Phillip C. Saunders, "Chinese Civilian Foreign Policy Research Institutes: Evolving Roles and Increasing Influence", *The China Quarterly*, 171, September 2002, p. 600.
29 John L. Campbell, "Ideas, Politics and Public Policy", *Annual Review of Sociology*, 28, 2002, p. 31.
30 Erin Zimmerman, *Think Tanks and Non-Traditional Security: Governance Entrepreneurs in Asia* (Basingstoke: Palgrave MacMillan, 2016), p. 31.
31 ibid.
32 Peter M. Haas, "Introduction: Epistemic Communities and International Policy Coordination", *International Organization*, 46:1, Winter 1992, p. 2.
33 Vivien A. Schmidt, "Discursive Institutionalism: The Explanatory Power of Ideas and Discourse", *Annual Review of Political Science*, 11, 2008, p. 309.
34 ibid.
35 Vivien A. Schmidt, "Discursive Institutionalism: Scope, Dynamics and Philosophical Underpinnings", in Frank Fischer and Herbert Gottweis (eds.) *The Argumentative Turn Revisited: Public Policy as Communicative Practice* (Durham and London: Duke University Press, 2012), p. 86.
36 ibid.
37 ibid., p. 57.
38 Vivien Schmidt, "Reconciling Ideas and Institutions through Discursive Institutionalism", in Daniel Beland and Robert Cox (eds.) *Ideas and Politics in Social Science Research* (New York: Oxford University Press, 2011), p. 57.
39 ibid.
40 Vivien A. Schmidt, "Discursive Institutionalism: Scope, Dynamics and Philosophical Underpinnings", in Frank Fischer and Herbert Gottweis (eds.) *The Argumentative Turn Revisited: Public Policy as Communicative Practice* (Durham and London: Duke University Press, 2012), p. 87.
41 Erin Zimmerman, *Think Tanks and Non-Traditional Security: Governance Entrepreneurs in Asia* (Basingstoke: Palgrave MacMillan, 2016), p. 29.

42 ibid.
43 Vivien A. Schmidt, "Taking Ideas and Discourse Seriously: Explaining Change through Discursive Institutionalism as the Fourth 'New Institutionalism'", *European Political Science Review*, 2:1, 2010, pp. 1–25.
44 Stella Ladi, "Think Tanks, Discursive Institutionalism and Policy Change", in Georgios Papanagnou (ed.) *Social Science and Policy Change: Democracy, Values and Capacities* (Paris: UNESCO, 2011), pp. 205–220; Thomas Medvetz, *Think Tanks in America* (Chicago: University of Chicago Press, 2012).
45 Mat Hope and Ringa Raudla, "Discursive Institutionalism and Policy Stasis in Simple and Compound Polities: The Cases of Estonian Fiscal Policy and United States Climate Change Policy", *Policy Studies*, 33:5, September 2012, pp. 399–418.
46 For an analysis of think tanks using the DI framework, see Stella Ladi, "Think Tanks, Discursive Institutionalism and Policy Change", in Georgios Papanagnou (ed.) *Social Science and Policy Challenges: Democracy, Values and Capacities* (Paris: UNESCO, 2011), pp. 205–220; Diane Stone, "The ASEAN-ISIS Network: Interpretive Communities, Informal Diplomacy and Discourses of Region", *Minerva*, 49, 2011, pp. 241–262 and Erin Zimmerman, *Think Tanks and Non-Traditional Security: Governance Entrepreneurs in Asia* (Basingstoke: Palgrave MacMillan, 2016).
47 See Sudha Pai and Pradeep Sharma, "New Institutionalism and Legislative Governance in the Indian States: A Comparative Study of West Bengal and Uttar Pradesh", *Working Paper Series* (New Delhi: Centre for the Study of Law and Governance, JNU, March 2005); Aseema Sinha, "The Changing Political Economy of Federalism in India: A Historical Institutionalist Approach", *India Review*, 3:1, 2004, pp. 25–63.
48 It has been noted that the two countries came very close to resolving the Kashmir dispute in 2007 through what is popularly often called "the back-channel." While this was a secret group, members are known to be sourced from the NSAB in India and the foreign and armed services from Pakistan. The deal, however, could not be carried forward, and with the change in government on both sides and the revival of tensions owing to the Mumbai attacks in 2008, it has been forgotten. The NSAB, as will be highlighted in the next chapter, is a crucial arena for the induction of think tank expertise into formal policy making in India.
49 Stella Ladi, "Think Tanks, Discursive Institutionalism and Policy Change", in Georgios Papanagnou (ed.) *Social Science and Policy Challenges: Democracy, Values and Capacities* (Paris: UNESCO, 2011), p. 208.
50 Hartwig Pautz, *Think Tanks, Social Democracy and Social Policy* (London: Palgrave MacMillan, 2012), p. 4.
51 Todd Landman and Neil Robinson, *The SAGE Handbook of Comparative Politics* (London: Sage, 2009).
52 Stephen Bell, "The Power of Ideas: The Ideational Shaping of the Structural Power of Business", *International Studies Quarterly*, 56, 2012, p. 663.
53 Thomas Medvetz, *Think Tanks in America* (Chicago: University of Chicago Press, 2012), p. 14.
54 B. Guy Peters, *Institutional Theory in Political Science* (London and New York: Bloomsbury Publishing, 2011).
55 Vivien A. Schmidt, "Discursive Institutionalism: The Explanatory Power of Ideas and Discourse", *Annual Review of Political Science*, 11, 2008, p. 306.
56 ibid.
57 Stella Ladi, "Think Tanks, Discursive Institutionalism and Policy Change", in Georgios Papanagnou (ed.) *Social Science and Policy Challenges: Democracy, Values and Capacities* (Paris: UNESCO, 2011), p. 207.
58 ibid., p. 208.
59 John L. Campbell, "Ideas, Politics and Public Policy", *Annual Review of Sociology*, 28, 2002, p. 31.
60 Erin Zimmerman, *Think Tanks and Non-Traditional Security: Governance Entrepreneurs in Asia* (Basingstoke: Palgrave MacMillan, 2016), p. 41.

61 ibid.
62 ibid., p. 30.
63 Daniel Drezner, "Ideas, Bureaucratic Politics and the Crafting of Foreign Policy", *American Journal of Political Science*, 44:4, October 2000, p. 734.
64 Richard Higgott and Diane Stone, "The Limits of Influence: Foreign Policy Think Tanks in Britain and the USA", *Review of International Studies*, 20:1, January 1994, p. 28.
65 Hartwig Pautz, *Think Tanks, Social Democracy and Social Policy* (London: Palgrave MacMillan, 2012), p. 7.
66 Thomas R. Bates, "Gramsci and the Theory of Hegemony", *Journal of the History of Ideas*, 36:2, 1975, p. 353.
67 Hartwig Pautz, "Revisiting the Think Tank Phenomenon", *Public Policy and Administration*, 26:4, 2011, p. 425.
68 Thomas R. Bates, "Gramsci and the Theory of Hegemony", *Journal of the History of Ideas*, 36:2, 1975, p. 353.
69 Hartwig Pautz, "Revisiting the Think Tank Phenomenon", *Public Policy and Administration*, 26:4, 2011, p. 425.
70 Andreas Bieler, "Questioning Cognitivism and Constructivism in IR Theory: Reflections on the Material Structure of Ideas", *Politics*, 21:2, 2001, p. 99.
71 Antonio Gramsci, *Selections from the Prison Notebooks*. Edited and translated by Quintin Hoare and Geoffrey Nowell Smith (New York: International Publishers, 1971), p. 3.
72 C. Raja Mohan, "The Making of Indian Foreign Policy: The Role of Scholarship and Public Opinion", *ISAS Working Paper* (National University of Singapore), 73, July 13, 2009.
73 ibid., p. 11.
74 Inderjeet Parmar, *Think Tanks and Power in Foreign Policy* (New York: Palgrave MacMillan, 2004), p. 119.
75 ibid., p. 219.
76 ibid., p. 106.
77 Diane Stone, "Recycling Bins, Garbage Cans or Think Tanks? Three Myths Regarding Policy Analysis Institutes", *Public Administration*, 85:2, 2007, pp. 259–278.
78 ibid.

3
THINK TANKS AND INDIAN FOREIGN POLICY

An overview

The preceding chapter has outlined the role of ideas and discourse in the formulation of foreign policy, examining international scholarship that identifies think tanks as ideational actors. It also introduced the DI-Gramscian perspective and its reflection on state-society relations, the nature of the foreign policy elite and its relationship to non-state policy actors such as think tanks. DI provided a methodological tool to examine think tank interactions and interface with policymakers, both through their coordinative and communicative discourse. Yet it was found to be insufficient in explaining the material interests of think tanks and the evident bargaining that think tanks are involved in to retain their institutional relevance. Also problematic was the over-emphasis on ideas and over-simplification of structural constraints, curtailing think tank ability in getting involved in the policy process. This was the rationale for the emphasis on Gramsci that enabled an understanding of the nature of interactions between think tank intellectuals and policy elites and their existing symbiotic relationship.

An important aspect that emerged from the examination was that think tanks are better defined by taking into account the context in which they operate. For discursive institutionalists thus, "discursive processes help explain why certain ideas succeed and others fail because of the ways in which they are projected to whom and where."[1] A Gramscian understanding, however, appreciates the independence of ideas and material conditions. In the context of India then, the place of think tanks as discursive actors is also a reflection of state-society relations, which in turn has had an impact on the relevance and acceptance of their ideas.

Analyses of India's foreign policy, its transitions from idealism to pragmatism, grand strategy and the role of important personalities all form a substantial part of the literature on foreign policy.[2] What is missing, however, is a comprehensive exploration of the policy process, the actors and institutions involved, and the path that the policy-making process takes, though Bandyopadhyaya and recently Bajpai and Chong are notable exceptions.[3] They too, however, give little credence to the role of think tanks. While the relevance and central position of the Ministry of External Affairs (MEA) is clearly articulated, it is not clear how ideas move across the policy process. The literature on Indian think tanks is even more ambiguous. The effort in this chapter is thus to draw attention to how literature on Indian foreign policy considers the role of think tanks as viable foreign policy actors. This chapter considers the trajectory of the foreign policy planning process and examines the top-down policy-making process and the elite engagement with civil society and grassroots actors.

The comparative analysis of think tanks in India considers their activities and analyses their discourse, highlighting funding patterns and affiliation with the government of India. This is done by critically evaluating the organisational membership, leadership and worldviews; the institutional associations with the foreign policy establishment; and the think tank role both as policy actors and as influencers of public opinion. Using the DI-Gramscian framework, think tank discourse on India's policy towards Pakistan is analysed. Additionally, Gramsci's analytic tools examine power and policy making, providing a commentary on state-society relations in India, foreign policy institutions and the relative position of think tanks within the policy landscape. The first section explains the origins and development of think tanks in India and their changing relevance and position as agents within the policy-making system. Emphasis is on the existing linkages between the think tank elite and the foreign policy elite in India. Taking a cue from DI and its emphasis on discourse, the second part of this chapter discusses India's foreign policy discourse towards Pakistan, focusing particularly on the structured dialogue process initiated by the CD in 2004. It emphasises how this period expanded the space for think tanks in India, particularly those that dealt with foreign and security policy, signifying Ladi's "critical juncture." The peacebuilding process also reflected the growth of smaller think tanks with peacebuilding as their focus, with substantial attention to issues under consideration within the India–Pakistan dialogue.

Foreign policy making in India – key institutions

Dominant scholarship on Indian foreign policy has focused on events, landmarks and India's external relations with its South Asian neighbourhood and its engagement with the global superpowers.[4] A study of Indian foreign policy has usually remained limited to a study of India's bilateral relations, its national security concerns vis-à-vis its South Asian environment and most recently on the economic rise of India and the global interest that it has created. Very few have undertaken a more nuanced understanding of Indian foreign policy that is focused on the making of Indian foreign policy – its institutions, its frameworks and its leadership.[5] Who makes India's foreign policy? What constitutes what is often referred to as the "policy-making establishment".[6] Who are the actors and agents responsible for formulating foreign policy in India and their relative relevance are crucial questions that this book addresses.

It is important to shift attention to some of the prominent institutions responsible for the formulation of foreign policy in India and their engagement with key issues. As Harsh Pant argues, "a nation's foreign policy flows from several sources – from the international system; to its domestic political imperatives; to the cultural factors that underlie its society; to the personal characteristics and perceptions of individual decision-makers."[7] With both formal and informal linkages, India's foreign policy establishment – key institutions that are highlighted in the following section – form an essential component in the creation of a coherent foreign policy discourse.

Policy planning in India is based on issue areas, leading to a subsequent division of authority. Three bodies in the Indian government primarily work together to make foreign policy: the Prime Minister's Office (PMO), the National Security Council (NSC) led by a powerful National Security Advisor (NSA), and the Ministry of External Affairs (MEA), not necessarily in this order.[8] Other affiliated institutions include the Cabinet and its Committee on Security, the Ministry of Home Affairs, various economic ministries and the foreign affairs committee of Parliament. Within all these institutions, the elite from the Indian Foreign Service (IFS) are a significant part. Even though it is argued that the value of the service has declined, the MEA continues to be the primary institution responsible for the planning and implementation of India's foreign policy and deals directly with the PMO on crucial matters of concern.[9] The position of the Foreign Secretary is particularly crucial.

There have been debates on the comparative role of this elite in India, namely the IFS, the MEA and the PMO. Much like international scholarship, the relevance of institutions to policy has been considered through a pluralist and statist perspective with varying degrees of state control. The focus has been on leadership and the evolving role and relevance of these institutions to the formulation of foreign policy in India. While some have focused on the dominant role of successive Prime Ministers who have held the portfolio of foreign minister and set the tone for the discourse on foreign policy, others have dealt with the highly centralised bureaucracy, which has made it fairly independent of the electoral process. India's first Prime Minister Jawaharlal Nehru held both the foreign and defence portfolio as did his successors Indira Gandhi, Rajiv Gandhi, V.P. Singh and P.V. Narasimha Rao. Furthermore, Rao, I. K. Gujral and Atal Bihari Vajpayee made their mark as foreign ministers before becoming prime ministers.[10]

In contrast, others have argued in favour of the centralised bureaucratic structure and its relative freedom from politicised patronage. The bipartisan nature of bureaucracy has also been highlighted.[11] Arguments have emphasised the significant leeway that bureaucrats in India have in crafting policy. Manjari Chatterjee Miller highlights a lack of top-down planning in India on its long-term foreign policy goals and argues that civil servants are often responsible for convincing the leadership of particular policy decisions.[12] Though convinced of the bureaucracy's prominence in policy making, Narang however argues that:

> unlike other democracies such as the United States, where public opinion and executive bodies such as the State and Defense Departments exert tremendous ideational and bureaucratic gravity in foreign policy, policy formulation in India is restricted to a handful of individuals and, particularly, the Prime Minister, who with a stable government has significant freedom to manoeuvre in international affairs.[13]

There is also emphasis on the dynamics between foreign policy and domestic policy and the specific nature of federal and state politics in India.[14] Other analysis has also considered the civil and military cooperation in the formulation of foreign and defence policy.[15]

The inherently conservative, insular and "closed shop" bureaucracy has been the centre of much controversy and criticism in India.[16] Echoing this sentiment, Raja Mohan and Miller also highlight that the IFS are insulated from outside influences and make little room for other services into its fold:[17] "The monopoly of information on world affairs, and the development of specialists reinforced the condescension in South Block that they had little to learn from outsiders."[18] Refuting this claim, Shashi Tharoor argues that where the situation warrants the need for outside expertise, the IFS doesn't hesitate to consult, for instance, experts on trade issues, who have been taken on board for short periods.[19] Such interaction, however, is limited. In addition to their exclusivist attitude, the Official Secrets Act also imposes penalties on former policymakers for the public disclosure of information.[20] While the MEA's archives are now available in the National Archives of India, the process of accessing them is arduous. Popular histories are thus penned by retired officials rather than policy analysts or historians.[21] Thus, state control on the policy sphere is emphasised, with information limited to the policy elites.

Yet, despite the "closed shop," "insulated" bureaucracy, there is also emerging a gradual change to accommodate global and regional realities brought about by globalisation, the changing nature of conflicts, developments in the field of information and technology and the growing relevance of multi-track diplomacy. These have created what Raja Mohan refers to as a "different template for the South Block to deal with."[22] Thus, in addition to strengthening capacity in foreign policy, there have also been calls for a robust national security policy in India.[23] Responding to this call, in 1998, the NDA government led by Atal Bihari Vajpayee established the National Security Council (NSC) and the post of the National Security Advisor (NSA). The NSA is assisted by a Deputy NSA and a dedicated National Security Council Secretariat (NSCS). This has allowed limited involvement of outside experts into the formal policy-making apparatus. Reporting to the NSC is the National Security Advisory Board (NSAB) that includes experts from various fields: ex-diplomats and foreign and defence service officials, members of the academia, media as well as think tanks, and also some representation from the business community.[24] After the Vajpayee government lost power in 2004, the new UPA government led by the Congress party initiated a process of economic reforms alongside an expansion of welfare programmes to be designed in consultation with civil society representatives in a novel institution, the National Advisory Council (NAC).[25] The openness to civil society engagement was also evident in the realm of foreign policy and the government's approach to Kashmir as part of the India–Pakistan dialogue, details of which will be elaborated on further in this volume. On foreign policy, the office of the NSA has been considered very crucial owing to its unrestricted access to the PMO and its supervisory role in handling matters related to foreign affairs and coordinating with the Ministry of Defence (MoD) and other key departments. Yet, here too, the role of leadership is important; for instance, the NSA under Modi plays a different role to the NSA under Manmohan Singh. Even though the NSA under Manmohan Singh performed a significant part in decision making,[26] under the Modi administration that assumed power in 2014, NSA Ajit Doval enjoys a very close relationship with the Prime Minister and a more influential role in foreign policy decision making that is now centred in the NSC and the PMO.[27]

In addition to these formal governmental agencies, there exist in India a network of think tanks that engage with India's foreign policy and strategic doctrines. Since they are relatively new actors, however, research on their role and relevance is limited. While sometimes identified as civil society actors, arguments largely call for the need to strengthen the think tank role in policy making.[28] India's foreign policy, it is argued, "must be seen as a shared partnership across departments within the government of India, and academia and think tanks outside the traditional corridors of power."[29]

Think tanks and Indian foreign policy

Reiterating the definition of think tanks as used in the last chapter, the attention here is on institutions that have been focused on research-based policy planning and advocacy in India, particularly on foreign policy. The previous segment has highlighted governmental institutions responsible for formulating foreign policy and their declining expertise or incapacity to deal with new foreign policy environments. This has foregrounded the need to shift focus to other institutions, including think tanks in India, and examine their rising relevance to the formulation of discourse.

Over the years, the evaluation of foreign policy institutions has taken into account the role of these non-state actors and intellectual elites associated with them. Alagappa identifies think tanks as an integral part of the architecture of international relations (IR) studies in India and argues that "the output of research institutes can contribute to academic inquiry and knowledge accumulation as well as inform public opinion and policy formulation."[30] However, he also argues that:

> often government funded and/or staffed by retired diplomats and military officers, the foreign and security policy institutions have by and large followed the government line rather than providing deep analysis of policy alternatives. The interests and priorities of funders appear to have been limiting factors for institutions financed by private sector companies.[31]

Yet, the particular role that think tanks play in the promotion of ideas and policy alternatives in India remains uncertain. Also ambiguous is the changing relevance of think tanks and with it the changing strategies that think tanks have employed in seeking to have an impact on policy.

Within South Asia, India has one of the oldest histories of think tanks or policy research institutions that includes the Gokhale Institute of Politics and Economics in Pune established in 1930, the Indian Statistical Institute established in 1931 and the Indian Council of World Affairs (ICWA) established in 1943. While the Indian Statistical Institute is not necessarily a conventional think tank, it has a notable history of promoting research, teaching and application of statistics, natural sciences and social sciences since 1931. Yet, it is argued that in the early years of independence, there was less attention to policy processes, and centralised planning and development goals were predominantly set by the state. "Research institutes that emerged during this period supplemented the work of the government by filling gaps in analysis and providing alternative sources of data."[32] This appears to fit in with elite theorists' conceptualisation of think tanks as "instruments deployed in the service of a ruling class political agenda."[33] The sole purpose of think tanks at this stage was therefore to assist in the business of top-down policy making.

Thus, while some early think tanks emerged, they remained limited in their scope and the ability to influence discourse, and policy making remained the exclusive domain of the formal governmental machinery. Nehru's individualistic style has also been linked to the development of the policy planning apparatus in India, particularly with reference to foreign policy. Arguments focus on Nehru's preference for economic planning over planning on foreign policy.[34] Nehru's perceived preference for handling matters of foreign policy on his own without relying on outside expertise was also linked to the inadequate development of proficiency in the disciplines of international relations and strategic policy. While Nehru was considered responsible for training and inspiring a generation of diplomats who shaped foreign policy, his personalised conduct of foreign policy affected foreign policy institutions, and the "personalised basis" was carried forward to other generations of Indian leaders.[35] Thus, while economic planning was opened up for alternative thinking, parallel efforts were not made for foreign and strategic policy. Foreign policy formulation in the formative years of Indian independence was the domain of the MEA led by Nehru himself (from 1947–1964) and influenced by Foreign Service diplomats, notably Krishna Menon and Vijayalakshmi Pandit, who advocated for prominent foreign policy decisions including the decision to pursue non-alignment and the support for decolonisation and nuclear disarmament.

One think tank that enjoyed Nehru's support, however, was the ICWA established in 1943 – perhaps the only policy research institution that focused on international studies and concentrated on building expertise on foreign policy issues at the time. Led by intellectuals including M.S. Rajan, A. Appadorai or Tej Bahadur Sapru in 1955, as part of the ICWA, the Indian School of International Studies (later renamed School of International Studies, SIS) was set up and later incorporated into the Jawaharlal Nehru University (JNU) established in 1970. Bringing together intellectuals, bureaucrats, professionals, businessmen, scholars and journalists, the ICWA continued with its activities in the field of international relations and foreign affairs, experiencing a heyday in its first two decades, with speeches given by the likes of Margaret Thatcher and Kurt Waldheim and patronage from stalwarts such as Sarojini Naidu and S. Radhakrishnan.[36] In 1947, it organised the Asian Relations Conference, one of the earliest attempts at regional multilateralism initiated by India.[37]

Institutions such as the ICWA were seen as a possible arena for mutual cooperation between the MEA and the research community. Debates around that time also advocated for an exchange program between the MEA and academia, where roles were reversed and each was given an opportunity to influence policy – through research and practice of foreign policy respectively. There was, however, no such provision in the MEA, and such a practice was not encouraged.[38] This resonates with the international debate marking think tanks as a bridge between knowledge and policy that has been highlighted in the previous chapter. The ICWA, however, remains one of the key foreign policy think tanks in India, and its interactions with the policy process and its institutional relevance have evolved through the years – as is discussed in the following chapter.

The development of policy research institutes also received an impetus in the 1960s. The absence of Nehru, India's defeat by China and India's war with Pakistan in 1965, in addition to the intensification of cold war politics, created an interest in research on defence and strategic studies. In 1965, therefore, the Institute for Defence Studies and Analyses (IDSA) was set up by the MoD, headed by K. Subrahmanyam and his acknowledged expertise in strategic affairs. In addition, recognising the need for research expertise in other parts of the country, the Indian Council for Social Science Research (ICSSR) was established in 1969 to promote and develop regional institutions.[39]

The creation of the IDSA and institutions in other states, along with the development of an independent media, "offered a nucleus around which a strong and influential community of IR professionals might have been built."[40] In addition, the Indian elite were plugged into the IR community around the world, published in international journals and hosted research scholars from abroad.

Whether or not it influenced early India's external relations, literature has focused on the dynamism of India's intellectual discourse on world affairs during the 1950s and the 1960s.[41] The IDSA's influence on policy, particularly the high-profile leadership of Subrahmanyam, form a significant part of the scholarship on think tanks.[42] While the debate until then had focused on the dominating influence of the MEA and the Prime Ministerial leadership on foreign policy, the literature gradually began to take notice of these "policy experts." Yet, the role of the state remained central to the construction of foreign policy.

The next phase of think tank development, one that has been described as that of "second wave institutes," appeared in the 1980s with an increase in funding – both governmental and external – as India began to bring down the barriers to external funding.[43] Thus, the Centre for Policy Research (CPR) was established in 1973, the Indian Council for Research on International Economic Relations (ICRIER) in 1981 and the Research and Information Systems (RIS), the think tank set up by the MEA, in 1983. However, while new organisations continued to emerge, the domestic political discourse became more centralised under the leadership of Indira Gandhi and, according to Raja Mohan, "foreign policy began to acquire a monochromatic hue and there was a general disempowerment of the older centres of foreign policy discourse in the region."[44]

The development of India's nuclear weapons program, however, stands out as an exception to this disempowerment, and think tanks such as the IDSA and CPR and intellectuals – namely K. Subrahmanyam and Brahma Chellaney – were lauded for their "advocatory role."[45] They have been accredited for suggesting an alternative policy discourse, especially with regard to debates on disarmament versus development of weapons, rejecting the Comprehensive Nuclear-Test-Ban-Treaty and proposing testing. With little access to official information and communiques, however, the accounts on the nuclear debate tend to derive more from personal interpretations and reflections of those involved, thus making it difficult to ascertain concrete influence in policy making. It does, however, indicate the changing policy landscape in India, as ideas from private organisations outside of government began to be acknowledged and appreciated. Subrahmanyam is credited with making policy-relevant research a goal worth pursuing for many younger researchers. Also, in the absence of common knowledge on military and strategic affairs, Subrahmanyam's writings in the media contributed to the shaping of public discourse as well as "a tool to mobilize pressure on the politicians and bureaucrats deciding on foreign and national security affairs."[46]

With the economic liberalisation of India and the global shift in power, demands for expertise on a new foreign policy, articulating the interests of India's changing global and regional position emerged. New institutions included Bangalore's National Institute of Advanced Studies set up in 1988, the Centre for Contemporary Studies in 1990, the Observer Research Foundation (ORF) in 1990 and the Delhi Policy Group (DPG) in 1994. In addition, due to the increasing interest in South Asian neighbours and new possibilities for peace and cooperation, a number of think tanks focused on conflict and peace studies also developed. This was also a reflection of the changing nature of conflict globally and the development of new formulations on security policy along with a newfound focus on non-traditional aspects of security. Some of the noteworthy research institutions in this regard were the Institute of Peace and Conflict Studies (IPCS) established in 1996, the Institute of Conflict Management in 1997, the Centre for Dialogue and Reconciliation (CDR) in 2000 and Women in Security, Conflict Management and Peace (WISCOMP) in 1999. Not limited to the national capital, new think tanks were also instituted in other parts of India, including the Centre for Security Analysis (2002) and the Takshashila Institution (2009) in Chennai. Additionally, the armed forces also set up their own specialised think tanks, namely the Centre for Air Power Studies (CAPS) in 2001, the Centre for Land Warfare Studies (CLAWS) in 2004 and the National Maritime Foundation (NMF) in 2005.

To this growing landscape, a new crop of think tanks supported by political parties also emerged. Thus, while the Rajiv Gandhi Institute for Contemporary Studies was affiliated to the Congress Party, the Syama Prasad Mookerjee Research Foundation (SPMRF), Vivekananda International Foundation (VIF) and the India Foundation (IF) have emerged with visible support from the Bharatiya Janata Party (BJP). Further, new US-styled think tanks also now occupy the think tank landscape in India. The Gateway House: Indian Council on Global Relations was set up in 2009 inspired by the Council on Foreign Relations (CFR) in the US. The Brookings Institution and the Carnegie Endowment for International Peace – both well-known American think tanks – have also established branches in India. Recognising the growing strength of Indian think tanks, in January 2020, Indian think tanks featured in the list of top non-US think tanks in the *Global Go To Think Tank Index Report* published by the University of Pennsylvania. At rank 15 was the ORF, followed by the ICRIER at 51, the Centre for Civil Society at 71, the Energy and Resources Institute at 91, Brookings India at 100, Gateway House at 124, IDSA at 139, USI at 148, VIF at 149 and CLAWS at 157.[47]

The growth in the number of think tanks has been attributed to several factors. While the need to engage with new issues of foreign policy required an increase in knowledge and expertise – a service that this growing number of think tanks provided – liberalisation and the increased interest of international agencies in policy research have also made the institution of these civil society and advocacy groups possible.[48] Weaver and Stares suggest that this also reflected the changing nature of representative governments and the rise of coalition governments, which led to the fracturing of democratic processes and an increasing demand for alternative policy advice.[49] The cumulative effect of a class of leadership "non-dynastic" in nature, including Narasimha Rao, I.K. Gujral, Vajpayee, and Manmohan Singh, has also had an impact. Their tenures, it has been argued, moved India towards a more academic and structured approach to foreign policy.[50]

While leadership changed, the funding structure for think tanks also transformed. Many were still funded by the government, but others found sources of substantial foreign contributions, thereby reducing their dependence on government funding. Yet, the government also played an indirect enabling role here, by relaxing rules regarding international partnerships and the receipt of foreign contribution. It retained control on the regulation of foreign funding through the Foreign Contribution (Regulation) Act (1976, FCRA). The FCRA and its application has been known for its "arbitrariness of procedure."[51] Other ways in which the government exercises what is termed "despotic influence" is the donation of land or sale of land at concessional rates for the construction of think tank offices and income tax exemptions.[52] For instance, the offices of IDSA and the other three defence policy think tanks (CLAWS, CAPS and NMF) are located on land under the jurisdiction of the MoD. The use of the FCRA by governments, led by either the Congress party or the BJP, have played a role in both enabling foreign contributions and also significantly restricting the ability of civil society actors including think tanks from pursuing specific projects.

By control of funding, the influence of the government on the ideology and impact of think tanks is therefore debatable in India.[53] Also, while economic research has benefitted from foreign funding, the argument is that by their very nature, the Indian foreign and strategic policy establishments would be wary of externally funded study, and the avenue of external capital is thus not an easy option for international relations and strategic affairs institutions.[54] Further, while liberalisation and privatisation policies in the 1990s improved private donor involvement in think tanks, they also raised crucial concerns regarding independence of thought and objective analysis. Though they occupied the space freed by the state in supporting think tanks, the grants were often project-driven and the limited research agenda, it is argued, "obstructed the emergence of an independent and critical research agenda."[55] The sponsors' direction of research agendas was also a factor irrespective of whether they were public agencies, private foundations or international organisations.[56] Though foreign contributions can be controlled by government regulation, domestic private sector funding for research is also a new phenomenon in India. It is, however, pointed out that the "private sector is yet to make any serious long-term investment in developing think tanks and research institutions in the field."[57]

Theorising think tanks in India

The previous section has highlighted the emergence of think tanks into the foreign policy-making landscape, demonstrating that their development has followed crucial transitions in India's domestic and foreign policy directions. So far, the literature examining think tanks in India takes a statist and elitist position and seems to place think tanks as secondary actors in the policy process. Indian think tanks are represented as a part of the foreign policy machinery; however, focus has remained on formal institutions and their centrality to policy making. The literature lacks a detailed analysis of think tank actors' and their institutional as well as informal linkages with the policy-making elite in India.

Examining broader institutional positions and worldviews first, think tanks in India are found to focus on a variety of issues including social and political policy, issues of the environment such as environmental pollution and climate change, socio-economic development and political participation. Foreign policy think tanks in India have commissioned a broad range of research studies, examining India's geostrategic position, bilateral relations with its South Asian neighbours, international trade and development, and India's multi-lateral engagements. In addition, non-traditional security issues related to drug and human trafficking, terrorism and other human security issues are also now being increasingly researched.

In terms of membership, much like the MEA, while "first-hand" policy-making expertise is plentiful in India, such expertise is possessed almost exclusively by retired ambassadors and other post-career government officials. Indian think tanks are "characterised by a sharply bifurcated personnel structure that privileges senior staff and does not offer younger scholars a ready path for career advancement, through either government service or research."[58] Though many employ fresh graduates, the hierarchical structure is very similar to the Indian bureaucracy. Critics calling for capacity building within think tanks have also highlighted the elite privileged backgrounds of retired public and military officials and the lack of full-time research staff with strong applied theoretical and methodological skills in international studies.[59] There has also been a trend of prominent personalities with good official linkages that have helped to raise the profile of some of these think tanks. Intellectuals including K. Subrahmanyam (IDSA), Brahma Chellaney (CPR), Pratap Bhanu Mehta (CPR) and retired army officials including V.R. Raghavan (DPG and CSA), Jasjit Singh (IDSA and CAPS) and Dipankar Banerjee (IPCS) are just a few of the prominent names. In addition to their intellectual capability, these elite represent a privileged socio-political background and have held senior positions in their specific spheres of expertise.

Debates regarding membership, however, do not consider effectively the linkages that these knowledge elites build with policy elites – both in the MEA and in the PMO. The arguments continue to reflect the disconnect between policy making and research.[60] Yet, the way this elitist composition of think tanks benefits or challenges their institutional capacity to impact policy is not considered. The examination of think tank leadership and membership in detail to underscore the manifestation of the "knowledge/power nexus" between think tanks and policy elites is the endeavour of this volume. This is done through a critical examination of think tank involvement in the policy formulation process, especially on the discourse on Pakistan. For DI, two elements that highlight think tank influence are the coordinative and communicative discourse and the ability of think tanks to "transfer knowledge to discourse and act as carriers of coordinative and communicative discourse."[61] Think tanks can also "promote specific ideas, specific framing of policy issues and provide arguments for the debate by participating in advocacy coalitions."[62]

Previous sections of this chapter have highlighted that scholarship on Indian think tanks has considered them to have limited political power or authority, working primarily as experts offering second opinions or specialised knowledge. The highly bureaucratic and exclusive political culture in India has been blamed for limited avenues for think tank involvement. Policy-relevant ideas put forward by think tanks have also often been found to be too theoretical in their scope. As Sanjaya Baru maintains, "officials in government argue that the so-called experts are far too theoretical in their approach, unwilling to be realists and that area studies have very little ground level understanding of their areas."[63] From the perspective of think tanks though, K. Subrahmanyam argued that:

> in foreign and strategic affairs, bureaucrats continue to retain their relevance and power by withholding information to outside scholars and experts. Consequently, when a non-governmental analyst comes up with a viewpoint unacceptable to the government, the bureaucracy dismisses it merely on the grounds that the viewpoint is not grounded in reality.[64]

Still perceived of as an American conception, think tank influence is restricted by bureaucrats, who are reluctant to build viable networks with them.[65] However, while the literature has treated policy elites (such as bureaucrats) and knowledge elites at think tanks as mutually exclusive entities, this book explores their symbiotic relationship. It investigates if policy elites in the government use the resources of think tanks – their discourse and their ability to generate public opinion – to privilege a particular understanding of a foreign policy issue. Inversely, it examines adjustments made by think tanks to maintain their research relevance to suit government policy directions and balance their research autonomy by offering new policy ideas.

In recent years, the capacity of think tanks to offer policy-relevant research has begun to be recognised, and the government has invited the expertise of some of these organisations. For instance, as the designated Indian Track II coordinator for BRICS and a member of the BRICS Think Tanks Council, ORF has provided knowledge inputs and helped to strengthen research collaboration with the other nodal BRICS coordinating institutions in the member countries.[66] Similarly, in March 2013, CPR, in collaboration with the Brookings Institution and the China Institute of Contemporary International Relations, hosted a Track-II Trialogue among India, the USA and China in New Delhi. The conference was the third in a series of meetings that had been initiated in 2012. New developments in the region and the need for alternative research have also prompted several new initiatives. Thus, in May 2013, an ORF-commissioned project on the 'Future of Afghanistan Post-NATO Withdrawal and its Implications for India' presented its research to the MoD. Similarly, the DPG's

"Afghanistan–India–Pakistan trialogue" initiated in 2009 brought together policymakers, analysts and Track II representatives from Afghanistan, India and Pakistan, to review changes and progress in Afghanistan, India and Pakistan relations, and to see whether there were new opportunities for the three countries to work together trilaterally, or in parallel bilaterals, to spur stalled and/or obstacle-strewn peace processes among them.[67]

Working closely with government ministries on particular issues has broadened the scope of the "coordinative discourse" of Indian think tanks. These dialogue forums and focused research on new issues concerning Indian foreign policy have provided think tanks with an opportunity to interact with actors at the centre of policy construction. However, as has been highlighted in the previous chapter, in a polity like India, foreign policy formulation is controlled by top leadership and the foreign policy bureaucracy. The broader literature presented earlier has also indicated this trend. What opportunities then do think tanks in India have to act as foreign policy actors? Are Indian think tanks able to transform into "sentient agents" of Schmidt's understanding, "who articulate and communicate their ideas through discourse in exchanges that may involve discussion, deliberation, negotiation and contestation"?[68]

It is also important here to mention DI's emphasis on the potential of agents as having both "background ideational abilities" and "foreground discursive abilities." The concept of "foreground discursive abilities" refers to the importance of discourse and deliberative argumentation in breaking the elite monopoly on national and supranational decision making while ensuring democratic access to such decision making.[69] Only a very detailed analysis of the discourse developed by Indian think tanks would be able to provide evidence of their foreground and background ideational abilities, something that the current literature on think tanks does not tell us.

Another component for DI is the "communicative discourse perpetuated by individuals and groups involved in the presentation, deliberation and legitimation of political ideas to the general public (leaders, social activists, think tanks)."[70] The emphasis here is on the use of ideas for public persuasion through deliberations in policy forums of informed publics about the ongoing policy initiatives of governments.[71] As carriers of communicative discourse, think tank research on government policies, meetings and conferences completes the cycle – disseminating government policy to the wider public arena. Think tanks in India have been argued to have influence in shaping and gauging public opinion.[72] Also, while it is claimed that they serve a purpose in transactional issues, think tanks are involved in preparing the ground for public opinion for paradigmatic changes to policy.[73]

Yet, while a preliminary analysis might give evidence of the think tank role in both "coordinative" and "communicative" discourse in India, the particular linkages between think tank research and their policy impact is unclear. While informal linkages are evident, the institutional role of think tanks is uncertain owing to the structure of policy making in India. This is particularly relevant in the light of think tank financial dependence on the government and the inability to disassociate government discourse from alternative discourse from think tanks. While elitists argue for state control over the conduct on foreign policy, the constructivist understanding of "research communities" and "interpretive communities" are also not visible in India.

The DI approach used elsewhere has highlighted the creation of ideational networks and their transformative influence on policy. In South East Asia, for instance, Zimmerman has highlighted the agenda-setting and problem-framing role of think tanks in placing the NTS agenda onto the official policy frames.[74] In India, however, these institutional networks are not visible, and the aspect of influence on policy is even murkier. The relationship between think tanks and policymakers has been described as "informal" and "un-institutionalised."[75] While the MEA and MoD have been known to support a handful of think tanks and sometimes contract policy studies from think tanks, universities and individuals, this is done on an ad hoc basis rather than as part of a systematic programme.[76] In the Indian system, foreign and security policy remain the government's "domain" and funded primarily by the government, think tanks are perceived to be "an extension of government thinking."[77]

Yet, while policy impact is difficult to ascertain, think tanks in India are notable for their knowledge elites. A small strategic elite concentrated primarily in New Delhi dominates expertise on foreign and security policy.[78] Members of this elite have included experts such as K. Subrahmanyam, with his acknowledged role in producing a Draft Nuclear Doctrine (DND) and contributing crucially to the Kargil Review Committee (KRC). Others such as Shyam Saran (former Foreign Secretary) have been involved in the policy process through various institutional engagements, as a Research Fellow at CPR and as the Chairman of the RIS. Saran is also co-chairman of the India-ASEAN Eminent Person's group established to review the ASEAN-India dialogue and explore ways to widen and deepen existing cooperation towards a long-term strategic partnership between ASEAN and India.[79] Others at CPR, including until recently Pratap Bhanu Mehta and Srinath Raghavan, have also been involved with the NSAB that offered a key interface between policy makers and experts from beyond the bureaucratic set-up.[80] Key policy positions at the official level are now occupied by Ajit Doval (NSA) and until recently Arvind Gupta (Deputy NSA), both closely associated with think tanks.[81] The role of these knowledge elites within the think tank community has often come under critical scrutiny for providing a narrow and limited engagement.

Even though expertise on foreign policy exists in abundance in India, the arguments in favour of a disconnect between an 'ivory tower' academia and the 'real world' of public policy making persists. Think tanks in India also reflect some of the predicaments of the Indian bureaucratic structure such as understaffing, over-reliance on senior researchers and a high-profile leadership, the importance of personal linkages and issues related to the declining quality of research on international relations. If a brief comparison is undertaken between think tanks in India and their counterparts in China and South East Asia, though some aspects of informal and positional influence are similar, a crucial aspect found missing is that of "horizontal linkages" or "horizontal communications."[82]

With limited political authority and significant lack of access to official documents, the policy impact of Indian think tanks remains questionable. There is, however, a general recognition in India that the growing numbers of Indian think tanks strengthens India's strategic discourse and thus increases the quality and effectiveness of the policy-making process. The role of intellectual capital at Indian think tanks is also important. There have been some arguments about a possible division of labour, wherein

> while decision makers behave along an established pattern without necessarily realising that their behaviour conform to a certain pattern, it is researchers and academics who often uncover these patterns, or say, provide a certain big picture argument to their actions.[83]

In addition, it is argued that "at their best, they can play a big role in advising governments on sound policy, enabling increasingly important dialogue with a variety of stakeholders and interpreting obscure policy issues for the broader public."[84]

The aspect of state–think tank cooperation is expanded in later chapters through the examination of think tank linkages with the foreign policy establishment in India. This is done through an examination of the role of think tanks in perhaps one of the most recurrent and problematic issues of India's foreign policy – that is, its relations with Pakistan. Think tanks have devoted significant attention to the dynamics of the India–Pakistan conflict and have been active participants in the development of the peace process and India's Pakistan policy. In providing a neutral space for the articulation of ideas on contentious issues, including Kashmir and supporting the CD process initiated by the two governments, think tanks have engaged with the element of incrementalism within the process and were influential in the multi-track dialogue processes that were crucial for the sustainability of the peace process.

The India–Pakistan Composite Dialogue

While clearly a crucial concern for Indian foreign policy, relations with Pakistan also represent a significant area of interest for Indian think tanks. As mentioned earlier, the security dynamics in the 1960s and the India–Pakistan war in 1965 in particular, prompted an emphasis on research on security and strategic policy. The IDSA was also established in 1965 and continues to be a key forum for research and policy-relevant analysis on India's security concerns. India's Pakistan policy has prompted significant research both in official and unofficial circles and presents a good test case to examine the interaction between think tanks and policy. In this book I focus on a critical analysis of think tank discourse on

Pakistan as well as their role in mobilising public opinion in support of the Indian government's dialogue with Pakistan.

A comprehensive analysis of the nuanced nature of India–Pakistan relations is beyond the purview of this research project; however, a historical background is of necessity here. Since 1947, India's relations with Pakistan have been characterised by several disputes and differing consensus on some key issues, the two most often disputed elements being the struggle over Kashmir and the contested borders, complicated further by four wars fought in 1948, 1965, 1971 and most recently in 1999 in Kargil. Pakistan's support of extremist and separatist groups in Kashmir, which have allegedly carried out acts of terrorism in India and have strengthened the secessionist elements in Indian Kashmir, are a big concern for India. In addition, other problems – including the sharing of river waters, drug trafficking, territorial disputes in Sir Creek and Siachen, disagreements regarding the economic arrangements required for trade cooperation and above all a general perception of mistrust on both sides of the border owing to a troubled history – continue to be crucial.

While resolution of some operational issues such as the advance notification of military exercises, non-violation of each other's air spaces, a formal agreement on exchange of information regarding nuclear power research facilities and a commitment not to attack each other's nuclear installations and a hotline between the Indian and Pakistan Director General of Military Operations (DGMOs) were established in 1990, India's relations with Pakistan have remained largely troublesome. Nuclear tests by both India and Pakistan led to a further escalation of tensions, leading to the Kargil war in 1999 and a military stand-off on the borders in 2002.

By 2002, India–Pakistan tensions had "reached levels unseen since the early 1970s."[85] Yet, in 2004, a comprehensive peace process known as the Composite Dialogue (CD) was initiated, representing a significant change in India–Pakistan relations. In the past, Pakistan had been unwilling to engage in discussions with India unless a resolution to the Kashmir dispute was prioritised, while India had insisted on an end to cross-border attacks by Pakistan-based militant groups before peace talks could be considered. For India, the CD meant a change in its negotiating style with Pakistan, a new approach to regional relations and opportunities for non-state actors, including think tanks, to engage with policy development. Specifically, the multi-stakeholder approach of the CD process strengthened think tank capacity to engage with critical aspects of policy discourse on India's relations with Pakistan.

The impetus for a structured dialogue process with Pakistan emerged from India's broader policy directions during this period that espoused regional cooperation within South Asia. To further regional cooperation, India's then-Minister for External Affairs, I.K. Gujral, mooted a 'Gujral Doctrine' in a speech at Chatham House in 1992 that espoused generosity and the principle of non-reciprocity towards India's smaller South Asian neighbours. When political churning unexpectedly led to Gujral becoming Prime Minister, he was given an opportunity to enact his doctrine. Pakistan was offered dialogue and unilateral goodwill and, in 1997, together with the Pakistani Prime Minister, Nawaz Sharif, Gujral announced that India would seek to resolve neighbourhood conflicts without insisting on reciprocity.[86] This represented an emerging political consensus on the benefits of regional economic trade and cooperation to both India's economy and global standing, crucial to which was peace in South Asia.[87] The outreach towards Pakistan was subsequently adopted by the NDA government led by Vajpayee, reflected in the Lahore Declaration signed in 1999 and the invitation to Pakistan's President Musharraf for the Agra Summit in 2001. While the Kargil war in 1999 and the ensuing border stand-off in 2002 were setbacks, the desire for dialogue with Pakistan was reflected in Indian policy in the following years. Vajpayee's encouragement to the process was motivated by the desire to craft a policy of strategic restraint that was "uncompromising on Indian security interests" while seeking "conciliation and lasting peace" with Pakistan.[88]

The Composite Dialogue formalised in 2004 was the longest sustained and institutionalised effort at peace between India and Pakistan and continued until 2013 with some periods of disruption. The CD framework comprised discussions on the following issues:

1. Peace and security
2. Jammu and Kashmir
3. Sir Creek
4. Siachen
5. Terrorism
6. Drug trafficking
7. Wullar Barrage/Tulbul navigation project
8. Promotion of friendly exchanges in various fields

The dialogue was structured on an incremental approach – a "two plus six formula."[89] With working groups constituted for each of the issues, the Kashmir issue and peace and security were to be handled at the level of foreign secretaries, while the rest of the six issues would be handled by other relevant secretaries and technical committees. The CD represented a significant step towards normalisation of India–Pakistan relations, and it was argued that it "provided the framework within which it became possible for the first time to talk about a 'peace process' between India and Pakistan."[90] The CD also highlighted the different levels at which the peace process operated. Underlining the importance of political will, Gopinath writes:

> the political leadership in this instance was ahead of their security and foreign policy establishments to grapple with the "trust deficit" between the two countries, stake their reputations, and take on the ire of the recalcitrant domestic communities and critics to invest in peace.[91]

Even though the Vajpayee government unexpectedly lost power in 2004, the CD process was retained by the new UPA government led by the Congress under the leadership of Manmohan Singh. The Congress was elected on a platform of 'inclusive growth' and placed significant emphasis on the creation of "a South Asia free of violence, poverty, disease and ignorance, in which there is a free movement of ideas, people, goods and services."[92] Thus, the broader goals of the CD that were to lead to a conducive atmosphere that encouraged regional economic development were central to the UPA's policy.

The change in policy towards Pakistan generated both official and unofficial interest, and while governments and bureaucracies dealt with the process at an official level, research institutions and think tanks also took a keen interest. Most foreign and security policy think tanks in India have had an active research and advocacy component centred on policy towards Pakistan. The initiation of the formal dialogue created further interest in the research community, and in addition to providing research insights, allowed think tanks to interface with the formal processes from time to time, provide advisory policy ideas and become active participants in the multi-track initiatives.

The period when the CD was most active created new spaces for out-of-the-box thinking on India–Pakistan relations, creating an atmosphere that was conducive for new think tanks and research organisations to emerge, concurrent with greater availability of foreign funding. The process itself, from the perception of the Indian government, took note of the multiple stakeholders in the conflict and displayed an orientation to work with different levels of state and civil society. The dialogue structure represented a considerably new approach. In 2005, Manmohan Singh requested a meeting with prominent journalists, academics and think tank members with expertise on Kashmir to, as his media advisor Sanjaya Baru put it, "break the mold and seek an 'out-of-box' solution to a problem to which the governmental system was unable to find a solution."[93] Unlike previous attempts at dialogue that faltered owing to the dynamics of the specific dispute in Kashmir, the CD placed Kashmir at the centre of the dialogue. By doing so and by building a new strategic relationship with Pakistan based on trading and people-to-people interaction, it was hoped that a security spill-over could be created, making negotiations on other long-standing disputes easier.[94] The dialogue therefore included significant confidence-building measures (CBMs) to bolster formal negotiations and seek reconciliation through an active engagement with civil society.

Other noteworthy initiatives as part of the dialogue included a first-of-its-kind roundtable with prominent Kashmiris in academia, political parties and separatist groups at the Prime Minister's residence in 2006. Following the roundtable, five working groups were established to depoliticise the conflict in Kashmir and attempt reconciliation. The working groups were: Strengthening relations across the LoC; Center-State Relations; Good Governance; Infrastructure and Economic Development; and CBMs within Jammu and Kashmir, including for widows and orphans of violence, return of displaced persons and return of people who crossed over during the insurgency. Think tank intellectuals also engaged with these working groups and their specific debates. In addition to a more general focus on strengthening economic cooperation with Pakistan, Singh also convened an Economic Advisory Council for the development of Jammu and Kashmir (J&K) which involved business leaders, Kashmiri economists and the heads of public sector enterprises. A back-channel was established to prepare for public summits and a framework agreement between the Indian and Pakistani leaderships. The initiatives that were given priority included the opening of cross-border trade and travel, a strengthening of self-government and the creation of cooperative governance institutions.[95] The focus on economic cooperation led to establishment of the India–Pakistan Joint Study Group, in February 2005, and the Jammu and Kashmir Joint Chamber of Commerce and Industry, in 2008. The latter is a non-governmental organisation that brings together traders from both sides of the Line of Control (LoC), the de facto border demarcation between the India- and Pakistan-administered parts of Kashmir.[96]

The dialogue on Kashmir also introduced some new policy ideas put forth by Manmohan Singh and Pervez Musharraf that found further voice through think tank engagement. In enabling travel and trade through Kashmir, the Manmohan Singh government also proposed setting up "cooperative and consultative mechanisms between the two Kashmirs in order to improve the human condition in both parts of the Kashmir."[97] Musharraf's four-point proposal also acknowledged the centrality of the J&K dispute to Indo-Pak relations and called for official talks to commence based on the best solution acceptable to all parties and the rejection of any solution that is not acceptable to the Kashmiris.[98]

As representatives of civil society, the dialogue provided Indian think tanks an opportunity to engage with the policy debates and possibilities for resolution of the conflict with Pakistan. Think tank interpretations of India's relationship with Pakistan during this period were reflected in their adopted agendas and institutional positions, their specific peacebuilding-related research projects and in their research outputs – publications, policy recommendations and particular policy briefs to the MEA and MoD. In addition to developing discourse, think tanks also conducted feasibility studies of key governmental initiatives adopted within the CD.[99] Intellectual elites through the platform provided to them by think tanks were also involved in multi-track processes initiated between the two countries during the CD.

It was argued earlier that think tanks that developed in the 1960s and 1970s focused on India's strategic narrative, its defence preparedness and the challenges of a turbulent neighbourhood.[100] The CD, however, created the space for think tanks with peacebuilding as their focus to emerge. This was reflected in the establishment of the IPCS, the DPG and the Centre for Dialogue and Reconciliation (CDR). Their research agendas displayed a focus on subjects with specific bearing on Indo-Pak relations, including the dispute in Kashmir, trade relations between India and Pakistan, the examination of causes of militancy and extremism and options for counter-terrorism, and strategic military relations with a very specifically defined focus on nuclear security issues.[101] The dialogue process also echoed a focus on people's security, strengthening people-to-people contact and working specifically to address the trust deficit between the people of India and Pakistan. Therefore, many of these think tanks ran programmes on youth exchanges, interactive workshop formats for civil society participants and small peacebuilding training modules.

The CBMs instituted as part of the CD succeeded in building trust and addressing some of the emotional and psychological baggage of the conflict, especially for divided families in Kashmir. The period between 2004 and 2007 saw significant people-to-people exchanges. From 30 visas being processed in June 2003, it is reported that the Indian missions in Pakistan processed over 30,000 visas; by early 2007, an average of 12,000 visas had been issued for Pakistani visits to India in that year.[102] This positive atmosphere also enabled think tanks to establish cross-border networks, which were crucial for deepening economic links. The liberalised visa regime enabled think tanks to reach out to social groups beyond the border, adding to their institutional relevance as well. The forum provided by think tank events enabled what came to be known as Track III interactions among scholars, media persons, artists, women and other civil society networks in India and Pakistan.[103] Together they reflected an increased tolerance for alternative approaches on Kashmir that went beyond national security concerns. As a result of trade-related CBMs, official trade between India and Pakistan increased from US$300 million in 2003–2004 to US$2.1 billion in 2008–2009.[104]

The relevance and position of think tanks within the policy process and their ability to assume importance during "critical junctures" is an important aspect here. Critical junctures, as described in the previous chapter, "refer to particular historical moments that have lasting consequences and can provoke changes in policy."[105] The positive atmosphere of the CD can thus be perceived as a "critical juncture," wherein avenues for policy change in India's relations with Pakistan were available and active civil society engagement was encouraged. Further, on the relevance of think tanks as actors in the formulation of India's Pakistan policy, this book critically examines the way in which think tanks – both governmental and non-governmental – expanded on the agenda of India's Pakistan policy independent of their funding concerns. Did they seek to set the agenda by introducing new interpretations of the India–Pakistan conflict or did they reproduce the government's assumptions and strategies? While Zimmerman and others have highlighted think tank potential in responding to emerging policy challenges and giving them the opportunity to supply the conceptual language and paradigms for emerging security problems facing Asia, this book argues differently.[106] In India, as the evidence presented shows, particularly with respect to India–Pakistan relations, paradigms were established by the state and were subsequently adopted, refined and articulated by think tank research and analysis. This was despite the new avenues made available by the CD process and reflected in the Indian state's continued influence on policy directions.

The aspect of think tank relevance and capacity to work within structural constraints visible in India's policy-making apparatus has also involved the specific position and significance of intellectual elites within think tanks. While DI provides key tools to analyse discursive processes to problematise the relationship between the state and independent agents such as think tanks, Gramsci's emphasis on the "organic intellectuals" – where specific sets of ideas are funded, generated and disseminated by foundations, think tanks, publishing houses and NGOs – is of particular relevance to this research project. In examining the relationship between civil society and political society, the Gramscian perspective offers an explanation for the role that intellectuals can play through "active political strategies" to forge historic blocs.[107] In this constant negotiation between civil society and the state, the "organic intellectuals" and their social backgrounds and institutional positions in the formal foreign policy establishment are important. For Gramsci, the role of organic intellectuals "in directing the ideas and aspirations of the class to which they organically belong" is crucial.[108] Parmar argues that a strong state is required to mobilise organic intellectuals and to legitimise its own foreign policy reform programmes. Thus, the discourse generated by intellectuals owing to their class positions and their relationship with state managers becomes important. At think tanks, these intellectuals are the "knowledge elites" who, owing to their cooperative engagement with the state and their ability to shape policy ideas, identified intricately with and subsequently promoted the interests of the state.

Conclusion

To summarise, the literature on Indian think tanks so far has examined their bridging role in providing policy analysis, and while think tanks have been identified within the policy space, their discourse is seen to be lacking in applicability to policy. Indian think tanks are seen as secondary actors and the state-centric foreign policy-making structure has been emphasised. What has also come to light is the unique role of the intellectual elite in India – represented both in their proximity to formal government structures as well as their role in articulating think tank policy positions. This aspect of state-elite collaboration provides a better understanding of think tanks' place in policy structures while also accounting for their structural challenges. The emphasis on examining discourse on India's Pakistan policy will provide further clues into this collaborative and symbiotic relationship.

This chapter has highlighted the trajectory of the foreign policy planning process in India and the engagement with civil society and grassroots actors. In elaborating on the structure of policy making, it has taken into account the origins and development of think tanks in India and their changing relevance and position. Furthermore, the chapter has discussed India's policy discourse towards Pakistan, focusing particularly on the structured dialogue process initiated by the CD in 2004. The emphasis has been on the period of the CD as a 'critical juncture' that enabled an expansion of the space for think tanks in India, particularly those dealing with foreign and security policy. From the general, the discussion on Indian think tanks will now move into the particular. The following chapters provide a comparative analysis of the different categories of Indian think tanks demarcated on the basis of affiliation and support from the Indian government. The analysis entails a comparison of membership, leadership and worldviews in addition to differences in the focus of policy ideas and the specific role in generating public opinion on key policy changes. Through the use of the DI-Gramscian framework, discursive processes – both coordinate and communicative – are highlighted, underscoring the role of the intellectual elite within Indian think tanks.

Notes

1 Vivien A. Schmidt, "Discursive Institutionalism: The Explanatory Power of Ideas and Discourse", *Annual Review of Political Science*, 11, 2008, p. 309.
2 Some notable works on Indian foreign policy include Harsh V. Pant, "A Rising India's Search for a Foreign Policy", *Orbis*, 53:2, 2009a, pp. 250–254; Sumit Ganguly and Manjeet Pardesi, "Sixty Years of India's Foreign Policy", *India Review*, 8:1, 2009, pp. 4–19; C. Raja Mohan, *Crossing the Rubicon: The Shaping of India's New Foreign Policy* (New Delhi: Penguin Viking, 2003); Amrita Narlikar, "Peculiar Chauvinism or Strategic Calculation? Explaining the Negotiating Strategy of a Rising India", *International Affairs*, 82:1, 2006, pp. 59–76; George Tanham, *Indian Strategic Thought: An Interpretive Essay* (Santa Monica, CA: Rand Corporation, 1992).
3 J. Bandyopadhyaya, *The Making of India's Foreign Policy: Determinants, Institutions, Processes, and Personalities* (Bombay: Allied Publishers, 1970); Kanti Bajpai and Byron Chong, "India's Foreign Policy Capacity", *Policy Design and Practice*, 2019, DOI: 10.1080/25741292.2019.1615164
4 C. Raja Mohan, *Crossing the Rubicon: The Shaping of India's New Foreign Policy* (New Delhi: Penguin Viking, 2003); Sumit Ganguly (ed.), *India's Foreign Policy: Retrospect and Prospect* (New Delhi: Oxford University Press, 2010); Rajiv Sikri, *Challenge and Strategy: Rethinking India's Foreign Policy* (New Delhi: Sage Publications, 2009); C. Raja Mohan and Ajai Sahni, *India's Security Challenges at Home and Abroad* (Washington: The National Bureau of Asian Research, 2012); David M. Malone, *Does the Elephant Dance? Contemporary Indian Foreign Policy* (Oxford: Oxford University Press, 2011).
5 Taking an alternative view and providing a broader understanding of Indian foreign policy moving away from the constricting binary approach are Pratap Bhanu Mehta, "Still under Nehru's Shadow? The Absence of Foreign Policy Frameworks in India", *India Review*, 8:3, July–September 2009, pp. 209–233; Priya Chacko, *Indian Foreign Policy: The Politics of Postcolonial Identity* (London: Routledge, 2012); Radha Kumar, "India as a Foreign Policy Actor: Normative Redux", *CEPS Working Document*, 285, February 2008; Amitabh Mattoo and Happymon Jacob (eds.), *India and the Contemporary International System* (New Delhi: Manohar Press, 2014); Happymon Jacob, *Does India Think Strategically?* (New Delhi: Manohar Press, 2014); Shivshankar Menon, *Choices: Inside the Making of India's Foreign Policy* (New Delhi: Penguin Random House India, 2016).
6 Parmar identifies with Godfrey Hodgson's definition of an American foreign policy establishment as a "history, a policy, an aspiration, an instinct, and a technique." To this Parmar adds the aspect of "social background." For more see: Inderjeet Parmar, *Think Tanks and Power in Foreign Policy* (New York: Palgrave MacMillan, 2004), p. 5.
7 Harsh V. Pant, "A Rising India's Search for a Foreign Policy", *Orbis*, 53:2, 2009a, p. 251.
8 K. P. Saksena, "India's Foreign Policy: The Decisionmaking Process", *International Studies*, 33:4, 1996, pp. 391–405; Vipin Narang and Paul Staniland, "Institutions and Worldviews in Indian Foreign Security Policy", *India Review*, 11:2, 2012, 76–94;

Manjari Chatterjee Miller, "India's Feeble Foreign Policy", *Foreign Affairs*, May/June 2013, pp. 14–19.
9 Shashi Tharoor, "Our Diplomatic Deficit", *Indian Express*, August 24, 2012, http://archive.indianexpress.com/news/our-diplomatic-deficit/992257/; Kanti Bajpai and Byron Chong, "India's Foreign Policy Capacity", *Policy Design and Practice*, 2019, DOI: 10.1080/25741292.2019.1615164
10 D. Shyam Babu, "India's National Security Council: Stuck in the Cradle?", *Security Dialogue*, 34:2, 2003, p. 219.
11 Vipin Narang and Paul Staniland, "Institutions and Worldviews in Indian Foreign Security Policy", *India Review*, 11:2, 2012, p. 78.
12 Manjari Chatterjee Miller, "India's Feeble Foreign Policy", *Foreign Affairs*, May/June 2013, p. 16.
13 Vipin Narang and Paul Staniland, "Institutions and Worldviews in Indian Foreign Security Policy", *India Review*, 11:2, 2012, p. 78.
14 Varghese K. George, "Domestic Politics of India's Foreign Policy Decision-Making", in Amitabh Mattoo and Happymon Jacob (eds.) *India and the Contemporary International System* (New Delhi: Manohar Press, 2014), pp. 125–156; Teresita C. Schaffer and Howard Schaffer, "When India's Foreign Policy Is Domestic", *The Brookings Institution*, April 2, 2013, www.brookings.edu/blog/up-front/2013/04/02/when-indias-foreign-policy-is-domestic/; Sukhwant S. Bindra, "Domestic Milieu of India and Foreign Policy Making Process: A Theoretical Perspective", *The Indian Journal of Political Science*, 65:2, April–June 2004, pp. 245–258.
15 Srinath Raghavan, "Civil-Military Relations in India: The China Crisis and After", *Journal of Strategic Studies*, 32:1, 2009, pp. 149–175; Apurba Kundu, *Militarism in India: The Army and Civil Society in Consensus* (London: I.B. Tauris, 1998), pp. 100–121; Harsh Pant, "India's Nuclear Doctrine and Command Structure: Implications for Civil-Military Relations in India", *Armed Forces & Society*, 33:2, January 2007, pp. 238–264.
16 Daniel Markey, "Developing India's Foreign Policy 'Software'", *Asia Policy*, 8, July 2009, pp. 73–96.
17 Manjari Chatterjee Miller, "India's Feeble Foreign Policy", *Foreign Affairs*, May/June 2013, p. 16.
18 C. Raja Mohan, "The Re-Making of Indian Foreign Policy: Ending the Marginalization of the International Relations Community", *International Studies*, 46:1 & 2, 2009, p. 157.
19 Shashi Tharoor, *Pax Indica: India and the World of the 21st Century* (New Delhi: Penguin, 2012).
20 In 2015, a high-level government committee was set up to review the Official Secrets Act (1923) in light of the now operational Right to Information (RTI) Act. Jatin Gandhi, "Govt. Forms Panel to Review Official Secrets Act", *The Hindu*, April 15, 2015, www.thehindu.com/news/national/govt-forms-panel-to-review-official-secrets-act/article7105495.ece
21 Several retired officials have recently released their memoirs, providing insights into foreign policy decisions taken during their years of service. Some examples include: A. S. Dulat, *Kashmir: The Vajpayee Years* (Noida: HarperCollins, 2015) – Dulat is the former chief of India's Research and Analysis Wing (RAW); Shyam Saran, *How India Sees the World: From Kautilya to the 21st Century* (New Delhi: Juggernaut, 2017); Maharaja Krishan Rasgotra, *A Life in Diplomacy* (New Delhi: Penguin, 2016) – both Saran and Rasgotra are former Foreign Secretaries.
22 C. Raja Mohan, "The Re-Making of Indian Foreign Policy: Ending the Marginalization of the International Relations Community", *International Studies*, 46:1 & 2, 2009, pp. 147–163.
23 The comparatively smaller size of the IFS as compared to the diplomatic corps of other countries like China and the US, with fewer than 900 diplomats, has led to calls for expansion.

24 The role of the NSAB has undergone a change under the Modi administration since 2014. A new board was reconstituted in October 2016 after a gap of two years. "NSAB Reconstituted with Ex-Envoy P S Raghavan as Head", *Indian Express*, October 9, 2016, http://indianexpress.com/article/india/india-news-india/nsab-national-security-advisory-board-p-s-raghavan-3073906/
25 Priya Chacko, "The Right Turn in India: Authoritarianism, Populism and Neoliberalisation", *Journal of Contemporary Asia*, 48:4, 2018, pp. 541–565.
26 Prakash Nanda, "Indian Foreign Policy under Modi", *Fearless Nadia Occasional Papers* (Australia-India Institute), 3, Winter 2014, p. 8.
27 Several analytical reports on the Modi government's foreign policy have indicated this trend. For more, see Suhasini Haidar, "South Block in the Shade", *The Hindu*, May 13, 2016, www.thehindu.com/opinion/op-ed/south-block-in-the-shade/article8591271.ece; Sumit Ganguly, "Has Modi Truly Changed India's Foreign Policy?", *The Washington Quarterly*, 40:2, 2017, pp. 131–143; Natalie Obiko Pearson, "India's 007, Former Super Spy, Is Shaping Modi's Foreign Policy", *Bloomberg*, September 19, 2016, www.bloomberg.com/news/articles/2016-09-18/india-s-007-former-super-spy-is-shaping-modi-s-foreign-policy; Praveen Donthi, "Undercover: Ajit Doval in Theory and Practice", *The Caravan*, September 1, 2017, www.caravanmagazine.in/reportage/ajit-doval-theory-practice
28 Daniel Markey, "Developing India's Foreign Policy 'Software'", *Asia Policy*, 8, July 2009, pp. 73–96.
29 Amitabh Mattoo, "A New Foreign Policy Agenda", *The Hindu*, April 8, 2014, www.thehindu.com/opinion/lead/a-new-foreign-policy-agenda/article5883940.ece
30 Muthiah Alagappa, "Galvanising International Studies", *Pragati: The Indian National Interest Review*, 30, September 2009, pp. 11–16.
31 ibid.
32 Kuldeep Mathur, *Public Policy and Politics in India: How Institutions Matter* (New Delhi: Oxford University Press, 2013), p. 9.
33 Thomas Medvetz, *Think Tanks in America* (Chicago: University of Chicago Press, 2012), p. 8.
34 According to Mathur, the Planning Commission recognised in its First Five Year Plan that there is "the need to strengthen capabilities of institutions outside the government in the field of economics in order to provide independent sources of economic data and evaluation of policies." The development of economic planning institutions was visible in the legacy of institution building in the decade of 1956–1965 and the establishment of many institutions including the National Council of Applied Economic Research in 1956, Institute of Economic Growth in 1958 and the Centre for the Study of Developing Societies in 1962. For this and other research on economic think tanks in India, see Sanjaya Baru, "Can Indian Think Tanks and Research Institutes Cope with the Rising Demand for Foreign and Security Policy Research", *ISAS Working Paper* (National University of Singapore), 67, June 16, 2009; Kuldeep Mathur, *Public Policy and Politics in India: How Institutions Matter* (New Delhi: Oxford University Press, 2013).
35 Rajiv Sikri, *Challenge and Strategy: Rethinking India's Foreign Policy* (New Delhi: Sage Publications, 2009), p. 260.
36 Jayati Srivastava, *Think Tanks in South Asia: Analysing the Knowledge-Power Interface* (London: Overseas Development Institute, December 2011), p. 12.
37 Headed by Nehru, the conference brought together leaders of the other independence movements in Asia and represented the first attempt to assert Asian unity. With its focus on five major themes concerning Asia (i.e. national freedom movements, racial and migration related issues, socio-economic development, culture, and women's issues), it established the Asian Relations Organisation as a permanent secretariat in New Delhi. The goals of Asian unity, however, could not move forward owing to cold war dynamics, placing newly independent Asian nations in contesting alliances. For more, see Sankalp Gurjar, "Time to Resurrect the Asian Relations

Conference", *The Diplomat*, April 18, 2017, https://thediplomat.com/2017/04/time-to-resurrect-the-asian-relations-conference/
38 A. Appadorai, "International and Area Studies in India", *International Studies (JNU)*, 24:2, 1987, p. 142.
39 Through its grant-in-aid, ICSSR has supported 27 think tanks across India. These are located in only 12 states and two union territories (of 28/7). Jayati Srivastava, *Think Tanks in South Asia: Analysing the Knowledge-Power Interface* (London: Overseas Development Institute, December 2011), p. 14.
40 C. Raja Mohan, "The Re-Making of Indian Foreign Policy: Ending the Marginalization of the International Relations Community", *International Studies*, 46:1 & 2, 2009, pp. 147–163.
41 ibid.
42 Muthiah Alagappa, "Galvanising International Studies", *Pragati: The Indian National Interest Review*, 30, September 2009, pp. 11–16; Sanjaya Baru, "Can Indian Think Tanks and Research Institutes Cope with the Rising Demand for Foreign and Security Policy Research", *ISAS Working Paper* (National University of Singapore), 67, June 16, 2009.
43 Contributing to this growth of "second wave institutes" was the "availability of a generation of Indians who had been involved in policy making by post-independence governments." Kuldeep Mathur, *Public Policy and Politics in India: How Institutions Matter* (New Delhi: Oxford University Press, 2013), p. 86.
44 C. Raja Mohan, "The Re-Making of Indian Foreign Policy: Ending the Marginalization of the International Relations Community", *International Studies*, 46:1 & 2, 2009, p. 152.
45 Constantino Xavier and Stephen Cohen, "The Career and Ideas of K. Subrahmanyam", *Event Summary Brookings Institution*, February 2011, www.brookings.edu/events/2011/02/18-india-subrahmanyam, accessed on March 5, 2015.
46 C. Raja Mohan, "The Re-Making of Indian Foreign Policy: Ending the Marginalization of the International Relations Community", *International Studies*, 46:1 & 2, 2009, pp. 147–163.
47 James G. McGann, "2019 Global Go to Think Tank Index Report", *TTCSP Global Go to Think Tank Index Reports*, 17, 2020, https://repository.upenn.edu/think_tanks/17
48 Kuldeep Mathur, "Policy Research Organizations in South Asia", *Working Paper Series: Centre for the Study of Law and Governance* (New Delhi: CSLG, April 2009).
49 Kent R. Weaver and Paul B. Stares (eds.), *Guidance for Governance Comparing Alternative Sources of Public Policy Advice* (Tokyo: Japan Centre for International Exchange, 2001).
50 Suhasini Haider, "Foreign Policy Making in India: An Institutional Perspective", in Amitabh Mattoo and Happymon Jacob (eds.) *India and the Contemporary International System* (New Delhi: Manohar Press, 2014), p. 102.
51 Jayati Srivastava, *Think Tanks in South Asia: Analysing the Knowledge-Power Interface* (London: Overseas Development Institute, December 2011), p. 19.
52 ibid.
53 For instance, think tanks like the IDSA are funded primarily by the MoD, thereby raising questions about the independent nature of its research programs. In addition, new names including the VIF face allegations regarding their allegiance to Hindu nationalist groups like the Rashtriya Swayamsewak Sangh (RSS) known to be a key ally of the current government at the centre. It is due to VIF's affiliation with the Vivekananda Kendra set up by RSS ideologue Eknath Ranade that leads to claims of proximity to the BJP-RSS agenda. For more, see "From Vivekananda to PMO Stars: Meet Modi's Favourite Think Tank", *Firstpost*, June 17, 2014, www.firstpost.com/politics/from-vivekananda-to-pmo-stars-meet-modis-favourite-think-tank-1574369.html;LolaNayar, "Those Hard Thinking Caps Realigned", *Outlook*, June 9, 2014, www.outlookindia.com/magazine/story/those-hard-thinking-caps-realigned/290876

54 Sanjaya Baru, "Can Indian Think Tanks and Research Institutes Cope with the Rising Demand for Foreign and Security Policy Research", *ISAS Working Paper* (National University of Singapore), 67, June 16, 2009.
55 T. S. Papola, "Social Science Research in Globalising India: Historical Development and Recent Trends", *ISID Working Paper* (Institute for Studies in Industrial Development, Delhi), May 2010, p. 9.
56 ibid.
57 ibid.
58 Daniel Markey, "Developing India's Foreign Policy 'Software'", *Asia Policy*, 8, July 2009, pp. 73–96.
59 Sanjaya Baru, "Can Indian Think Tanks and Research Institutes Cope with the Rising Demand for Foreign and Security Policy Research", *ISAS Working Paper* (National University of Singapore), 67, June 16, 2009, p. 7.
60 ibid.
61 Stella Ladi, "Think Tanks, Discursive Institutionalism and Policy Change", in Georgios Papanagnou (ed.) *Social Science and Policy Challenges: Democracy, Values and Capacities* (Paris: UNESCO, 2011), p. 212.
62 ibid.
63 Sanjaya Baru, "Can Indian Think Tanks and Research Institutes Cope with the Rising Demand for Foreign and Security Policy Research", *ISAS Working Paper* (National University of Singapore), 67, p. 8.
64 ibid.
65 Personal communication with senior academic at WISCOMP in New Delhi on September 7, 2015.
66 ORF also hosted the BRICS Academic Forums in 2009 and 2012 and helped in the drafting of a Long-Term Vision for BRICS along with several relevant research publications. It coordinates with the other Track II partners to inform the wider research community and key stakeholders on the relevance, significance and expected output from BRICS. For more, see *The ORF BRICS Compilation* (New Delhi: Observer Research Foundation, 2013), www.orfonline.org
67 www.delhipolicygroup.com
68 Vivien A. Schmidt, "Discursive Institutionalism: Scope, Dynamics and Philosophical Underpinnings", in Frank Fischer and Herbert Gottweis (eds.) *The Argumentative Turn Revisited: Public Policy as Communicative Practice* (Durham and London: Duke University Press, 2012), p. 91.
69 Vivien A. Schmidt, "Discursive Institutionalism: The Explanatory Power of Ideas and Discourse", *Annual Review of Political Science*, 11, 2008, p. 315.
70 Vivien A. Schmidt, "Discursive Institutionalism: Scope, Dynamics and Philosophical Underpinnings", in Frank Fischer and Herbert Gottweis (eds.) *The Argumentative Turn Revisited: Public Policy as Communicative Practice* (Durham and London: Duke University Press, 2012), p. 86.
71 ibid., p. 56.
72 Personal communication with senior researcher and former Diplomat at VIF in New Delhi on October 14, 2015.
73 Personal communication with senior researcher at VIF, New Delhi on October 5, 2015.
74 Erin Zimmerman, *Think Tanks and Non-Traditional Security: Governance Entrepreneurs in Asia* (Basingstoke: Palgrave MacMillan, 2016).
75 Personal communication with senior member and a former bureaucrat at Research and Information Systems (RIS) in New Delhi on September 4, 2015.
76 Rajiv Sikri, *Challenge and Strategy: Rethinking India's Foreign Policy* (New Delhi: Sage Publications, 2009), p. 275.
77 Personal communication with senior researchers at ORF and IPCS, New Delhi in September 2015.

78 Vipin Narang and Paul Staniland, "Institutions and Worldviews in Indian Foreign Security Policy", *India Review*, 11:2, 2012, pp. 76–94, 80.
79 *ASEAN-India Eminent Persons' Report to the Leaders* (Indonesia: ASEAN Secretariat, 2012).
80 The NDA government led by PM Narendra Modi has significantly reduced the NSAB. A new board was reconstituted in October 2016 after a gap of two years. "NSAB Reconstituted with Ex-Envoy P S Raghavan as Head", *Indian Express*, October 9, 2016, http://indianexpress.com/article/india/india-news-india/nsab-national-security-advisory-board-p-s-raghavan-3073906/
81 Arvind Gupta is currently Director of Vivekananda International Foundation (VIF).
82 David Shambaugh, "China's International Relations Think Tanks: Evolving Structure and Process", *The China Quarterly*, 171, September 2002, p. 580; Bonnie S. Glaser and Phillip C. Saunders, "Chinese Civilian Foreign Policy Research Institutes: Evolving Roles and Increasing Influence", *The China Quarterly*, 171, September 2002, p. 600.
83 Happymon Jacob, *Does India Think Strategically?* (New Delhi: Manohar Press, 2014), p. 14.
84 Dhruv Jaishankar, "Can India's Think Tanks Be Truly Effective?", *The Huffington Post India*, April 15, 2016, www.huffingtonpost.in/dhruva-jaishankar/can-indias-think-tanks-be_b_9688434.html
85 Paul S. Kapur, "Ten Year of Instability in a Nuclear South Asia", *International Security*, 33:2, 2008, pp. 71–94, DOI: 10.1162/isec.2008.33.2.71
86 Priya Chacko, *Indian Foreign Policy: The Politics of Postcolonial Identity from 1947 to 2004* (London and New York: Routledge, 2012), p. 163.
87 C. Raja Mohan, *Crossing the Rubicon: The Shaping of India's New Foreign Policy* (New Delhi: Penguin Viking, 2003).
88 Shekhar Gupta, "Modi Is Wise to Return to Vajpayee's Pakistan Policy", *Indian Defense News*, December 9, 2015, www.indiandefensenews.in/2015/12/modi-is-wise-to-return-to-vajpayees.html, accessed August 2017.
89 Sumona DasGupta, "Kashmir and the India-Pakistan Composite Dialogue Process", *RSIS Working Paper*, 291, May 21, 2015, p. 2.
90 Meenakshi Gopinath, "Processing Peace: To Speak in a Different Voice", *Peace Prints: South Asian Journal of Peacebuilding*, 4:2, Winter 2012, p. 4.
91 ibid.
92 Shivshankar Menon, *India and the Global Scene: Prem Bhatia Memorial Lecture*, August 11, 2011, National Maritime Foundation, http://maritimeindia.org/article/india-and-global-scene
93 Sanjaya Baru, *The Accidental Prime Minister: The Making and Unmaking of Manmohan Singh* (London: Penguin, Kindle Edition, 2014), p. 2315.
94 E. Sridharan, "Improving Indo-Pakistan Relations: International Relations Theory, Nuclear Deterrence and Possibilities for Economic Cooperation", *Contemporary South Asia*, 14:3, 2005, pp. 321–339, DOI: 10.1080/09584930500463768
95 Sanjaya Baru, *The Accidental Prime Minister: The Making and Unmaking of Manmohan Singh* (London: Penguin, Kindle Edition, 2014), pp. 3062–3120; Ashutosh Misra, "An Audit of the India-Pakistan Peace Process", *Australian Journal of International Affairs*, 61:4, 2007, pp. 506–528; C. Raja Mohan, "Soft Borders and Cooperative Frontiers: India's Changing Territorial Diplomacy towards Pakistan and China", *Strategic Analysis*, 31:1, 2007, p. 17.
96 Sajjad Padder, "The Composite Dialogue between India and Pakistan: Structure, Process and Agency", *Heidelberg Papers in South Asian and Comparative Politics*, Working Paper, 65, February 2012, p. 11.
97 C. Raja Mohan, "Soft Borders and Cooperative Frontiers: India's Changing Territorial Diplomacy towards Pakistan and China", *Strategic Analysis*, 31:1, January–February 2007, p. 9.
98 Ashok K. Behuria, "Pakistan's Approach to Kashmir Since the Lahore Agreement: Is There Any Change?", *Strategic Analysis*, 33:3, May 2009, p. 440.

99 Given the need for better understanding of developments in Pakistan, the IDSA launched its Pakistan Project in the year 2009. The report was reviewed by a panel of experts in January 2010 and finalised with their inputs and suggestions. The fact that the report was prepared under the leadership of Arvind Gupta is significant as he was former Deputy NSA in India. Further, initiated by the MEA, in 2009 a field study in J&K evaluated progress on cross-LoC CBMs adopted as part of the CD.
100 Personal communication with a senior academic and strategic analyst in New Delhi on October 7, 2015.
101 Karthika Sasikumar has identified that the Draft Nuclear Doctrine (DND) created by the NSAB after the Kargil war was the beginning of India "seeking to change its informal strategic culture to a more institutionalised one." The NSAB was a crucial forum where think tank elite could interact directly with the policy processes. Karthika Sasikumar, "Learning to Play the Game: Strategic Culture and Nuclear Learning", in Happymon Jacob (ed.) *Does India Think Strategically?* (New Delhi: Manohar Press, 2014), p. 34.
102 Meenakshi Gopinath, "Processing Peace: To Speak in a Different Voice", *Peace Prints: South Asian Journal of Peacebuilding*, 4:2, Winter 2012, p. 5.
103 ibid., pp. 5, 6; Smitu Kothari and Zia Mian (eds.), *Bridging Partition: Peoples' Initiatives for Peace between India and Pakistan* (Hyderabad: Orient Blackswan, 2010).
104 Ishrat Husain, "Managing India-Pakistan Trade Relations", in Michael Kugelman and Robert M. Hathaway (eds.) *Pakistan-India Trade: What Needs to Be Done? What Does It Matter?* (Washington: Wilson Center, 2013), p. 60.
105 Stella Ladi, "Think Tanks, Discursive Institutionalism and Policy Change", in Georgios Papanagnou (ed.) *Social Science and Policy Challenges: Democracy, Values and Capacities* (Paris: UNESCO, 2011), p. 208.
106 Erin Zimmerman, *Think Tanks and Non-Traditional Security: Governance Entrepreneurs in Asia* (Basingstoke: Palgrave MacMillan, 2016), p. 30.
107 Hartwig Pautz, "Revisiting the Think Tank Phenomenon", *Public Policy and Administration*, 26:4, 2011, p. 425.
108 Antonio Gramsci, *Selections from the Prison Notebooks*. Edited and translated by Quintin Hoare and Geoffrey Nowell Smith (New York: International Publishers, 1971), p. 3.

4
GOVERNMENT THINK TANKS
Promoting security-centred government narratives on Pakistan

The analysis so far has considered the merits of using Gramsci's examination of intellectual elites and DI's emphasis on think tanks as discursive actors. While DI provides a methodological tool to examine think tank interactions, Gramsci enables an understanding of the nature of interactions between intellectuals and policy elites, highlighting the specific collaboration between state and non-state actors such as think tanks. In bringing these arguments to the literature on Indian think tanks and its attention to their bridging role in providing policy analysis, Chapter 3 has highlighted the dominant arguments regarding think tanks as actors in the policy space. The discourse at think tanks, however, has largely been seen to be lacking in policy relevance, and though increasingly perceived as secondary actors, the state-centric foreign policy-making structure has been emphasised in India. This chapter and the following two further problematise the role of Indian think tanks – by critically analysing their role and influence on policy making and public opinion mobilisation, particularly towards their discourse on Pakistan.

As the evidence in the following sections indicates, the establishment of these think tanks and the Indian government's support to a body of elites with similar worldviews represents an effort to create consensus on policy directions. This is reminiscent of Gramsci's emphasis on the state's ideological and political power to construct and reconstruct society, politics and economy in the light of changing conditions and crises of social order.[1] In the Indian case too, the need for sustained research on security and strategic studies motivated the institutionalisation of think tanks. Further, the Indian state has collaborated with these actors to create consensus on its policy directions towards Pakistan. This, however, differs from state control as understood by elitist or statist conceptions. The discursive interactions between these think tanks and the Indian government indicate that think tanks also benefit from this collaboration – to promote their interests and retain their institutional relevance as outside policy actors. Also of particular significance is the nature of intellectual elites at government-sponsored think tanks. Displaying a certain fluidity, as they move from one think tank to the other, shaped by their need to retain their research and policy relevance, this elite see themselves as part of the state itself, embodying Gramsci's "state spirit."

The element of policy relevance and the construction of popular consensus is also exhibited in think tank discourse on India–Pakistan relations. Research interests and policy outlooks exhibited by these think tanks reflect dominant state narratives on Pakistan, particularly those held by India's defence community and the Foreign Ministry. Government funding sourced from the MEA and the MoD assures close interaction with policymakers and practitioners. Further, think tanks in this category – namely, the Indian Council of World Affairs (ICWA), the Institute for Defence Studies and Analyses (IDSA), the Centre for Air Power Studies (CAPS), the Centre for Land Warfare Studies (CLAWS) and the National Maritime Foundation (NMF) – are staffed by serving officers from each of the three forces and former bureaucrats from the MEA and MoD. Thus, both membership and source of funding comes directly from the government. While government funding addresses resource limitations, it raises questions regarding research autonomy and the expansion of government agendas. Questions also arise on the efficacy of these think tanks in breaking the barriers that government bureaucracies create owing to their futuristic approach or their ability to introduce fresh policy agendas and enable better collaboration and dissemination of relevant policy research to policy elites, media and the public.[2]

The analysis of the IDSA, ICWA, CAPS, CLAWS and NMF begins with a focus on the nature of the intellectual elite through a closer examination of membership patterns and institutional worldviews. Elite composition highlights partnerships and networks, indicating inroads into formal policy making as well as government influence on think tank institutional agendas. It further highlights in detail the exchange of ideas on India's short- and long-term policy goals towards Pakistan, between policy elite and think tank intellectuals and the presence of overlapping ideas centred on national security. Further, through a critical examination of policy discourse on Pakistan, dominant narratives on key issues identified within the CD are considered. The enquiry into discourses brings to light think tank contribution as communicative actors, generating public opinion on prominent issues by critically analysing and popularising significant government initiatives.

Nature of intellectual elite – patterns in institutional worldviews and collaborations with the state

The literature as elaborated in Chapter 3 provides evidence of opening up the Indian policy space to accommodate sustained research on new security concerns, particularly after the 1965 war with Pakistan. The first such attempt was to support the institution of new think tanks that addressed India's lack of focus on strategic affairs and security policy. The following section provides insights into the institutional worldviews and membership patterns, highlighting first the creation of these think tanks with government support and the continued partnerships with the MEA and the MoD – their principal financial sponsors. Secondly, through an examination of the nature and composition of intellectual elites, the similarities in training and intellectual viewpoints are addressed.

Though operating within their own institutional worldviews and agendas, there does exist an overlap in discourse at government think tanks, as later sections of this chapter highlight. While a common funding agency (i.e. the MoD) is a probable cause, another contributing factor is the similarity in membership patterns visible when the nature and composition of the intellectual elite is examined. Intellectual elites at government think tanks come from similar professional backgrounds and have experienced common training methods. The government's role in supporting these elites and institutionalising foreign policy think tanks is also visible. With active interest from Prime Minister Nehru, as early as the 1950s, there was "an attempt to structure a loose foreign policy establishment that sought to bring together public intellectuals, bureaucrats, professionals, businessmen, scholars and journalists under the rubric of ICWA in New Delhi."[3] Members of the ICWA governing body have included former vice presidents, foreign ministers and senior members of India's bureaucracy. The body of intellectual elites including Tej Bahadur Sapru, H.N. Kunzru, Sardar Swaran Singh, Jaswant Singh, M.S. Rajan and A. Appadorai have been notable for their contributions to India's foreign policy in the early years. While initially an active forum for debate on foreign policy issues, the ICWA declined in influence after Kunzru's death in 1978, and while attempts to revive the institution continued through the 1980s, it did not return to its predominant place.[4] The council was taken over by the MEA in 2001 and now serves as a platform for the MEA to host foreign dignitaries, in addition to involvement in several initiatives.[5] Its association with the MEA assures regular interaction with the foreign policy machinery, and the ICWA continues to maintain a close relationship with the Jawaharlal Nehru University, with academic staff predominantly sourced from there.[6] The ICWA is currently led by former diplomat T.C.A. Raghavan, who has served as the Indian High Commissioner to Pakistan from 2013 to 2015.

Through a similar initiative by the Ministry of Defence, the IDSA was established in 1965 with then Defence Minister Yeshwantrao Chavan as one of its founding members. Unlike the ICWA, the IDSA is funded by the MoD, and the President of the Institute is the Defence Minister himself. Initially ambivalent about including active serving officers, retired armed forces personnel and civil servants associated with the defence ministry were inducted into the new organisation to be joined later by active service officers when the ban was lifted.[7] "In a mutually beneficial arrangement, the armed forces now send three to four research fellows every year to the IDSA, and the civil services are following suit."[8] The induction of serving officers from the armed forces helped to bridge the gap between a theoretical understanding of security and practitioner experience. Former Director K. Subrahmanyam, for instance, "combined civil service, journalism, government consulting, and think tank analysis to become a hugely influential figure over decades," while Jasjit Singh and Uday Bhaskar brought their military experience on board.[9]

At the IDSA, the role of this "elite," capable of providing thinking on defence and security issues, was important from the beginning. The personal commitment of Chavan, K.C. Pant and other bureaucrats was also responsible for procuring annual grants from the government.[10] The prominence of intellectuals has been important for the IDSA's evolution and credibility as a think tank and represented by former Directors Subrahmanyam, Jasjit Singh, P.R. Chari, N.S. Sisodia, K. Santhanam, Uday Bhaskar, Arvind Gupta and Jayanta Prasad, to name a few, these elites have been known to be involved in shaping defence policy in India.[11] Subrahmanyam's important place in lifting the profile of the IDSA has been highlighted very often, in addition to his potential to encourage policy-relevant research.[12] This resonates with the larger understanding of think tanks as actors bridging knowledge and policy, as discussed in previous chapters.

Unlike Subrahmanyam, Jasjit Singh's background was from the Air Force and has often been credited to have given the IDSA a strong international profile in addition to a focus on national security structures in India.[13] Michael Krepon, for instance, has argued that Singh was "a rite of passage for US strategic analysts venturing into the subcontinent."[14] Further,

> during his last few years at IDSA, he instituted the Asian Security Conference, an annual gathering of national and international security experts from all over the world, deliberating on the role of Asia in the changing global order.[15]

While it has been suggested that the concept of a revolving door (i.e. the appointment of think tank staff into the policy administration), of the kind that is visible in American think tanks needs to be encouraged in India,[16] membership patterns and the trajectory of think tank elites presents evidence of such a practice already in place, albeit of a different kind. IDSA leadership patterns indicate that a non-institutionalised revolving door exists as several members have held senior government positions subsequent to their engagement with the Institute. For instance, former D.G. Jayanta Prasad appointed in 2015 held key diplomatic positions and was a part of the Indo-Pak Chaophraya Track II dialogue.[17] In addition, serving officials from the MEA have served on deputation at the IDSA at senior leadership positions.[18] Experts such as K. Santhanam, who directed the IDSA from 2001–2004, continued to provide scientific inputs as Scientific Advisor to the MEA and as Additional Secretary of the newly constituted NSCS.[19] Former Director N.S. Sisodia was also closely associated with the NSC, the Strategic Policy Group and the NSAB. More recently, Arvind Gupta who headed the South Asia and Internal Security Centres at the IDSA was appointed as the Deputy NSA in PM Narendra Modi's administration and subsequently moved to the Vivekananda International Foundation as Director in 2017. Current Director General Sujan Chinoy is also a career diplomat with particular expertise on China.

The IDSA was instituted during a phase when a need for defence and strategic planning was emphasised, particularly after the 1962 and 1965 wars. While it provided a broad understanding of India's national security concerns, there was also a developing need for specialised research on military strategy. To fulfil this, each of the armed forces in India set up their own think tanks with a specialised and limited agenda. The first among these, the CAPS was established in 2001 as an autonomous defence research and analysis body focusing particularly on aerospace and airpower. Run by a trust, the CAPS receives funding from the IAF and the MoD and also conducts research projects for the Defence Research and Development Organisation (DRDO) on aspects such as UAVs, cruise missiles and ballistic missiles. Its board members include former bureaucrats and retired and serving air force officers with "50 percent of the research staff comprising serving IAF officers thereby creating a good mix of research and operational experience."[20] This is true for the CLAWS and the NMF as well. The initiative to create the CAPS came from Jasjit Singh, former Director at the IDSA, and it flourished under his leadership and the support of the IAF. As a prominent representative of India's intellectual elite, his contributions to the understanding of "Joint Operations in the 1980s and 1990s exhorted the Indian Army to understand air power better and recognise its war-winning potential in battles of the future."[21] Further leadership at the CAPS has also been from within the Air Force.[22]

The CLAWS was similarly led by Vijay Oberoi, former Vice Chief of the Indian Army with operational experience and a distinguished military career. Senior researchers at the CLAWS have included Gurmeet Kanwal,[23] Dhruv Katoch[24] and former director B.S. Nagal[25] with similar professional backgrounds. Affiliated with the Indian Navy, the NMF's board and staff are also predominantly serving or retired naval officers, with research staff consisting of students and young researchers with varied profiles, specialising in different aspects of India's maritime policy. While former Director Vijay Sakhuja is a former navy officer and was Director (Research) at the ICWA from 2009–2014,[26] former Executive Director Gurpreet Khurana, a missile specialist at the Indian Navy, was also associated with the IDSA.[27] Strategic experts including C. Uday Bhaskar, currently an Honorary Fellow, a prolific writer and commentator on nuclear, maritime and international security-related issues, have also been associated with the NMF.[28]

As the older organisation in the group, the IDSA has contributed significantly to the evolution of this body of elites and security analysts. The fluidity of the elite in moving from one think tank to another has often involved an association with the IDSA, the first of its kind to encourage sustained policy-relevant research. The attention to developing specialised policy research capacity also encouraged the institution of the CAPS, the CLAWS and the NMF and the presence of serving defence service professionals provided inroads into contemporary policy frameworks with an understanding of operational and ground realities. The institution of these think tanks has represented the Indian government's efforts to create consensus on defence policy. The Indian state's collaboration with private forces is also reflective of "Gramsci's notion of 'state spirit' – of a feeling among certain leading private figures and organisations that they bear a grave responsibility to promote a historical process through positive political and intellectual activity."[29]

Think tank contribution to policy discourse

While funding and membership patterns are similar, a closer look at the discourse emerging from these think tanks is also important, particularly with regard to India–Pakistan relations. Dominant discourse, reflected in research projects and policy recommendations, centres on national security with a focus on threats from a failing Pakistani state with basic irreconcilable ideological differences with India. The interest that each think tank displays towards relations with Pakistan is also based on its own specialised research agenda and the interest of donor agencies. It is also reflective of the similarity in viewpoints with the defence and foreign policy community in India from which these government think tanks receive their funding and patronage. As mentioned earlier, the structure of the CD provided space for alternative thinking on Pakistan, creating the opportunity to expand on the government agenda. Government-affiliated think tank discourse, however, as the evidence points out, perpetuated security-centred narratives on Pakistan, side-lining and under-emphasising alternative conceptualisations on resolution of key conflicts. Government think tanks have also not engaged substantially with issues of trade, people-to-people contact or the Sir Creek dispute, even though it concerns India's maritime borders – a key security focus particularly since the Mumbai attacks – reflecting again their dependence on cues from funding agencies. The following sections critically analyse policy discourse from these think tanks, elaborating on policy ideas and dominant narratives on the basket of issues under consideration in the CD. Significant issues under consideration have been the debate on nuclear doctrines, the conflict in Jammu and Kashmir including but not limited to ideas on political status and the specificities of the dispute regarding Indus Waters, Siachen and the recurring problem of cross-border terrorism – a considerable issue of concern between India and Pakistan.

Nuclear Security – The IDSA, the CAPS and the NMF have all considered the debate on India's national security doctrine. Dominant arguments have focused on the predominant and detrimental role played by the Pakistan army and doctrinal and operational distinctions between India and Pakistan's nuclear doctrine that have the potential to negatively impact the nuclear CBMs proposed within the CD. The discourse that emerged perpetuated dominant state narratives of a nuclear threat from Pakistan and, while critical of any dilution of India's position and its nuclear capabilities, did offer some suggestions for the expansion of the dialogue agenda on nuclear issues. Intellectual elite, particularly Subrahmanyam and Jasjit Singh, were involved in debates on India's acquisition of nuclear weapons, and the concept of 'minimum credible deterrence' as a viable nuclear policy alternative for India was advocated extensively by the IDSA.[30]

The subversion of India's nuclear deterrence doctrine to Pakistan's use of proxy wars and sub-conventional warfare is also amply highlighted in the discourse, in addition to narratives that highlighted Pakistan's use of nuclear weapons as a strategy of "offensive-defence."[31] Nuclear threats from Pakistan and linkages between terrorism and nuclear weapons were further emphasised in the CAPS discourse. It was argued that Pakistan's policy of "terrorism under a nuclear umbrella" was further "legitimised in Pakistani military as sanctioned by religion."[32] The fact that this viewpoint came from the founder of the organisation is notable. Further arguments highlighted Pakistan's strategy of "using its nuclear weapons for decades – but in a covert, politico-diplomatic manner against the whole world – and India in particular," while India's 'no-first use' doctrine led to a dilution of its strategic advantage.[33]

Discourse has also elaborated on the nuclear CBMs adopted within the CD and articulated the reframing of the nuclear dialogue to include "appropriate consultative mechanisms to monitor and ensure implementation of CBMs" and to establish a strategic dialogue mechanism.[34] Indian policy should also, it was argued, take "immediate measures at least in the sphere of short-range and tactical ballistic missiles,"[35] both as a diplomatic strategy as well as levelling the lacunae in the nuclear doctrines between India and Pakistan. Policy recommendations also stressed the need to amend the "massive punitive retaliation" clause in the nuclear doctrine review of 2003 to one of "flexible punitive retaliation," keeping in mind the "failed state" status of Pakistan and its implications on India's security."[36]

A noteworthy idea that was popularised in think tank discourse was the connection between China and the development of Pakistan's nuclear programme – an aspect that has gained significant traction in Indian policy narratives over the years. A strategic dialogue with Pakistan and China was thus recommended for clarity on concepts of nuclear deterrence.[37] The expansion of the nuclear dialogue to a trilateral India-Pakistan-China level was also suggested, keeping in mind China's nuclear weapons/missiles-related assistance to Pakistan.[38] Similar to assertions at the IDSA and the CAPS, China's nuclear capability was also of interest to the NMF, particularly its assistance to the Pakistan navy and its "plans for getting a nuclear submarine capability."[39] Thus, while the NMF and the CAPS stressed the relevance of the nuclear dialogue to its funding agencies, the Indian Navy and IAF respectively, the IDSA affiliated with the MoD adopted a broader perspective aimed at strengthening the government's formulations on nuclear CBMs with Pakistan.

Kashmir – The CD approach to the resolution of the Kashmir conflict was essentially two-pronged. First, it sought to address the cross-border element of the conflict exacerbated by Pakistani support, and second, the process aimed to tackle the considerable human security concerns within Kashmir and to rebuild trust and attempt reconciliation with the people. Think tank discourse also adopted this dual formulation, however, discourse continued to reflect the dominant policy narratives – thus the conflict in Kashmir was perceived first and foremost as a law-and-order situation that must be resolved primarily by continued Indian government and military control. There were suggestions that focused on humanitarian efforts, yet the predominant arguments were based on the politics of the conflict – both within Kashmir and with regard to Pakistan. As the two think tanks directly associated with the Indian Army, discourse at the CLAWS and the IDSA engaged significantly with the debates on the army's role in maintaining law and order in Kashmir. In addition to focusing on Pakistan's motivations for escalating the conflict in Kashmir, opinions at the CLAWS reflected a negative opinion of back-channel diplomacy, explained by the lack of control the government in Pakistan has over its foreign policy. The discourse at the CLAWS therefore focused significantly on the "deep state"[40] in Pakistan that exists beyond the civilian government and one that India needed to engage with, keeping lines of communication open.[41] On the political status of J&K and internal dissent, viewpoints at the IDSA too, remained firmly in support of the Indian government's policy, arguing that any concessions on *Azaadi* in Kashmir "will have a domino effect on other states seeking secession from the Indian state."[42] Other policy debates at the IDSA focused on Article 370 and its impact on integration in J&K; the use of force by the Indian government and possible attempts towards decentralisation through strengthening of local government institutions in the region. While implementation of CBMs with Pakistan was favoured, caution with regards to the pursuit of a soft-border policy was advised.[43]

The contact with the MoD and the army presented to both the IDSA and the CLAWS the ability to critically examine Kashmir CBMs with insights from the field. The research at IDSA, for instance, elaborated on the relevance of the Armed Forces Special Powers Act (AFSPA) and other counter-insurgency strategies, adding significantly to the public discourse on these complicated issues. The AFSPA study expanded on the debate from the human rights and international humanitarian law perspective and also offered policy recommendations on addressing grievances and improving available safeguards against misuse.[44] The IDSA also conducted a feasibility study on the adopted Cross LoC CBMs at the behest of the MoD and the MEA. Based on extensive fieldwork in J&K, it evaluated progress and argued that "the benefits of cross LoC CBMs outweighed the costs and there was a need to improve existing mechanisms and increase opportunities for more cross-LoC contacts."[45] Spanning all three regions of the state, the study was aimed at acquiring regional perspectives on the cross-LoC interactions and evaluating problems and prospects regarding its implementation. It also sought opinions on other proposed routes under consideration.[46] Thus, the government in this particular case used the IDSA as a tool to gather public opinion on a key policy.

The report also highlighted that the initiative achieved the humanitarian objective of enabling divided families to travel and visit each other but also served an "unintended purpose" of changing and demystifying perceptions about "bad India" and "good Pakistan,"[47] making "Pakistani propaganda untenable." The "continued need for stringent security measures to ensure that the LoC does not compromise India's security" was also reiterated.[48]

While the AFSPA was considered crucial, there were recommendations on reduced visibility of security forces and penalty against human rights violations. The army's humanitarian position was also popularised by the CLAWS through the promotion of the WHAM (Winning Hearts and Minds) strategy that introduced a "human-centric" approach and "enabled conflict zones to return to an environment where the political process can lead to conflict resolution and enablement of the civil administration to carry out its functions."[49] The research at the CLAWS also highlighted the role played by Operation *Sadhbhavana* initiated by the army in 1998 based on which the army provided health care to remote and inaccessible areas in addition to conducting medical camps, remote area support posts and mobile medical teams. The discourse at the IDSA also promoted both the WHAM strategy and Operation *Sadhbhavana* as essential for the promotion of goodwill for the army and for reducing the hostility towards the counter-insurgency operations.[50]

Even though policy discourse at both the CLAWS and the IDSA considered the army's role as essential in Kashmir, there were differences in their perspective on the dialogue process. While official dialogue too toyed with the idea of involving separatist leadership in the dialogue in Kashmir, the recommendations from the CLAWS called for restricting access of the separatist leaders to meet with Pakistani officials. During this period, however, the IDSA recommended Track II talks in the spirit of 'insaniyat' as professed by Vajpayee and maximum autonomy as considered by the UPA government. The role of the Hurriyat conference too, in contrast to the position held by CLAWS, was considered by the IDSA to be crucial to ensuring a lasting settlement of the Kashmir conflict. It was argued that to bridge the psychological and emotional disconnect, the "central and state leadership must take back the space that has been occupied by hard-line elements."[51] Discourse at the IDSA reflected a sustained engagement with the nuanced nature of civil-military dynamics in Kashmir and called for an all-party consensus on issues such as terrorism, in the national interest, without the interference of local politics.[52] In addition, the support to militants from the Kashmiri population was considered to be "a reality check both for the administrative machinery of the state and security forces" and considered crucial for the military response.[53] The changing dynamics after the Amarnath agitation[54] in 2008 further opened up the discourse, with policy ideas calling for "the revisiting of New Delhi's relationship with the Kashmir valley" and adopting new policy directions on Kashmir.[55] Policy ideas included:

> initiating less restrictive security policies, bettering human rights record of the security forces, ensuring that funds given to the state are utilised

in a manner that improves the standard of living of the common people, improving the connectivity of the state with India and with PoK and implementing the recommendations of the various working groups set up by the Prime Minister.[56]

The proximity to the MoD, however, assured an extensive focus on the security situation in Kashmir as well as military responses to "proxy war" by Pakistan. Policy recommendations therefore argued for possible military retaliation "through selective elimination of terrorist leaders across the border" and "maintaining the right of hot pursuit" and "destruction of terrorist launch pads in PoK."[57]

Disputes Around Indus Waters – The dispute over Indus Waters has several layers of complexity. While essentially an issue of resource politics, dominant perspectives have connected the debate with the political conflict in Kashmir. There is, however, a presumption that the Indus Waters Treaty (IWT) represents a success story in India–Pakistan negotiations and could form the basis for resolution of disputes such as the Wullar Barrage.[58] This aspect of successful negotiations was seen to be replicated within its inclusion into the CD. At defence policy think tanks, however, the debates around the IWT centred around water as a political tool, and the linkages with the Kashmir conflict took prominence.[59]

It was only at the IDSA that significant interest was taken in the provisions of the IWT and its utility considering changed hydrological circumstances and possibilities for renegotiation. This was motivated by the IDSA's researchers with specific expertise on South Asian water conflicts and their involvement in several government initiatives.[60] While the primary position was that the treaty provisions are more advantageous to Pakistani concerns as a lower riparian state, the terms for the modification of the treaty, however, were not implicitly addressed in the discourse.[61] Yet, the discourse emphasised that "given the nature of sub-continental politics, there will be an increasing use of water as a 'tool and a bargaining instrument' in the larger politico-strategic objective."[62] Indian policy directions therefore should include "inventive diplomacy based on linkages, trade-offs, bargains and delaying tactics."[63] In renegotiating the IWT, a potential joint mechanism to study the actual flow of water was recommended.[64]

Siachen – In addition to Sir Creek, the CD process also regarded the Siachen dispute as a "low hanging fruit" owing to the grave humanitarian costs of sustaining military deployment in the area. Yet, while the official dialogue failed to achieve a consensus on demilitarisation, government think tanks also remained sceptical with some debate on the humanitarian aspect of the dispute. The humanitarian arguments and the options for possible withdrawal were not encouraged, as they go against the dominant perspectives on Siachen seen primarily through a national security lens. Early writing at the IDSA refuted the Pakistani claims on Siachen and justified Indian military action in 1984 as a reaction to the Pakistani decision to send military patrols to the east of the Saltoro Ridge and on to the Siachen glaciers.[65] The IDSA's proximity to the MoD and the viewpoint of the Indian army was also reflected in the institutional discourse.

Broad perspectives identified Siachen as an issue of national security – ideational, cartographic and intimately linked to the unresolved issue of J&K. In addition, it was argued that while ecological and human security threats are real and could create incentives for resolution, "it is unlikely that policy elites will make any concession" on the dispute.[66] For dominant opinion at the CLAWS too, a withdrawal from Siachen represented a weakening of India's strategic and political position on Kashmir.

While the dispute remained unresolved after several rounds of negotiations, the 2012 Gayari avalanche reiterated the human cost arguments and indicated a softer stance from Pakistan with the Army Chief Ashfaq Parvez Kayani's emphasis on demilitarisation. Opinions at the IDSA appeared split on the possibility of demilitarisation. One view perceived it as an opportunity to "re-evaluate national security, ecological security and human security" and recommended for India and Pakistan "to conduct more joint scientific studies and without any loss of face on either side, put in place an AGPL [Actual Ground Position Line] agreement within a reasonable time frame."[67] The opposing perspective, relying primarily on Pakistani vernacular media reports, argued that the Pakistani intent is questionable and the onus "is squarely on Indian shoulders" to enable an environment suitable for resolution of thorny issues.[68] Further apprehensions characterised the Siachen issue as a "legacy of Partition and Pakistani aggression" and were critical of the UPA's decision to resume dialogue with Pakistan in early 2012.[69] This argument based on Pakistani objectives in the war effort in Afghanistan upheld the continued need for India to maintain military presence and not "throw away the strategic gains" in Siachen.[70] This viewpoint was also endorsed by the CLAWS that expanded on the ramifications of a possible withdrawal on cross-border infiltrations on the LoC and the prevalence of terrorist infrastructure in PoK, which was likely to become more emboldened with the changing political situation in Afghanistan.[71] Offering a nuanced perspective yet one that did not gain traction, former director at the CLAWS Gurmeet Kanwal was one of the few who highlighted that opposition and criticism to prospects for withdrawal were not understood and that since verification and monitoring would be jointly conducted, there were significant merits to such a policy.[72] Thus, even though there were dissenting voices both from the IDSA and the CLAWS that called for a studied understanding of a possible withdrawal, keeping in mind vigilant monitoring, these ideas were not incorporated into the discourse as squarely.

Terrorism – The analysis of Pakistan's proxy war in Kashmir and the use of terrorism as a political tool was a common yet predictable thread within think tank discourse, particularly when funding comes from the MoD and the MEA. There was no space in the discourse to refute this claim, but policy ideas instead engaged with possible responses from India. Analysing Pakistan's "deep state," for instance, the CLAWS discourse made a distinction between 'good terrorists' who were considered 'strategic assets' and were employed to destabilise neighbouring countries, such as the Lashkar-e-Taiba (LeT), Jaish-e-Mohammed (JeM), Lashkar-e-Jhangvi and the Haqqani network, and the 'bad terrorists' that included the Tehrik-e-Taliban considered as enemies of the state. It was asserted that "the roots of the conflict and insurgency in J & K were in PoK and India must be pro-active in launching trans-LoC operations against them."[73] The IDSA engagement too highlighted PoK as a safe haven for "a vast network of terrorist training camps, religious centres and schools and weapons stores."[74] It was also argued that the region was likely to emerge as what was referred to as "the epicentre of Global Jihad," particularly with regards to developments in Afghanistan.[75]

As the formal dialogue process took a turn for the worse after the Mumbai attacks in 2008, the efficacy of engagement with Pakistan and emphasis on tackling terrorism became pronounced. As public opinion shifted, in the IDSA discourse too, the resumption of the CD was perceived as "counterproductive if undertaken before it [Pakistan] has shown an inclination to wind down the infrastructure of terror."[76] It was recommended that:

> India should remain in touch with various constituencies in Pakistan, particularly in Sindh and Balochistan; develop long term contacts with *Shias, Ismailis, Barelvis, Sindhis and Mohajirs* to encourage them to take a firm stand against the Taliban; involve Indian Muslims, particularly the Barelvis and Shias to establish contacts in Pakistan.[77]

Additionally it was suggested that India should retain its "leverage particularly in the context of water and cyber issues and not give in to Pakistani blackmail on water and instead propose re-negotiation of the Indus Waters Treaty."[78] Although the IDSA discourse became critical of the efficacy of the promotion of people-to-people contact, its association with the MoD prompted suggestions for an engagement with Pakistan's military leadership.[79] It argued for the need

> to adopt a multi-track approach, a sort of "composite back-channel" in which the intelligence agencies comprise one track, the military leaders another track in which they discuss military and security related matters, while a third track can discuss larger strategic perceptions, outlooks and assessments. All these various tracks can then provide inputs to the political back-channel.[80]

In addition, the use of military force against further terrorist attacks coming from Pakistan was recommended even if "merely symbolic" and limited in nature.[81] Recommendations also suggested a "tactically agile diplomatic offensive" that should also "encompass the Track II realm, where the services of the retired government officials as well as that of academics and think tanks could be utilised."[82] At the CLAWS too, the military option as well as a focus on rising fundamentalism in Pakistan and its repercussions on India was articulated.

Policy inputs discussed in this section hence indicate that the focus at these think tanks was on dominant state narratives on Pakistan. Even though some alternate and new policy ideas were put forward, think tank discourse largely preferred to set them aside, and any paradigmatic change in India's policy towards Pakistan was not articulated. The proximity to funding bodies, namely the MoD and the MEA, meant that research agendas continued to be informed by sponsors. This was also due to similarities in membership patterns and institutional worldviews analysed in previous sections. The government in India, therefore, as argued by DI-Gramscian perspective, attempted to create a consensus on policy directions on Pakistan. Yet, close cooperation with government thinking was also in the self-interest of these think tanks, who needed to retain their linkages and patronage from the government for their institutional policy relevance. Another critical aspect of policy making that these think tanks were involved in was the promotion of government policy, as highlighted in the next section through the consideration of their role as communicative actors that worked in collaboration with the state.

Think tank contribution as communicative actors

In addition to policy recommendations, the close proximity to policymakers meant that government think tanks also contributed to the mobilisation of public opinion, particularly on policy towards Pakistan. Practitioner experience and the role of the intellectual elite also enabled a close relationship with policymakers and an insight into government policy that was not commonly available. There was also an exchange of policy ideas through research publications, in addition to classified policy inputs relayed directly to the Policy Planning Division of the MEA. The government for its part has also used the research expertise from these think tanks to garner public opinion on new policy initiatives that were introduced as part of the CD.

The role of the IDSA was particularly significant in this regard. The specific studies on the AFSPA and the cross-LoC interactions that were highlighted in the previous section were initiated by the MEA, and in addition to generating a public debate on government policy, also enabled the government to gain insights from public discourse. The IDSA discourse thus contributed to the public understanding of debates on strategic issues, nuclear weapons doctrines as well as the finer points of the Siachen conflict. This role was particularly useful as there were limited avenues for insights into government policy in India, particularly on issues of defence policy. The IDSA's role, first visible in popularising the debate on nuclear weapons particularly by Subrahmanyan, has been discussed earlier. On the Indo-Pak dimension, the IDSA contributed to generating public opinion with comprehensive research projects that focused on the nature of the Pakistani state, its power structure, role of the military and religion in Pakistani politics and the political dynamics within PoK. To this end, the IDSA launched its Pakistan Project in the year 2009. The report of the project was prepared under the leadership of Arvind Gupta, then Director of the Institute and until recently the Deputy NSA. The report titled *Whither Pakistan? Growing Instability and Implications for India* finalised in 2010 and subsequent follow-up reports titled *Pakistan on the Edge* (December 2012) and *Unending Violence in Pakistan: Analysing the Trends, 2013–14* served a particular purpose. These studies generated significant interest in the internal dynamics in PoK – an aspect that previously remained out of popular opinion. The research and its wide dissemination elaborated on PoK's constitutional and political status and highlighted particularly the lack of human rights and ethnic tensions in the area. The public discussion around these reports helped to popularise the Indian government's position and the emphasis on the area as occupied Indian territory and gave support to arguments that called for highlighting human rights violations and the lack of democratic and political rights in the region.[83] The IDSA was a forum for debates on this issue as far back as 1995 and frequently reiterated the accepted government position on Kashmir.[84] In addition to the focus on Pakistan's proxy war, attention was drawn towards new negotiating patterns with "the new Indian focus on Gilgit and Baltistan and 'Azad Kashmir'."[85]

These debates were also initiated to bring attention to government programmes as part of the Kashmir CBMs, such as the opening of the Srinagar-Muzaffarabad and Kargil-Skardu bus routes. The narratives adopted appreciated these new policies but also highlighted that these initiatives have the potential to "expose the population of the region [PoK] to the freedom and democratic rights enjoyed by their ethnic kin across the Line of Control in Ladakh and Kargil."[86] The growing alienation within PoK was thus promoted as "valuable leverage" for India in negotiating with Pakistan.[87] Discourse popularised the idea that "the people of PoK should be regarded as citizens of India and special documents should be issued to them in this regard. They may be allowed to visit India after proper check of their antecedents."[88] The report was shared publicly in a roundtable[89] and further recommended that "India must engage the new emerging political leadership in PoK which is disillusioned with Pakistan's approach and is demanding genuine representation and a popular system of governance."[90] A similar position was taken at the CLAWS, citing videos and information regarding resistance within the PoK and the demand for "Balawaristan" by the Balawaristan National Front, which is a coalition of influential leaders in the northern areas.[91]

While reaching out to PoK/Gilgit Baltistan, the discourse reiterated the government's approach that regarded the subject of Indian Kashmir as an internal matter and emphasised the distinction between the problem 'in' Kashmir and the problem 'of' Kashmir.[92] This also created support for the Kashmir roundtables initiated by Manmohan Singh in 2006 that were seen to "trash General Musharraf's idea of 'self-governance' and 'demilitarisation'."[93]

The IDSA and other government think tanks also popularised the idea of "precision military strikes" to neutralise suspected terrorist threats from across the LoC.[94] Policy options for India coming from the CLAWS were also in favour of "covert action inside Pakistan to target terror leadership"[95] and further argued that ceasefire at the LoC has been advantageous to Pakistan and "has negated whatever little military dominance and advantage the Indian army had."[96] These ideas became more popular after the 26/11 Mumbai attacks that also brought attention to the need for an assessment of India's maritime and coastal security arrangements – with recommendations for improved infrastructure for the Border Security Force and Coast Guard.[97] Coastal security and maritime terrorism, for instance, was a subject of interest for the the NMF, and the emerging nexus between maritime terrorism and drug cartels, further accentuated by the presence of transnational criminal groups headed by Dawood Ibrahim for instance, was recognised.[98] The NMF also contributed substantially to the subject of High Risk Area piracy and argued for strengthening India's strategic outlook.[99] Popularising the concept of 'active' deterrence, the NMF highlighted the capability of the Indian navy to operate in international waters "by virtue of its inherent attributes of flexibility and poise offering a viable option to the political leadership shift from 'deterrence by denial' against Pakistan to deterrence by punishment."[100]

The focus once again was on niche areas of concern, thus while the NMF emphasised the role of the Indian navy, the discourse at the CAPS highlighted the need to augment the IAF capabilities to take into account the evolving cooperation between Pakistan and China and to "build adequate force levels to possess the capability and counter the adversaries in a two-front scenario for India."[101] Its close proximity to the MoD and the MEA meant that the IDSA's engagement with matters of coastal security coincided with government thinking at the time. While it cannot be ascertained if ideas put forward by the IDSA and the NMF contributed to policy, significant public opinion was built on the need to strengthen coastal security, and the GOI announced several measures to strengthen coastal and maritime security.[102] At the CAPS too, while limited, engagement with Indo-Pak issues remained critical of dialogue and emphasised the need to strengthen India's air supremacy. In the absence of policy inputs that are not available in the public domain, it is difficult to judge the CAPs' interactive discourse, yet its proximity to the MoD and IAF is fairly evident.

Government think tanks and India's Pakistan policy: a summary

A critical examination of policy discourse from government think tanks provides evidence that the emphasis of policy ideas was to highlight the dominant viewpoints of each of the defence forces from where these think tanks receive patronage and institutional relevance. On specific policy direction towards Pakistan, owing to their proximity to the Army and the MoD, research at both the IDSA and the CLAWS has highlighted issues of law and order, particularly on counter-insurgency in Kashmir. However, the NMF and the CAPS have focused on accentuating India's naval and air supremacy – key policy parameters for the Indian Navy and the IAF. The membership of serving and retired officers further indicates a balance of theory and practice, and research agendas informed by the MoD indicate a discursive process. There is also visible a role in generating public opinion, specifically on the nuclear doctrine debate and the army's counter-insurgency programmes in J&K as well as the Indian position on other crucial Indo-Pak issues. In all of these think tanks then, practitioner experience and the role of the intellectual elite points to a close relationship with policymakers. There is also an exchange of policy ideas through research publications and classified policy inputs relayed to the Policy Planning Division of the MEA.

Linking this to Gramsci then, the state, as Gramsci contends, tries to educate and mobilise the people in a variety of ways, often through collaboration with other social forces in order to construct a historic bloc. While this permits the state a high degree of autonomy, the arguments differ from the absolute exercise of power of the state as prescribed by statism. In India, while the government creates consensus on its policy directions on Pakistan through their support to this body of elites, close cooperation with government thinking is also in the self-interest of these institutions. Research interests at government think tanks have reflected the interests of India's defence community as well as the Foreign Ministry. While they may differ on specific operational details (the withdrawal from Siachen) or timing (post 26/11 dialogue) or tactics (use of force as a tool against counter-insurgency), policy outlooks coming from these think tanks were similar to official policy. They perpetuated dominant state perspectives centred on security and dissenting voices were sidelined, for instance, those that argued in favour of a demilitarisation in Siachen. Government think tanks in India expanded on state-led agendas, popularised them by generating opinion and also conducted a critical appraisal of government policy. They did not, however, effectively challenge government narratives or introduce new ideas into the discourse that could transform India's policy towards Pakistan – away from a merely security-centred understanding.

Conclusion

The attention in this chapter was on government think tanks in India, their specific interactions with policymakers and their policy discourse on India's Pakistan policy. Through the analysis of five government think tanks – namely the IDSA, the ICWA, the CAPS, the CLAWS and the NMF – using the DI-Gramscian approach, the chapter has highlighted membership patterns, funding arrangements and the nature and prominence of the intellectual elite in building significant institutional linkages with policy structures. The evidence presented in the prior sections has highlighted that think tanks supported financially by the MoD or the MEA have maintained a direct connection with policymakers, and there exists close interaction represented in an exchange of ideas on India's foreign policy goals towards Pakistan. The membership pattern at these think tanks also indicates common training, similar professional backgrounds and similar worldviews in addition to an active component of fluidity. Research agendas are also provided guidance and direction by the foreign policy bureaucracy,

78 Government think tanks

providing sufficient evidence of partnerships and networks indicating inroads into formal policy making. The institutionalisation and government patronage has therefore enabled the Indian government to build consensus on policy directions on Pakistan, further aided by similarities in membership and close collaboration with think tank intellectual elites. The direct support by the government has created a discourse that perpetuates government thinking on Pakistan, leaving little room for alternative perspectives.

Notes

1 Inderjeet Parmar, *Think Tanks and Power in Foreign Policy* (New York: Palgrave MacMillan, 2004), p. 18.
2 Gurmeet Kanwal, "Role of Think Tanks in National Security", *Forum for Strategic Initiatives*, January 12, 2015, www.fsidelhi.org
3 C. Raja Mohan, "The Making of Foreign Policy: The Role of Scholarship and Public Opinion", *ISAS Working Paper* (National University of Singapore), 73, July 13, 2009, p. 5.
4 B. Vivekanandan, "A Tribute to Life and Work of Professor M S Rajan", *International Studies*, 47:4, 2010, p. 103.
5 It serves as the Secretariat of the CSCAP India Committee (Council for Security Cooperation in the Asia Pacific) and leads the Delhi Dialogue with Federation of Indian Chambers of Commerce and Industry, a track 1.5 dialogue between India and ASEAN. Since 2015 it has also been recognised as a member by the UN Academic Impact, https://academicimpact.un.org/sites/academicimpact.un.org/files/Newsletter%20january%20.pdf
6 The School of International Studies that later merged with JNU was established in Sapru House, under the administration of ICWA.
7 K. Subrahmanyam, "The Birth of the IDSA and Early Years", in N. S. Sisodia and Sujit Datta (eds.) *India and the World*, Vol. 1 (New Delhi: IDSA, 2005), pp. 1–38.
8 Gurmeet Kanwal, "Role of Think Tanks in National Security", *Forum for Strategic Initiatives*, January 12, 2015, www.fsidelhi.org
9 Vipin Narang and Paul Staniland, "Institutions and Worldviews in Indian Foreign Security Policy", *India Review*, 11:2, 2012, p. 80.
10 K. Subrahmanyam, "The Birth of the IDSA and Early Years", in N. S. Sisodia and Sujit Datta (eds.) *India and the World*, Vol. 1 (New Delhi: IDSA, 2005), pp. 1–38.
11 It has been argued that "the IDSA, under his [Subrahmanyam's] leadership, was able to launch a national debate on nuclear policy at a time when the subject seemed so forbidding." Uday Bhaskar, for instance, has further argued that "through seminars, workshops, lectures and his steady stream of newspaper articles, K Subrahmanyam (KS) shaped the Indian response to the nettlesome nuclear issue and the media became a contested domain." For more on Subrahmanyam's role in India's nuclear debate, see C. Uday Bhaskar, "KS: Vamana of Indian Nuclear Theology?", in C. Uday Bhaskar (ed.) *Subbu at 75: A Bouquet of Tributes* (New Delhi: Shri Avtar Printing Press, 2004); C. Raja Mohan, "The Making of Foreign Policy: The Role of Scholarship and Public Opinion", *ISAS Working Paper* (National University of Singapore), 73, July 13, 2009, p. 8.
12 Subrahmanyam was a member of several key governmental committees and a member of a non-hierarchical 'think tank' of officials and non-officials that Verghese had put together as the Information Advisor to PM Indira Gandhi to devise India's response to China's nuclear tests in 1966. Even after retiring as Director, he continued to serve on several committees, notably as Chairman of India's Joint Intelligence Committee and Kargil Review Committee (KRC) constituted for reforming India's national security and defence structures in the aftermath of the 1999 Kargil War. For more,

Sanjaya Baru, "Can Indian Think Tanks and Research Institutions Cope with the Rising Demand for Foreign and Security Policy Research?", *ISAS Working Paper* (National University of Singapore), 67, June 16, 2009, p. 6.
13 Singh was one of the members of the K.C. Pant committee that visualised a robust national security structure for India. In addition, as a member of the first NSAB, Singh made important contributions to the national defence and national security reviews as well as to the DND for India. He was also involved with the Ministry of Human Resource Development to strengthen teaching of national security in Indian universities.
14 Michael Krepon, "Jasjit Singh", *Arms Control Wonk*, August 12, 2013, www.armscontrolwonk.com/archive/403863/jasjit-singh/
15 Arvind Gupta, "R.I.P. Air Commodore Jasjit Singh AVSM, VrC, VM, IAF (Retd) (1934–2013)", *Strategic Analysis*, 37:6, 2013, p. 765.
16 Personal communication with a senior researcher and Defence Personnel at the IDSA, New Delhi on September 26, 2015.
17 They began in 2009 with three meetings occurring each year. The Islamabad-based Jinnah Institute and the Melbourne-based Australia India Institute have provided support to the two-day meetings, which take place at neutral locations including Sri Lanka and Thailand. Each Track II meeting culminates in a joint declaration with policy recommendations on specific issues. www.chaophrayadialogue.net
18 For example, ambassador Virendra Gupta was Deputy DG at IDSA on deputation from 2006–2007.
19 He was conferred the Padma Bhushan award in recognition of contributions to the Shakti-98 series of nuclear tests conducted in Pokhran in May 1998.
20 Personal communication with a Senior Researcher at the CAPS, New Delhi on October 21, 2015.
21 Arjun Subramaniam, "Warrior, Pilot, Strategist, Scholar", *The Hindu*, August 7, 2013, www.thehindu.com/opinion/op-ed/warrior-pilot-strategist-scholar/article4996360.ece
22 Former Director General, Air Marshal Vinod Patney is a decorated Air Force officer, awarded the Sarvottam Yudh Seva Medal (SYSM) for leading the IAF in the Kargil war, which ultimately proved to be the turning point in Operation Vijay.
23 Prior to joining the CLAWS, Kanwal had operational experience in counter-insurgency in Kashmir and research experience from his work at the IDSA, the ORF and the CAPS.
24 Dhruv Katoch, who succeeded Kanwal, also has vast experience in sub-conventional conflict, having taken part in Indian Peace Keeping Force operations in Sri Lanka and against terrorists and insurgents in J&K and various states of North East India. He was awarded the Sena Medal while in command of his battalion in active operations on the LoC in J&K.
25 With 40 years of experience in the Army and two years at the PMO, Nagal is a war veteran of the 1971 Indo-Pak war, and his specific areas of interest include nuclear deterrence, doctrine, strategy and policy. At the PMO, Nagal was known to head a nuclear cell, an Indian version of the Pakistani nuclear secretariat – the Strategic Plans Division. For more, see www.claws.in/director.php; Bharat Karnad, "Dedicated Nuclear Cadre", *Security Wise*, August 16, 2012, https://bharatkarnad.com/2012/08/16/dedicated-nuclear-cadre/
26 He also has research experience at the Institute of Southeast Asian Studies, Singapore (2006–2014), the CAPS, the ORF, the USI and the IDSA.
27 Khurana is accredited with the first use of the term 'Indo-Pacific' (in 2006–07) in the context of strategic/geopolitical academic discourse in India. In early 2009, he joined the Maritime Doctrine and Concept Centre (MDCC) at Mumbai and was awarded the Naval Chief's Commendation for revision of Indian Maritime Doctrine (2009). At MDCC, he compiled the first-ever Handbook on the Law of Maritime Operations for the Indian Navy in three volumes.

28 Bhaskar served in the navy for 37 years and was also Deputy Director at the IDSA from 1996–2004. He was later appointed as secretary to the GOI's task force on *Global Strategic Developments*. He is currently Director, Society for Policy Studies, a new think tank in Delhi. http://spsindia.in/
29 Inderjeet Parmar, *Think Tanks and Power in Foreign Policy* (New York: Palgrave MacMillan, 2004), p. 18.
30 For more, see Anit Mukherjee, "K. Subrahmanyam and Indian Strategic Thought", *Strategic Analysis*, 35:4, 2011, pp. 710–713 and Gurmeet Kanwal, "Role of Think Tanks in National Security", *Forum for Strategic Initiatives*, January 12, 2015, www.fsidelhi.org
31 Shalini Chawla, "How Do We Deal with Pakistan?", *CAPS Issue Brief*, 93:13, August 13, 2013, p. 3.
32 Jasjit Singh, "War through Terror under the Nuclear Umbrella", *CAPS Issue Brief*, 1:2, December 5, 2008, p. 1.
33 C. Uday Bhaskar, "No Snakes in the Backyard: Clinton to Kayani", original article in Hindi in *Dainik Jagran*, October 22, 2011, http://post.jagran.com/no-snakes-in-the-backyard-1320489442
34 Ali Ahmed, "Reconciling Doctrines: Prerequisite for Peace in South Asia", *IDSA Monograph Series*, 3, September 2010.
35 Abhijit Iyer Mitra, "Long-Term Gain Must Be the Aim", *Nuclear Newsletter*, (CAPS) 7, July 17, 2013.
36 Ali Ahmed, "Pakistani Nuclear Use and Implications for India", *Strategic Analysis*, 34:4, 2010, pp. 531–544.
37 Ali Ahmed, "Reviewing India's Nuclear Doctrine", *IDSA Policy Brief*, April 24, 2009.
38 Sheel Kant Sharma, "Strategic Situation: India Pakistan", *CAPS Issue Brief*, 86:13, February 28, 2013, p. 1.
39 Abhijit Singh, "Pakistan Navy's 'Nuclear' Aspirations", *IDSA Comment*, June 29, 2012, www.idsa.in/idsacomments/PakistanNavysNuclearAspirations_AbhijitSingh_290612
40 The deep state in Kanwal's definition is the collective action of the Pakistan army and the Inter-Services Intelligence (ISI). For more see, Gurmeet Kanwal, "Pakistan's 'Deep State' Continues to Sponsor Terrorism", *CLAWS Article*, 1417, August 9, 2015, www.claws.in/1417/pakistans-deep-state-continues-to-sponsor-terrorism-brig-gurmeet-kanwal.html
41 Gurmeet Kanwal, "Pakistani Army Firing across LoC: Raising the Ante in Kashmir", *CLAWS Article*, 1271, October 18, 2014, www.claws.in/1271/pakistan-army-firing-across-loc-raising-the-ante-in-kashmir-brig-gurmeet-kanwal.html
42 Roundtable on "Current Developments in J & K" organised by IDSA, New Delhi, 28 August, 2008
43 "Internal Security", *IDSA Policy Brief*, June 2009.
44 Vivek Chadha (ed.), "Armed Forces Special Powers Act: The Debate", *IDSA Monograph Series*, 7, November 2012.
45 Arpita Anant and Smruti Pattanaik, "Cross-LoC Confidence Building Measures between India and Pakistan: A Giant Leap or a Small Step towards Peace?", *IDSA Issue Brief*, February 12, 2010, p. 1.
46 ibid.
47 ibid.
48 ibid.
49 WHAM is described as a process of seeking the consent of the population for armed forces presence by accepting its necessity due to disturbed conditions in the area. Rahul K. Bhonsle, "Winning Hearts and Minds: Lessons from Jammu and Kashmir", *Manekshaw Papers*, 14 (New Delhi: CLAWS, 2009).
50 For more, see Arpita Anant, "Counter-Insurgency and 'Op Sadhbhavana' in Jammu and Kashmir", *IDSA Occasional Paper*, 19, October 2011; Vivek Chadha, "Heart as a Weapon': A Fresh Approach to the Concept of Hearts and Minds", *IDSA Policy Brief*, November 16, 2011.
51 Vivek Chadha, "Kashmir: Finding Lasting Peace", *IDSA Policy Brief*, June 26, 2014, www.idsa.in/policybrief/KashmirFindingLastingPeace_vchadha_260614

52 Vivek Chadha, "Security Situation in J & K: A Reality Check", *IDSA Comment*, June 28, 2013, www.idsa.in/idsacomments/SecuritySituationinJandK_vchadha_280613
53 ibid.
54 In 2008, the decision of the GOI and the state government of J&K to allocate land to the Amarnath Shrine Board was met with protests from the valley. The plan to allocate land to build temporary shelters for pilgrims to the Shrine was however supported by populations in the Jammu region of the state. The mass protests brought out the difference in perceptions between the two regions and reignited debates on the political status of Kashmir.
55 "Internal Security", *IDSA Policy Brief*, June 2009.
56 ibid.
57 Ashwani Gupta, "Ballot Bites the Bullet: Pakistan's Desperate Tactics in Kashmir", *CLAWS Article*, 1300, December 9, 2014, www.claws.in/1300/ballot-bites-the-bullet-pakistans-desperate-tactics-in-kashmir-ashwani-gupta.html
58 The dispute was over a barrage or dam that India wanted to construct on the Jhelum River just below the Wullar Lake. Pakistan's contention is that the lake is not suitable for a dam of any size, as it would inundate Srinagar and the valley. The Indian argument is that it would be used to maintain navigability in the Jhelum River during lean months. The construction was abandoned once the dispute started, and ten rounds of talks have been held but with little progress. Pakistan has argued that India violated Article I (II) of the IWT, which prohibits both parties from undertaking any "man-made obstruction" that may cause change in the volume of the daily flow of waters unless it is of an insignificant amount.
59 Uttam Kumar Sinha, "Water a Pre-Eminent Political Issue between India and Pakistan", *Strategic Analysis*, 34:4, July 2010, p. 483.
60 Uttam Kumar Sinha has conducted significant research on the IWT. In addition, he is currently on the technical advisory board of the South Asia Water Governance Programme and a policy advisory role to the International Centre for Integrated Mountain Development in Kathmandu. He was also India's representative to the CSCAP Working Group on Water Resources Security and Chaired the Working Group on Water Dispute Resolution Mechanism of the Strategic Studies Network, National Defense University, Washington DC.
61 Uttam Kumar Sinha, "India and Pakistan: Introspecting the Indus Treaty", *Strategic Analysis*, 32:6, November 2008, pp. 961–967.
62 ibid., p. 962.
63 ibid., p. 966.
64 Uttam Kumar Sinha, "Water a Pre-Eminent Political Issue between India and Pakistan", *Strategic Analysis*, 34:4, July 2010, p. 485.
65 Jasjit Singh (ed.), *Pakistan Occupied Kashmir: Under the Jackboot* (New Delhi: Siddhi Books, 1995).
66 P. K. Gautam, "Issues of National, Ecological and Human Security in the Siachen Glacier Region", *IDSA Comment*, April 25, 2012, www.idsa.in/idsacomments/Issuesof-NationalEcologicalandHumanSecurityintheSiachenGlacierRegion_pkgautam_250412
67 ibid.
68 Ashok Behuria, "Deciphering Kayani-Speak: One Avalanche Leads to Another?", *IDSA Comment*, April 20, 2012.
69 Ramesh Phadke, "A Siachen Resolution: Why Now?", *IDSA Comment*, November 8, 2012, www.idsa.in/idsacomments/ASiachenResolutionWhyNow_rphadke_081112
70 ibid.
71 Rahul Singh, "Action Please Not Words", *CLAWS*, June 21, 2012, www.claws.in/855/action-please-not-words-rohit-singh.html
72 Gurmeet Kanwal, "Demilitarisation of the Siachen Conflict Zone: An Idea Whose Time Has Come", *CLAWS Journal*, Winter 2012, p. 85.
73 Gurmeet Kanwal, "Pakistan's 'Deep State' Continues to Sponsor Terrorism", *CLAWS Article*, 1417, August 9, 2015, www.claws.in/1417/pakistans-deep-state-continues-to-sponsor-terrorism-brig-gurmeet-kanwal.html

74 Wilson John, "Pakistan Occupied Kashmir: An Emerging Epicentre of Global Jihad", in K. Warikoo (ed.) *The Other Kashmir: Society, Culture and Politics in the Karakoram Himalayas* (New Delhi: IDSA, 2014), p. 307.
75 ibid.
76 "Brief on India's Neighbourhood", *IDSA Policy Brief*, May 28, 2009, p. 2.
77 ibid.
78 ibid.
79 Sushant Sareen, "Need for a Composite Back-Channel with Pakistan Army", *IDSA Comment*, January 7, 2011, www.idsa.in/idsacomments/Needforacompositebackchannel withPakistanarmy_ssareen_070111
80 ibid.
81 Arvind Gupta, S. Kalyanaraman and Ashok K. Behuria, "India-Pakistan Relations after the Mumbai Terror Attacks: What Should India Do?", *Strategic Analysis*, 33:3, May 2009, p. 322.
82 ibid.
83 "Pakistan Occupied Kashmir: Changing the Discourse", *PoK Project Report* (New Delhi: IDSA, May 2011), p. 37.
84 Jasjit Singh (ed.), *Pakistan Occupied Kashmir: Under the Jackboot* (New Delhi: Siddhi Books, 1995).
85 Alok Bansal, "The Growing Alienation in Gilgit-Baltistan: The Future Portents", in Virendra Gupta and Alok Bansal (eds.) *Pakistan Occupied Kashmir: An Untold Story* (New Delhi: IDSA, 2007), p. 224.
86 ibid., p. 225.
87 ibid., p. 226.
88 ibid.
89 *IDSA Roundtable* on "Pakistan Occupied Kashmir: Changing the Discourse", August 19, 2010.
90 "Pakistan Occupied Kashmir: Changing the Discourse", *PoK Project Report* (New Delhi: IDSA, May 2011), p. 38.
91 Gurmeet Kanwal, "Pakistan Atrocities in PoK and Gilgit-Baltistan", *CLAWS Article*, 1449, October 9, 2015, www.claws.in/1449/pakistan-atrocities-in-pok-and-gilgit-baltistan-brig-gurmeet-kanwal.html
92 Ashutosh Misra, "Unfazed New Delhi Continues the Dialogue Despite Hurriyat's Absence", *IDSA Comment*, March 3, 2006, www.idsa.in/idsastrategiccomments/Unfazed NewDelhiContinuestheDialogueProcessDespiteHurriyatsAbsence_AMisra_030306
93 ibid.
94 ibid.
95 Seminar on *Terrorism in the India-Pakistan-Afghanistan Region: Linkages and Responses* organised by CLAWS, February 17, 2009, www.claws.in/event-detail.php?eID=220
96 Seminar on *Situation in Jammu and Kashmir and Contours of Future Strategy* organised by CLAWS, January 2, 2008, www.claws.in/event-detail.php?eID=177
97 Pushpita Das, "Securing the Northern Coast of Gujarat: Challenges and Responses", *IDSA Fellows Seminar*, November 28, 2008, www.idsa.in/event/indiancoastline_pushpitadas_281108
98 Alok Bansal, "Maritime Threat Perceptions: Non-State Actors in the Indian Ocean Region", *Maritime Affairs: Journal of the National Maritime Foundation of India*, 6:1, Summer 2010, p. 15.
99 Personal communication with senior member and defence personnel at NMF in New Delhi on October 17, 2015.
100 Gurpreet Khurana, "India Needs Sea-Based 'Active' Deterrence against State-Sponsored Terrorism", *NMF Commentary*, March 25, 2015, www.maritimeindia.org/Commentry View.aspx?NMFCID=8397
101 Vikram Munshi, *Wars by Pakistan* (New Delhi: CAPS, 2014).
102 Following the attack, the Indian Navy was designated as "the authority responsible for overall maritime security which includes coastal security and offshore security,"

effectively relegating the Coast Guard from its primary coastal security role. Organisationally, a series of Joint Operations Centers were established with responsibility over the various coastal regions. The Navy and Coast Guard acquired hovercrafts and surveillance aircraft, and the Navy also set up a new coastal security unit, the Sagar Prahari Bal, with the mission of day/night operations and "seaward anti-terrorist patrols." For more, see Marc Munson, "Indian Maritime Security after Mumbai", *Capability Analysis* (Center for International Maritime Security), July 2, 2012, http://cimsec.org/indian-maritime-security-after-mumbai/1634

5
NON-GOVERNMENT POLICY THINK TANKS

Government think tanks examined in the previous chapter did not lack financial resources and enjoyed easy access to policymakers. The discursive interactions therefore remained strong and substantive. While their ideational independence could be questioned and there was a similar political narrative, policy inputs were clearly visible due to direct connections with the government. Both examples of coordinative and communicative discourse can be found in their engagement with foreign policy issues. On the other end of the spectrum are non-government think tanks that do not depend primarily on government sources for funding alone but managed to establish networks with international funding organisations. While funding has been diversified, this chapter seeks answers to other crucial questions: did their relative independence from government funding enable independent thinking? how did they engage with formal policy-making mechanisms in India? what was the level of access to policymakers? Were non-government think tanks conditioned by the research agendas of donor organisations, particularly on India–Pakistan relations?

As in the previous chapter, this chapter also emphasises the role of intellectual elites in generating public opinion and interacting with policy-making mechanisms, particularly on relations with Pakistan. This chapter and the next are linked. While the first part focuses the attention on some of the big players in this category that include the Observer Research Foundation (ORF), the Centre for Policy Research (CPR), the Vivekananda International Foundation (VIF) and the India Foundation (IF) with broad research agendas, in the second part the focus is on non-government think tanks with research agendas specifically focused on peacebuilding and reconciliation. These include the Institute of Peace and Conflict Studies (IPCS), the Delhi Policy Group (DPG), the Women in Security, Conflict Management and Peace (WISCOMP) and the Centre for Dialogue and Reconciliation (CDR).

It was argued in the previous chapter that the creation of think tanks and support to intellectual elites was an attempt by the government of India to institutionalise consensus on policy directions. This was reflective of the Gramscian notion of state spirit where intellectual elites at government think tanks created consensus for government policy on Pakistan, highlighting dominant government narratives focused on national security and strategic strength. This chapter takes this argument further through an analysis of the intellectual membership and policy discourse of non-government think tanks. With relative freedom from government funding brought about by India's liberalisation process, these think tanks were able to expand the scope of ideas on Pakistan. Yet, access to funding was also enabled by government support and was a reflection of India's expanding international interests and the need to enhance the bureaucracy's capacity in dealing with new security issues.

The tools provided by DI have been useful to highlight the interactive processes that have enabled the ORF, the VIF, the IF and the CPR to be actors within the foreign policy process. The involvement of elites in government committees and specific project funding aimed at providing policy expertise in areas where the MEA lacks capacity are indications of their interactions and the creation of a "discursive sphere."[1] Through their research outreach they have thus been involved in the promotion, advocacy and articulation of foreign policy towards Pakistan during the CD period.

Yet, the place of non-government think tanks within policy structures is something that DI doesn't adequately explain. Several viewpoints expressed in the interview process highlighted that in the restrictive and bureaucratic set-up of India, think tank involvement has been limited to suggesting policy options and adding to the public discourse on foreign policy, rather than a direct involvement in the policy formulation processes. Respondents also argued that the adoption of think tank ideas on Pakistan remained dependent on the particular political atmosphere, and think tanks performed better on "functional issues" and were not as relevant to "bilateral issues" or "paradigm issues" that impacted the relationship with Pakistan.[2] It was also claimed that "the India-Pakistan relationship is not a foreign policy issue but a domestic political issue in both countries."[3] The resolution of the conflict is therefore dependent on the equation between various power centres in both countries – the army in Pakistan and the political leadership in India. The foreign ministry and diplomats are argued to have no role. Within this scenario then, policy ideas from non-government think tanks communicated to the foreign ministry would presumably have no role.

There do exist contrary opinions as well, which argued that "think tanks are useful when government wants to mould or inform public debate."[4] They also "gauge public opinion," thus fulfilling their role as a bridge between policy making and civil society.[5] There is very little evidence of specific inputs that have been implemented as policy. There is, however, an evolving consultative role for think tanks in India that is highlighted in the following chapter. Think tanks created an avenue for "more informed public debate" on key issues.[6] As a former diplomat noted, "I have done much more in the past 15 years since retirement in influencing the public discourse than I did in 36 years in the government."[7] Government funding indicates a significant interest in a broader research agenda by the government seeking specific research expertise from non-government think tanks.

Notwithstanding broad opinions, non-government think tanks have engaged considerably with the policy debate on Pakistan, as the evidence in the following sections shows. They have offered policy recommendations in addition to promoting the dialogue and debating the various formulations for resolution of key disputes. There was, however, a change in the interest on India–Pakistan issues, visible particularly after the suspension of the CD, with policy ideas becoming restricted and less amenable to dialogue. While this reflected the changed geopolitical circumstances and the broken bilateral relationship with Pakistan, it can also be explained by the process of bargaining and "research brokerage" that think tanks practice to maintain their policy relevance and remain viable actors.[8] Non-government think tanks analysed in this chapter can be described as "embedded institutions," which over time can spread ideas but are more likely to get ideologically absorbed into the stronger bureaucratic frameworks.[9] Drezner, for instance, argues that the "placement of institutions vis-à-vis the rest of the foreign policy apparatus determines the ability of these institutions to survive and thrive."[10]

Examining think tank policy narratives on Pakistan, this chapter therefore makes the argument that even though non-government think tanks were funded externally, there remained a certain dependence on government narratives and investment in the dialogue process owing to project funding. However, differences in the nature of the intellectual elite and institutional agendas that focus more on academic research expanded the understanding of issues. This contributed to their evolving role in the development and mobilisation of public opinion. The first section of this chapter looks at the diversity of intellectual elites and worldviews at non-government think tanks and explores their linkages with policy making. While drawing comparisons with government think tanks examined earlier, later sections consider the policy discourse on Pakistan as well as the role of these think tanks as communicative actors relaying information on government initiatives through their contribution to public discourse.

Nature of intellectual elite – patterns in institutional worldviews and collaborations with the state

Institutional structures at government think tanks closely resembled the government, and the presence of former bureaucrats and retired armed forces personnel, while providing access to policy makers, also created a replication of official policy narratives. However, at non-government think tanks, while linkages with policy making became unclear, there was a broader academic understanding of India–Pakistan issues. While former bureaucrats and military practitioners continued to make up the intellectual elite, the CPR, the ORF, the VIF and the IF also encouraged academic expertise. The following section details the professional background of the intellectual elites at these think tanks, highlighting linkages with official policy-making bodies as well as their crucial role in shaping public discourse on Pakistan. The aspect of diversified funding is also considered, yet the implicit government support to these think tanks – if not directly then through the approval of external funding and limited project funding – is also visible. The government in India also played a crucial part in the regulation of foreign funding through the FCRA, known for its "arbitrariness of procedure."[11]

The oldest in this ilk is the Centre for Policy Research (CPR), one of the "second wave institutes" that appeared with an increase in funding as India began to bring down the barriers on foreign funding.[12] With a particular focus on academic research, the CPR's evolution in 1973 began with government funding primarily from the Indian Council for Social Science Research (ICSSR) and project-specific funding from the MEA, yet sources of funding have since been diversified to include foreign donations/project funding from the World Bank, the International Development Research Centre (IDRC) Canada, the Ford Foundation, the Asia Foundation and the Bill and Melinda Gates Foundation, to name a few.

The inclusion of business funding and corporate interest in policy making is perhaps more easily visible in the Observer Research Foundation (ORF), established in 1990 with close linkages to the Reliance group of companies.[13] The ORF's establishment was also supported by government leadership, particularly former Prime Minister Atal Bihari Vajpayee, with research agendas aimed at encouraging the liberalisation process in India.[14] Focus has since expanded to subjects such as climate change, global governance, strategic studies, national security and space studies. According to the declaration of contributions, core funding continues to come from Reliance Industries, along with project funding from the MEA and other funding agencies.[15] Funding from Reliance accounts for around 65%, with the foundation diversifying its sources to include support from the government, private corporates, foreign foundations and others.[16]

While the source of funding is very clear in the cases of both the CPR and the ORF, in the other two think tanks in this category, the lines blur. Formed in December 2009, the Vivekananda International Foundation (VIF) identifies itself as "an independent, non-partisan institution" focused on academic research and additionally as a "platform for dialogue and conflict resolution."[17] Recognised as a Trust affiliated with the Vivekananda Kendra, funding for the VIF supposedly comes from the trust fund, though the official documents (annual reports, website) do not provide a detailed account of donations received and their allocation to specific projects and programmes. There is very little evidence also on the funding patterns of the India Foundation (IF) established in 2000.

While funding forms one part of the story, the nature of intellectual elites at think tanks is also relevant here. The previous chapter found evidence of an overlap in membership patterns and political narratives on Pakistan based on similarities in funding, professional backgrounds of the elite and fluidity in the movement of intellectual elites both within think tanks as well as the revolving door between think tanks and formal institutions of policy making. The membership pattern in the ORF, the CPR, the VIF and the IF is also similar, yet there is an increased attention to academic research. There are also linkages to business interests, particularly at the ORF, reflected both in affiliations and research focus on India's economic policy. The initiative to form the ORF came from R.K. Mishra, a former journalist with close linkages with policy makers and former Prime Ministers Indira Gandhi and Rajiv Gandhi. Mishra, along with Vivek Katju (former Head- PAI division, MEA) and Brajesh Mishra (former NSA), was also involved in the back-channel negotiations with Pakistan at the behest of Prime Minister Vajpayee during the Kargil war.[18] This role was acknowledged by the MEA and his close relationship with key policymakers and with Vajpayee himself also provided early support for the ORF.[19] Mishra was also able to secure financial support for the ORF from the Reliance group in perhaps the first instance of corporate interest in Indian think tanks.

The ORF is currently led by Chairman Sunjoy Joshi, a former bureaucrat, and President Samir Saran, a former employee of Reliance Industries. In addition, the ORF's membership has been a mix of former government and defence officials including General V.P. Malik (former Army chief), former foreign secretary M.K. Rasgotra, former chief of RAW Vikram Sood, as well as academic and media specialists, namely C. Raja Mohan, Manoj Joshi and Rajeswari Rajagopalan, reflecting a combination of academic and practitioner knowledge. Younger researchers, among them students of international studies from leading universities, add to the component of academic research, building capacity for IR research in India. The ORF has established its regional presence with branches in Mumbai, Kolkata and Chennai. The ORF's Mumbai chapter is led by Sudheendra Kulkarni, who served as a special aide to Vajpayee between 1998 and 2004. Apart from serving as Vajpayee's speech-writer, Kulkarni is known to have played an active role in conceptualising and driving several landmark initiatives of the Vajpayee government.

The ORF elites' linkages with the Indian foreign policy establishment are also visible. For instance, in addition to adding to the public discourse through his journalistic writings on Kashmir, Pakistan and Siachen, Manoj Joshi has served on the Naresh Chandra Committee to propose security reforms; former diplomat Rakesh Sood set up the Disarmament and International Security Affairs Division in the MEA, which he led for eight years till the end of 2000; Brajesh Mishra, India's first NSA and later trustee at the ORF has often been credited with influence on India's policy towards Pakistan in the Vajpayee years. Mishra's diplomatic imprint on India's Pakistan policy was seen in the Agra summit (2002) and gaining President Musharraf's commitment that Pakistan will not allow the use of its territory for terrorist activity (2004).[20]

Former bureaucrats, in addition to expertise on economics and politics, also form the core of intellectual elites at the CPR. The bureaucracy is represented by former Foreign Secretary Shyam Saran, who in addition to being a senior fellow at the CPR was also Chairman of the Research and Information System for Developing Countries (RIS) – the think tank of the MEA. Seasoned diplomats including G. Parthasarathy, with considerable experience in Indo-Pak issues, and a member of several Indo-Pak Track II initiatives also add to the CPR's discourse. There is a significant focus on academic research at the CPR led until recently by President Pratap Bhanu Mehta, who in addition to being a prolific writer, has contributed significantly to the public discourse on Indian foreign and domestic policy and has also served on many central government committees.[21] Other intellectuals such as Bharat Karnad and Brahma Chellaney, as described by Mehta

> [have] continued to lend their weight to CPR's status as one of a handful of modern think tanks steeped in the realist tradition, while Nimmi Kurian and Bibek Debroy provided the perfect counter balance through their focus on conflict resolution, sub-regional issues, trade and political economy.[22]

Chellaney, who until January 2000 was an advisor to India's NSC and convener of the External Security Group of the NSAB, has been notable for his advocatory role, along with K. Subrahmanyam, in the drafting of India's nuclear doctrine.[23] Bharat Karnad was also a member of the first NSAB, where he participated in the Nuclear Doctrine Drafting Group and the external security and technology security groups of the Strategic Review. In addition, Karnad has been commissioned by the Headquarters of the Integrated Defence Staff to conduct a strategic nuclear orientation course for senior military officers and to conceptualise and conduct a series of inter-agency wargames on the nuclear tripwire.[24]

While funding for all of these think tanks is diversified, there are visible linkages with the policy establishment, both direct and indirect. As argued earlier, each was established at a particular time in India's growing economic and political trajectory, thus both the ORF and the CPR receive project-specific funding from the MEA. In addition to enabling foreign contributions, the government of India has also involved these think tanks in specific policy initiatives. For instance, the ORF is the official Track II research coordinator for India at the BRICS. It is also a member of the BRICS Think Tanks Council set up in 2013.[25] The CPR in 2008 also organised with the MEA the third IBSA (India, Brazil, South Africa) Editors' Conference. In addition, the ORF's programmes on climate change and Indian Ocean security have captured the attention of the government, and in October 2014, it became a partner organisation for the sixth core group meeting of the Munich Security Conference with the MEA.[26] In March 2016, the ORF launched the Raisina Dialogue in collaboration with the MEA – "an annual conference serving as a platform for multi-stakeholder interactions on foreign policy in keeping with the MEA's approach to seek wider inputs for policy making."[27] Modelled along Singapore's Shangri-La Dialogue, the Raisina Dialogue is now a notable platform for policy promotion, with active involvement of senior policy elites from the MEA and the government of India.

The thematic clusters at the CPR have included a focus on both research and advocacy, and some of the specific research initiatives with active components of policy interface, demonstrating coordinative discourse among policy elites, have been the first of its kind in India. Notable among these are the Parliamentary Research Service initiated in 2005 that aimed at establishing linkages with legislative processes in India. The MP Policy Dialogue series initiated in 2009 is also a novel initiative envisaged as "a forum for Members of Parliament to discuss topical policy-related issues with an academic expert."[28] Other research initiatives include the Climate Change Initiative (2009) funded by the MacArthur Foundation with policy interface at several levels with the UNFCCC and the Copenhagen process and with the Ministry of Environment and Forests and the Planning Commission task force for low carbon growth. In addition to policy-relevant research, policy promotion has also been a key element, as represented in the wide array of published research reports and other policy-relevant writing. In 2012, the CPR faculty members, Pratap Bhanu Mehta, Shyam Saran and Srinath Raghavan, participated in the preparation of a document titled *Non Alignment 2.0: A Foreign and Strategic Policy for India in the Twenty First Century*. The document was the product of collective deliberation and was released at the CPR in 2012 by then NSA Shiv Shankar Menon.[29] In 2013, with funding from the Asia Foundation, the CPR also launched its online portal – the SARCist[30] – South Asia Regional Cooperation, with a special focus on trade and investment issues.

Known to be ideologically close to the BJP-RSS, a key objective identified at the VIF is to "reassess, formulate and develop India's civilizational and cultural imperatives."[31] The organisational impetus was provided by Ajit Doval, the former Intelligence Bureau Chief and Founder Director from 2009–2014. Doval was also one of the negotiators during the Kandahar hijacking case in 1999 and has considerable experience with militancy in the Kashmir valley. In 2014, Doval was appointed as India's NSA by the Modi government, a position to which he was reappointed in the new Modi government in 2019. Much of the initial policy direction at the VIF is known to have been the brainchild of Doval, and his induction into the prime position of foreign policy making in India makes this a unique characteristic of the revolving door policy. It has also significantly enhanced the VIF's coordinative discourse with direct and sustained linkages with the foreign policy establishment in India. In addition to Doval, other members at the VIF include Nripendra Misra (now Principal Secretary to PM Modi) and Ata Hasnain, who retired as GOC in Kashmir and has significant field experience working on the LoC. Hasnain has also been credited for having conceived and operationalised the "Hearts Doctrine" in J&K as an effort towards perception management regarding army operations in the valley.[32] The VIF is currently led by Arvind Gupta, former DG at IDSA and former Deputy NSA in the Modi government from 2014 to 2017. Other members on the VIF's advisory board and executive council include former Foreign Secretary Kanwal Sibal (member NSAB 2008–2010); former Secretary RAW A.K. Verma; former Cabinet Minister Arif Mohammad Khan; former army chiefs Shankar

Roy Chowdhury, V.N. Sharma, N.C. Vij; and senior diplomat Satish Chandra, to name a few. Former director N.C. Vij was DGMO during the Kargil War and briefed Vajpayee at the BJP National Executive Meeting on the progress of operations, breaking from military tradition.[33]

While the VIF is known to be close to the BJP, the IF has direct linkages with the BJP and the Modi government. Notable members of the Modi administration, including Nirmala Sitharaman (Current Finance Minister) and Suresh Prabhu (former Minister of Civil Aviation and current Member of Rajya Sabha), have been associated with the IF. In addition, Ram Madhav, the National General Secretary of the BJP, and Shaurya Doval, the son of NSA Ajit Doval, are on the IF governing board. Madhav has been a Member of the BJP National Executive and in charge of the media and public relations of the RSS. The research component within the IF comes from Executive Director Alok Bansal, a former Naval officer with research experience on India's strategic security and formerly associated with the IDSA and the NMF. Prominent political columnists Ashok Malik and Swapan Dasgupta are also affiliated with the IF, in addition to research staff composed of university students and researchers.

Thus, even though funding for non-government think tanks is diversified and there is distance from official policy making, there exist significant linkages with the policy establishment. These are both official and unofficial, yet relatively less institutionalised, as in the case of government think tanks. The nature of intellectuals, however, is more diversified with an additional emphasis on academic research. How this translated into policy ideas on Pakistan is the focus of the following sections that also elaborate on the influence of elites in framing and mobilising public opinion and raising awareness on the elements of India's dialogue with Pakistan.

Think tank contribution to policy discourse

The similarities in the policy discourse adopted by government think tanks were found to be due to similar membership styles and institutional worldviews derived from patronage from the government. Political narratives on Pakistan emphasised national security as the predominant theme, and prevailing narratives on Pakistan were encouraged while dissenting voices (particularly those calling for concessions to Pakistan) were undermined or ignored. This chapter examines if there is any deviation from that trend at non-government think tanks. When think tanks are able to supplement government funding through a reliance on private donors, does the nature of discourse undergo a change? Are think tanks then able to expand on the agenda and ideas beyond government narratives on relations with Pakistan? Further, the oft-argued "consultative role" in policy formulation is explored, with a particular focus on "orienting public opinion."[34]

The reliance on private sources for funding also raises questions about the relative independence of research agendas. Additionally, owing to the sensitive nature of the issues at hand, the Indian foreign policy establishment would be wary of externally funded research on international relations and strategic affairs."[35] Sponsors too are in a position to dictate their own research agendas irrespective of whether they are public agencies, private foundations or international organisations.[36] Samir Saran from the ORF, for instance, argues that:

> we are acutely aware of the need to balance a proximate relationship with the government that would allow enough distance to be able to conduct research freely and yet be cordial enough so that we would be able to share insights and ideas with institutions that are best placed to make use of them.[37]

This need to balance the sharing of policy ideas while striving to maintain independent research agendas becomes further complicated in the case of a high-profile and highly volatile relationship as with Pakistan. Policy inputs into India's relations with Pakistan are curtailed by the continually changing bilateral relationship and the overwhelming primacy of political will as the main driving force for change. It is within this dynamic that the CD process provided a "critical juncture" – offering space and power to think tanks – to transfer knowledge (in this case on specific issues that impacted India–Pakistan relations) and then act as carriers of coordinative and communicative discourse.[38] Think tank traction on "functional issues" and mobilisation of public opinion in support of government policy on Pakistan is thus crucial to understanding their place in the policy process.[39]

Non-government think tanks – namely the ORF, the CPR, the VIF and the IF – have all engaged with dynamics within the India–Pakistan relationship, to varying degrees. Research agendas at the ORF are comprehensive, and the engagement with India–Pakistan relations represents just one aspect. Discourse on India–Pakistan relations was strongest in the period while the official CD process was ongoing and there was focused attention on issues including Kashmir, Siachen and terrorism. What is surprising though is that being an organisation with an articulated focus on India's economic policies, the ORF's engagement with aspects of India's economic cooperation with Pakistan has been very limited, even though broader economic programmes undertaken by India have been considered.

At the CPR too, research on Pakistan is undertaken within the thematic cluster of International Relations and Security. Intellectuals including Brahma Chellaney, Bharat Karnad, G. Parthasarathy, B.G. Verghese and Ramaswamy Iyer have contributed to the discourse on nuclear security and Kashmir and India's position on river water disputes with Pakistan. There has also been an engagement with dialogue on Kashmir at the Track II level with participation in the Neemrana Dialogue, Pugwash initiatives and the Chaophraya dialogues. As early as 2003, the late B.G. Verghese was associated with the Task Force on Inter-Linking of Rivers and later between 2013–2014, was a part of three World

Bank study groups working on resolving conflicts in the Indus, Ganges and Brahmaputra basins.[40]

Initiated in 2009, the VIF arrived on the think tank landscape during a crucial phase for India–Pakistan relations. The formal CD was suspended and the post-Mumbai scenario was very different from the years preceding it. Most of the issues under consideration in the CD had collapsed by 2009, and VIF viewpoints have often reflected cynicism in the process and the futility of continuing a dialogue process with Pakistan. Research at the VIF has therefore been squarely focused on the dispute in J&K and the problem of terrorism emanating from Pakistan. The IF's policy discourse, however, is difficult to gauge as they "provide inputs directly to the government through policy briefs that are classified"[41] and other research outputs are limited, even though it is often a forum for discussions on foreign policy.[42] The following section highlights policy discourse from non-government think tanks on issues as addressed in the CD. It also reflects the government's collaboration with these non-state actors aimed at building consensus on its official positions.

Kashmir: expanding the debate – Much like narratives at government think tanks that analysed the conflict in Kashmir primarily through the national security paradigm, non-government think tanks have also highlighted the necessity of maintaining law and order in the state. They however expanded the scope of their policy ideas with an increased focus on civil society engagements in Kashmir as well as additional policy ideas on AFSPA and water conflicts impacting the dispute. Substantial attention in the discourse was on the delineation of the dispute first as a problem 'of' Kashmir, which relates to the relationship with Pakistan, and second as the problem 'in' Kashmir that refers to the internal dynamics within the Indian state of J&K. This approach resonated with the direction of the official dialogue adopted by the Indian government. In his closing remarks at the second Jammu and Kashmir Roundtable in May 2006, Manmohan Singh reiterated that the dispute in J&K has two dimensions – "one being the relationship between Delhi and Srinagar and the other, the relationship between Delhi and Islamabad."[43] Policy ideas from think tanks popularised this argument and further expanded it through their policy recommendations.

While attention to Kashmir was limited in the ORF discourse prior to the ceasefire in 2003, government initiatives including L.K. Advani's talks with separatists and Vajpayee's new peace initiatives with Pakistan were appreciated as a move beyond "traditionally stated positions."[44] As highlighted earlier, the ORF's R.K. Mishra and Brajesh Mishra were closely involved with Vajpayee's agenda in Kashmir. Opinions in the early stage of the process did, however, warn about the volatility of the issue and the "divergent" and "seemingly irreconcilable" positions of India and Pakistan as a deterrent to the larger process. However, reflecting the organisation's practice where research opinions are "not reconciled" into a common institutional position, the CD's engagement with Kashmir was understood in various ways at the ORF.[45] One opinion argued that the CD approach worked in "keeping Pakistan engaged on all matters except

Kashmir."[46] A differing perspective was that the unilateral ceasefire at the LoC was "inconvenient for the Indian army" and allowed the Pakistan army "the freedom to continue its nefarious activities in Kashmir without fear of Indian retribution," enabling Pakistan to "continue its low-cost, low-risk, high-payoff option of waging a proxy war against India."[47]

The "historical continuity" in Pakistan's Kashmir policy and the military-militant connection within Pakistan as a deterrent for peace was a dominant focus of the discourse. Musharraf's proclaimed commitment to destroy terrorist infrastructure within Pakistan was welcomed by the government, but opinions at the ORF argued that it was also

> a conscious decision on the part of his government to keep the Jihadi infrastructure alive as an insurance policy on Kashmir in case the peace process, especially the dialogue on Kashmir gets mired in bickering and protests, and fails to yield any tangible results for Pakistan.[48]

There was discussion at think tanks on the Kashmir proposals put forth by Pakistani President Musharraf. Reiterated in a TV interview during his visit to New Delhi in April 2005, Musharraf's four-point proposal sought a phased withdrawal of troops, local self-governance, free movement of Kashmiris across the LoC and a joint supervision mechanism in Jammu and Kashmir involving India, Pakistan and Kashmiris.[49] At ORF these ideas represented a "well-crafted and cleverly worded war game."[50] This perspective was similar to the CPR's where these proposals were seen merely as "public rhetoric" for domestic consumption.[51]

Even though there was some scepticism regarding the direction of the dialogue, the disagreement was mostly on the need for caution rather than a complete disregard for the process. Think tank discourse at this stage played a role in highlighting the nature of the dialogue as well as the significant government initiatives and proposals on Kashmir, including those set forth by Musharraf, were analysed in depth and introduced into the public domain. The CPR's opinion conceded that the four-point proposal signified a change in Pakistan's position of claiming "J&K by virtue of the two-nation ideology" and resembled the concept of a J&K with soft borders, leading to some kind of "confederation" that was canvassed with President Ayub and Abdul Qayyum Khan by Jawaharlal Nehru and Sheikh Abdullah as far back as 1964.[52] The idea of a "non-territorial" settlement aimed at "transforming the relationship across the LoC" was recommended as an advisable policy direction.[53] A more vigorous understanding of Musharraf's Kashmir proposals was also emphasised, particularly the concept of "self-governance" that brought to light the stark contrasts in the political and social realities between Indian Kashmir and Azad Jammu and Kashmir (AJK) on the Pakistani side.[54] The government's focus on cross-LoC interactions also found attention in think tank discourse, with recommendations to open up other cross-border routes including Jammu and Sialkot, Kargil and Skardu, Poonch and Rawalakot, Rajouri and Mirpur.[55] Travel between Kashmir was recommended to be used as an opportunity to build on the coordination and communication within an "informal co-federal relationship."[56] Think tank intellectuals at this stage were also directly engaged with the dialogue, for example, M.K. Rasgotra headed the working group on Strengthening Cross LoC Relationships set up by the UPA government, and Verghese at the CPR was a part of the Neemrana dialogue group, which is known to have contributed to the operationalities of cross-border travel.

In addition to a mere promotion of government policy, the ORF and the CPR also became forums for a studied critique of the initiatives in Kashmir. The academic discourse focused on the state of human rights in PAK often as a counter-tool to Pakistan's attention on Indian Kashmir. There was significant effort at these think tanks to highlight conditions in PAK, particularly after the Kashmir earthquake in 2005 that provided space to extremist organisations, including the Jamaat-ud Dawa (JuD), the parent organisation of the Lashkar-e-Taiba (LeT), in addition to a "coalition of various religious, secessionist and terrorist groups coming together in the aftermath of the earthquake."[57] In terms of policy implications, this collusion among various groups it was felt, would increase India's vulnerability at a time when the government was considering opening additional routes along the LoC. Questions were also raised on reconciling these new ideas with India's position on Kashmir adopted in the resolution of the parliament in 1994 and aspects of the 1972 Simla agreement.[58]

There was also a focus on evolving a military strategy with pro-actively aggressive trans-LoC operations in response to violations of ceasefire and attempts of infiltration.[59] The articulation of such a strategy gained momentum after 26/11. The VIF, for instance, was incessantly critical of Manmohan Singh's policy of engagement with Pakistan and argued that it failed to reduce the trust deficit and the continued LoC infiltrations. Terrorist attacks, movement of counterfeit currency and Pakistan's inactions against those involved in the Mumbai attacks were all considered a manifestation of this policy of appeasement. Policy ideas at this stage were also a reflection of the changing public opinion and the possible loss of the "critical juncture." Reflecting the growing cynicism with dialogue, recommendations from the VIF therefore included abandoning the CD, making trade liberalisation with Pakistan contingent upon the Most Favoured Nation status to India and curtailing visas till concerns related to terrorism were addressed.[60] In terms of offensive diplomatic action, recommendations suggested exploiting "Pakistan's faultlines" in Balochistan and highlighting cases of human rights violations, in addition to a recourse to covert and focused strikes against terrorists.[61] Any attempts by the foreign policy establishment under Manmohan Singh to resume dialogue with Pakistan were seen through this critical lens, whether it was the meeting between foreign ministers S.M. Krishna and Hina Rabbani Khar in 2012 or Pakistani Interior Minister Rehman Malik's visit to India in 2013.[62]

Think tank discourse also contributed to debates on resolving the internal conflict in Kashmir through specific discussions on maintaining law and order within the state, evaluating the presence of the Indian army and the execution of the AFSPA and the role of the separatists, particularly the Hurriyat. Additionally, efforts to work with civil society within Kashmir to address the alienation of populations was also a significant factor addressed in the discourse. Perspectives on these issues also reflected the difference of opinion among think tank intellectuals. At the ORF, for instance, while some arguments considered the Hurriyat a "marginal player," a "nuisance value" that would create domestic dissent, making it diplomatically easier for Pakistan to gain the upper hand, other opinions appreciated Manmohan Singh's invitation to the Hurriyat to be a part of the Roundtable Conferences and considered it "as a counter strategy to keep the Hurriyat from playing the role of a spoiler."[63]

At the CPR too, the Hurriyat's assumption as the "sole" representative of Kashmiri public opinion and its support for the Pakistani position on J&K was criticised.[64] The Prime Minister's roundtable, it was argued, was an opportunity for the government to keep the Hurriyat in check.[65] The UPA's initiatives on Kashmir were, however, given considerable value within the narratives. In considering the proposals on Kashmir, policy options recommended the creation of a "Union Territory comprising Srinagar, Baramullah, Anantnag, Kupwara, Pulwama and Budgam and giving it a semi-State status, much like what Delhi once had."[66] This, it was argued, would take into account the claims of all three regions of the state – namely, Jammu, Kashmir and Ladakh – giving them more autonomy and better opportunities for good governance. Arguments at the CPR also stressed the need for Indian public opinion to be made aware of the interests of the Indian government in giving concessions to J&K "from a position of moral strength and not be seen as shabby compromises that gloss over past guilt."[67] In addition to welcoming the PM's decision to meet with the Hurriyat, recommendations to consider a roundtable conference to address the alienation and return of the Pandits was also recommended as part of an internal settlement in parallel with a settlement with Pakistan.[68]

For the VIF, however, the dominant opinion was that separatists in Kashmir should not be allowed political space or the freedom to meet "external adversaries" for political or financial support and their "open alignment" with Pakistan should not be tolerated.[69] The criticism of India's Kashmir policy was not limited to the initiatives of the Manmohan Singh government alone. Earlier attempts by Vajpayee, including the visit to Lahore, the failure to "escalate" the Kargil conflict or the decision to seek a "political" resolution of the Kashmir conflict, were also critiqued.[70]

The changing dynamics in Kashmir visible after the Amarnath agitation in August 2008 brought to light the continued concerns of the Kashmiri youth. Policy recommendations from think tanks, for instance, articulated reaching out to disgruntled groups, including the Hurriyat, generating new employment opportunities and initiating direct dialogue with the people.[71] Discussions underlined "the need for sustained dialogue representing all stakeholders in Kashmir and underscored the criticality in maintaining law and order in the state and possible reduction in CRPF deployment in residential areas."[72] Introspection into government policy and highlighting significant shortcomings in the government's approach to internal dialogue was considered at think tanks. Ideas ranged from identifying underlying causes for mistrust in the Indian state to attributing this to the UPA's policy of appeasement of the separatists, "pampering the Kashmir valley with economic packages" and ignoring Pakistan's continued support to the insurgency, which was a significant cause for the disturbance.[73]

The fall-out of the Amarnath agitation was to redirect attention to the debate on Indian military presence in J&K, in particular the focus on the AFSPA. The AFSPA, as argued in the ORF discourse, represented "a legal protection to conduct effective operations." The focus remained on the need for the central government to undertake "counter alienation" policies to address the concerns of human rights violations that arose from the implementation of the AFSPA.[74] Yet, for the VIF, any dilution of the power wielded by state security forces in Kashmir was not recommended. One opinion stated that, "to utilize this public hyperventilation against localized perceptions of security forces' excesses [and] to justify and legitimise the separatist agenda in J&K is a serious and tragic mistake."[75] Instead, the need for a "bipartisan consensus" in J&K was recommended, although what this bipartisan consensus entailed was left unclear. There was no viable basis found for the dilution of the AFSPA provisions. Instead, the emphasis was on the return of Kashmiri pandits to the valley.[76] In addition, research at the VIF underscored the changing trends within militancy in Kashmir and articulated the need for new policy options, including counter-infiltration strategies and small trans-LoC strikes given the restrictions of waging conventional war. Perception management exercises were also suggested to be conducted internally to demonstrate the stronger position of the Indian army.[77] Understood collectively, these ideas represented a very visible change in dominant government narratives after the suspension of the CD and the continuing deterioration in India–Pakistan relations.

Siachen: from strategic value to International Peace Park – Government think tank discourse on Siachen was fairly split – between demilitarisation or the insistence on Siachen's strategic value for India. A similar perspective was visible in non-government think tanks, but much like formulations on Kashmir, policy ideas were expansive and more detailed. Ideas suggested caution yet recommended a phased demilitarisation from a 5–10-year period, going to a third party to secure guarantees against any possible Pakistani incursion, preparation of detailed maps by the MEA showing present positions and sharing them publicly.[78] Other tangible policy suggestions included the creation of a joint monitoring system. The viewpoint of the think tank intellectuals is also relevant here. Gurmeet Kanwal, Senior Fellow with the ORF at the time, positively perceived the demilitarisation of the region. Kanwal maintained this position during his subsequent association with the CLAWS and the CAPS, highlighted in the previous chapter. According to his arguments, a national consensus needed to be built around this issue, and the demilitarisation of Siachen represented a relatively low-risk option to test Pakistan's long-term intentions.[79] Similarly at the CPR, Verghese advocated for the establishment of an International Peace Park covering the entire region from the west of the Karakoram Pass up to K2 under joint management by India and Pakistan.[80] Subsequently, the Shaksgam region under Chinese control could also be included in the park. Verghese continued to support the recommendation of a peace park in 2007 and added further that:

> licensing a trekking expedition to Siachen, against Pakistan's hollow protest, could mark the beginning of converting the NJ 9842-Baltoro-Siachen triangle (or a wider arc extending to K2 in the northwest and the Pakistan "claim line" in the northeast) into a jointly controlled, demilitarised Peace Park.[81]

While the army's presence in Siachen forms one part, another part of the Siachen debate is the dispute regarding the AGPL. On this aspect too, opinions were divided. For Verghese (CPR) this could be easily resolved, through "a quiet authentication of the AGPL, if necessary through an annexed exchange of letters."[82] For sceptics, however, any kind of scaling back from India's strategic advantage in Siachen was not recommended "without an exchange of authenticated documents and carefully delineated positions."[83] These opinions found a further voice in the post-26/11 environment and a faltering peace process. In response to Kayani's calls for demilitarisation in 2012, opinions at the ORF also remained divided. For some, including former RAW chief Vikram Sood, the "strategic advantage in Siachen should not be given up for apparent short-term political gains."[84] While Verghese pushed for demilitarisation, the strategic value of the Siachen region was also emphasised at the CPR, and other opinions centred on Pakistani renouncement of terrorism and authentication of ground positions. A resolution of the Siachen region was also linked to an agreement on the resolution of the larger Kashmir dispute. It was therefore argued that any kind of demilitarisation or troop withdrawal from the glacier heights would put India at a strategic disadvantage.[85]

The strategic asset argument was also predominant at the VIF, and any kind of relinquishing of control was argued to be detrimental to Indian interests. Discourse urged that in the absence of Pakistan's redressal of terrorism concerns, any negotiation on Siachen was a moot point, and hence no policy recommendations for resolving Siachen were offered. Further, it was stressed that India's strategic advantage in Siachen is also important for its relationship with China.[86] Any demilitarisation of the region must therefore precede demarcation of the AGPL and should ideally consider Siachen as a part of the "overall settlement of the J&K issue."[87] It was argued that it is in India's interest to maintain its strategic presence in Siachen to circumvent any Kargil-like attack from Pakistan, which is highly likely owing to the trust deficit between the two.[88]

Nuclear Security: moving the discourse from doctrines to risk reduction measures – While it was a significant area of interest for non-government think tanks, the discourse went beyond an academic understanding of nuclear positions and doctrines to make policy recommendations, for instance on nuclear deterrence and risk reduction, even though an argument for discussions on Pakistan's nuclear 'first use' was recommended in the dialogue agenda. As early as June 2004, policy recommendations from the ORF suggested a possible agreement on "de-mating nuclear warheads from their delivery systems and storing warheads in a disassembled form."[89] Such a measure it was emphasised would reduce the risk of inadvertent or unauthorised use of nuclear weapons. In addition, "a possible agreement could be signed on the non-use of short-range ballistic missiles for nuclear deterrence."[90] During this time, the ORF also secured funding from the MEA for a project titled *India's Nuclear Diplomacy after Pokhran-II: its government and New Delhi* and thus became directly invested in the nuclear dialogue.[91] This also enhanced the possibilities of the ORF's policy narratives to make way into official discourse on the nuclear issue.

At the VIF, however, the increased asymmetry between India and Pakistan's nuclear doctrines was emphasised, and the need to enhance and upgrade India's nuclear weapons arsenal in the light of possible collusion between Pakistan and China was given prime place. There was considerable interest in the acquisition of Tactical Nuclear Weapons (TNW) by Pakistan and its challenges to India. India's recourse to TNWs was, however, not recommended.[92] The discourse at the VIF also recommended the creation of a Chief of Defence Staff position to provide guidance, particularly in the event of nuclear crises. One of the key recommendations in terms of reforming India's nuclear doctrine was to include a retaliatory second strike against an "abetting nuclear weapon state," once again with direct reference to Chinese support to Pakistan's nuclear weapons programme.[93]

Indus Waters Treaty: building public discourse – Previously examined government think tanks with the exception of the IDSA devoted little attention to the IWT and its application to water disputes between India and Pakistan. The perspective that Pakistan's concerns were ill-founded was also reflected in non-government think tanks, yet research and policy formulations were more detailed. There was also a difference in perceptions regarding this issue. At the VIF, for instance, the argument was that India should exercise full right over the Indus waters as legally permitted under the IWT, and the use of river water should be maximised within India, curtailing the amount of water released to Pakistan. Further, it was recommended that there should be more storage dams built in Kashmir. Additionally, the "IWT should be renegotiated with Pakistan to enable India to have access to 20 per cent of the waters and 40 per cent of the catchment area."[94]

However, while the VIF emerged on the scene during the later years of the CD, there was significant engagement with the issue at the CPR owing to the research expertise from B.G. Verghese and Ramaswamy Iyer – both of whom have contributed significantly to the academic understanding of the water debate. Iyer, for instance, was directly engaged with the GOI and on the directive of Manmohan Singh prepared a White Paper on the working of the IWT in 2010. The dominant policy narrative at the CPR was that the IWT represented a prime example of a successful agreement between India and Pakistan, and Pakistan's concerns as a lower riparian state were ill-founded. There were, however, noticeable differences in the positions of the two experts at the CPR on the future prospects of the treaty. While Verghese advocated for Indus II, Iyer was not in favour of the inclusion of water issues in future dialogues with Pakistan and held that the Treaty negotiated through a long and comprehensive process be left as it is, and India and Pakistan should continue to "operate it in a spirit of constructive cooperation."[95] Indus II, however, as Verghese argued, could be a viable trust-building exercise, and while the "Treaty has served its purpose, it leaves behind a possibly large untapped potential in the upper catchments of the three western rivers that are allocated to Pakistan but are under Indian control."[96] This potential, it was argued, could be "harnessed through joint investment, construction, management and control."[97] Further, owing to the effects of climate change and changing environmental conditions because of glacier melting, the need for an Indus II Treaty, which would also address Pakistan's water scarcity issues in a more efficient manner, was recognised.[98] The recommendation pushing for Indus II was reiterated following the ruling on the Baglihar Dam by the Neutral Expert in India's favour.[99] The controversy over Baglihar and other dam projects for Iyer were essentially "underlying lower-riparian anxiety and insecurity about upper-riparian control."[100] With the breakup of the CD after 2008, while security formulations became more sceptical, the CPR maintained that the Indian response to Pakistani paranoia over water security should be one of reassurance and within the provisions of the IWT.[101]

Terrorism – The aspect of terrorism is unique, as it is usually one where consensus is achieved in think tank formulations. Both before and after the events of 26/11, arguments from think tanks including the ORF were critical of the official dialogue's lack of focus on terrorism and the acknowledgement of Pakistan's position on Kashmir as an "unsettled issue," and any attempt to delink the dialogue with terrorism was criticised.[102] However, in addition to a general criticism, policy recommendations were made to improve India's counter-terrorism strategies and infrastructure. In July 2005, after the Mumbai blasts, the ORF recommended the formulation of a National Counter-Terrorism strategy that could include armed and punitive action against terrorist infrastructure and funding and specific recommendations centred on India's dialogue with Pakistan focused on making the issue of terrorism an integral part of the CD.[103] The demand for a viable counter-terrorism strategy also included the need to have a counter-terrorism legislation in India. The Mumbai blasts of 2005 also reflected the CPR's continued focus on academic research. In a comparative analysis of the NDA's anti-terror policy and the UPA's weak anti-terror response, Mehta argued for the need to develop a discourse that could "detach the issue of majority-minority distinction" and develop a political strategy towards terrorism in addition to a strategic one.[104] Critical of the UPA's lacklustre response to terrorism, former diplomat G. Parthasarathy was particularly critical of the Joint Anti-Terror Mechanism (JATM), which signified Indian inaction in exposing the involvement of Pakistan-based groups not just in India, but also in Afghanistan and western countries such as the US, UK and Australia.[105] The JATM, Parthasarathy argued, also conveyed the impression to Pakistan that it would discuss terrorism as an issue in other parts of India rather than in J&K.[106] Reflecting on his experience as India's High Commissioner in Pakistan at the time of the Kandahar hijacking incident, Parthasarathy recommended that a mere policy of "not yielding to terrorist demands" formulated in early 2008 was inadequate and must be backed by a parliament resolution, legislation, as well as a serious consideration to the possibility of covert action against terrorist infrastructure.[107]

The issue of terrorism was very often also linked to an analysis of Pakistan's position on Kashmir – particularly used as a political tool by the Pakistan army. The "historical continuity" in Pakistan's Kashmir policy, as demonstrated by Musharraf's refusal to deal sternly with terrorist infrastructure in Pakistan, was highlighted repeatedly.[108] The Pakistan Army, according to former RAW Chief Vikram Sood, "has a *Ghazwa-e-Hind* (the final battle for India) mindset," one not amenable to a peace process with India.[109] The VIF's policy discourse also maintained that the Deep State in Pakistan and the predominance of the Pakistani Army made for a distrustful ally. In the light of this, policy recommendations for India were to continue the dialogue but only after responding to ceasefire violations and infiltrations across the LoC in a "befitting" manner. The focus also remained on putting pressure on Pakistan to dismantle terror networks in its territory and act against terrorist groups, including the JuD and the LeT, primarily responsible for the 26/11 attacks and other terrorist acts in India.

This cynicism towards the peace process after 26/11 was also reflected in the ORF policy ideas, several of which focused on using a military option against Pakistan. Some of these ideas were new and countered the government policy to not internationalise the conflict. A detailed research report highlighted the continuing linkages between the LeT and the Pakistani establishment, and specific policy recommendations included setting up an international coalition of security experts under the UN umbrella to guide and monitor Pakistan's action against the LeT. International intervention to ensure the safety of nuclear weapons and installations within Pakistan and keeping active intelligence and military options to deal with any future terrorist attacks were also recommended.[110] Chellaney (CPR) also recommended that India must exert pressure on Pakistan to conform to international norms on terrorism, through the use of diplomatic and economic sanctions, and "waging [of] unconventional low intensity warfare."[111] The ORF and the CPR discourse, in general, recommended continued dialogue with a restructuring of the CD, with issues such as Siachen and Kashmir to be addressed through Joint Commissions institutionalised by the Parliament in the two countries and discussed on a long-term basis. The new agenda should also include more robust engagement with trade and commerce issues, and social-cultural-educational and health exchanges should be emphasised.[112]

While the expansion of the dialogue to the international level was a new policy direction suggested by non-government think tanks, discourse predominantly adopted the government position, particularly visible in the endorsement of the dual nature of the Kashmir dispute, the strategic value of Siachen and the need for an adequate response to terrorism. Policy ideas were, however, more elaborate in comparison to government think tanks with a specific focus on academic research. There was also a focus on civil society dialogue and especially the need to address humanitarian aspects of the relationship through soft borders and reconciliation policies in Kashmir. However, post-2008, the discourse became more status quoist, and think tank attention shifted away from a discussion on India–Pakistan relations. In keeping with their close association with the BJP – the chief opposition party at the time – the VIF and the IF remained critical and apprehensive of any future dialogue with Pakistan unless core conflicts were resolved. Since the BJP assumed power in India in 2014, there has been a further deterioration of relations with Pakistan, and several of the policy ideas discussed so far have become a part of official narratives. In line with the more hawkish views expressed in think tank discourse, the BJP has advocated a tougher stand on terrorism, and the growing discontent in the region has also led to a stronger reaction against the separatist movement in Kashmir. In addition, in response to ceasefire violations on the LoC, the BJP government in power has not shied away from publicising its offensive policies represented in military strikes conducted inside Pakistani territory, conducted first in September 2016 and more recently in February 2019. Thus, while the 2003 LoC ceasefire is continually challenged, formal dialogue with Pakistan has remained suspended with considerable escalation in tensions at the bilateral level.

Think tank contribution as communicative actors

As non-government think tanks vie for government patronage through the sharing of policy ideas, the government too has used them for consensus building on policy and specific initiatives related to the dialogue with Pakistan. Through their substantive research outputs – a combination of written publications and public events – these think tanks have also played a role in underlining the nature of the dialogue process with Pakistan and introduced its complex debates into the public domain. Furthermore, the body of intellectual elite in their personal capacities have written extensively on these debates and both through their repeated policy assertions and their direct engagement with government initiatives, they have popularised and promoted government policy. For instance, B.G. Verghese was associated with the Task Force on Inter-Linking of Rivers since 2003 and was also a part of a South Asians for Human Rights mission to Pakistan to report on minority rights in South Asia. Verghese's expertise on river water sharing also placed him in a critical position to contribute to the public discourse and with Ramaswamy Iyer, his writing contributed significantly to the academic understanding on river water disputes. The role played by R.K. Mishra and Brajesh Mishra and others including M.K. Rasgotra and G. Parthasarathy was also important, as they acted as a link between official policy and public intellectuals. Further, academic debates by Pratap Bhanu Mehta, Brahma Chellaney,

C. Raja Mohan and Manoj Joshi are abundantly available in the public domain for a better understanding of the complex government policy on Pakistan.

As communicative actors, think tanks brought attention to government initiatives and policy proposals on Kashmir, particularly those set forth by Musharraf and Manmohan Singh. which were analysed in depth and introduced into the public domain. The dual focus of the Kashmir conflict was endorsed by think tank policy discourse as examined in the previous section. Arguments in support of the government position were also popularised and expanded, and as official dialogue considered the conceptualisation of soft borders that brought relief to divided families in Kashmir, academic debates at think tanks also engaged with this idea. The ORF, for instance, became a forum for discussion with visits by prominent politicians, including by Sardar Abdul Qayyum Khan, former President and PM of PAK, who held discussions in September 2006 and again in April 2007. This coincided with the official Kashmir roundtables, thus the presence of PAK representation is notable here. Khan was received by M.K. Rasgotra, who headed one of the Working Groups (Strengthening Cross LoC relationships) established by Manmohan Singh to address internal dialogue in Kashmir.[113] The emphasis of the discussions remained on the need for Kashmiri leadership from both sides of the border to dialogue with each other.[114]

The government's continued focus on economic and humanitarian CBMs was also emphasised at an interaction with visiting former diplomats from Pakistan at the ORF in April 2005. Think tanks also performed an educative role. Changing dynamics in Kashmir visible after the Amarnath agitation in August 2008 brought to light the continued concerns of the Kashmiri youth. They also reflected the inadequacy in the government's understanding of the ground realities – a gap that research from think tanks could fill.[115] Publications such as Verghese's *J & K Primer* were therefore important for "demythifying" the conflict in J&K, and as a significant tool towards creating public awareness, it was "intended to educate ordinary people about the basics of the J&K question and to put various events and issues in context."[116] He also recommended "a unilateral suspension of operations" by Indian security forces under clearly specified terms, even if initially limited to designated areas and subject to periodic review".[117]

Furthermore, highlighting Pakistan's changed position in Siachen reflected in Army Chief Kayani's initiative to demilitarise the Siachen region following the Gayari avalanche, in May 2012, Verghese published *Siachen Follies: Defining Facts and Objectives* underscoring the key terms of the dispute and critical official agreements between India and Pakistan.[118] While Verghese contributed to the development of an academic perspective, expressed opinions by Ata Hasnain, Gurmeet Kanwal and Vikram Sood in the media, coupled with their operational experience in Kashmir and Siachen, provided a practitioner's analysis of the ground situation – enabled by the platform provided by think tanks. More recently, the VIF and the IF have become a platform for the articulation of ideas held by the BJP. Even though the party initiated the CD in 2004, it became a key opposition to the UPA's Pakistan policy in subsequent years – reflected in the opinions and perspectives highlighted by the VIF's policy discourse. In addition to the prolific writing in leading Indian newspapers and the new medium of the internet, think tanks and the analyses by elites thus became a channel for information on progress in the dialogue with Pakistan.

Non-government policy think tanks and India's Pakistan policy – a summary

The analysis of discourse on India's relations with Pakistan at the ORF, the CPR, the VIF and the IF has highlighted that during years when official dialogue was at its peak, there was robust research on bilateral issues and policy ideas were shared and articulated – some conforming to government policies and some pushing for change. The government also used think tanks as forums for discussion, for additional research and for creating awareness of its dialogue initiatives with Pakistan. Think tanks were involved in the promotion, advocacy and articulation of foreign policy towards Pakistan during the CD period. However, the restrictive and bureaucratic set-up in India has meant that think tank involvement was often limited to suggesting policy options and adding to the public discourse on foreign policy, rather than a visible and direct involvement in policy formulation processes. While funding was diversified, government control on funding legislation and project funding also demonstrated the Indian state's efforts to create a "historic bloc" – in this case, support for its dialogue with Pakistan in collaboration with think tanks. Think tank engagement with policy formulation is also reflected in the government's invitation to intellectual elites including Verghese, Rasgotra and others to become involved in subsidiary aspects of policy making. Further, in keeping with the DI-Gramscian framework, intellectuals in these think tanks played a role in mobilising public opinion and contributing to public debate on government policy, indicating significant collaboration between the civil society elite and the policy elite.

As formal dialogue derailed, the policy discourse at think tanks also reflected a change and became weaker and more status quoist. Thus, as dialogue faltered and the government and its policy directions on Pakistan changed, so did think tank interest. Broad institutional positions enabled a flexibility in policy thinking, and to retain their policy relevance and to balance proximity to policy elites, think tanks altered their research focus on Pakistan. The donor-driven agendas of these think tanks controlled by the tacit approval of the government also meant that while they had the ability to spread ideas over time, they were more likely to get ideologically absorbed into the stronger bureaucratic frameworks. This is also reflected in Schmidt's argument with respect to the influence of timing and the right audience on discursive interactions.[119] Thus, as dialogue was suspended, think tanks' agendas also adapted to the changing policy directions. The change is also reflective of the distinctions between think tank interaction with ruling coalitions. Presenting conflicting opinions, while some have argued that the new BJP government led by Narendra Modi was "more open to inputs from think tanks"[120] with a "general increase in receptivity,"[121] others have argued that the BJP is more open to "ideas similar to its own policy frames,"[122] and there is now "more traction for the IF and the VIF owing to their alignments with the government."[123] This is also acknowledged by the MEA, with the VIF now considered as one of the key forums for policy promotion.[124]

Conclusion

Through the analysis of non-government think tanks, this chapter has questioned their ability to challenge or endorse government policy narratives on Pakistan during the CD process. Particularly notable for their diversified funding structures and the varied membership patterns, think tanks in this category – namely, the ORF, the CPR, the VIF and the IF – have enjoyed relative freedom from government funding and direction to their research agendas. Encouraged by India's liberalisation process and the need to supplement government capacity on foreign policy, these think tanks were ideally placed to expand and challenge the policy discourse on Pakistan. While the greater emphasis on academic research and the informed discussion on India's Pakistan policy did enable some new thinking on key issues, the government control over funding legislation and the think tank need to retain policy relevance created significant challenges. Therefore, while providing support for government initiatives on dialogue with Pakistan, discourse has insufficiently challenged policy frameworks, and with the decline in official dialogue opportunities, think tank engagement with policy ideas on Pakistan have also declined, in favour of issues that enjoy continued government support.

Notes

1 Vivien A. Schmidt, "Discursive Institutionalism: Scope, Dynamics and Philosophical Underpinnings", in Frank Fischer and Herbert Gottweis (eds.) *The Argumentative Turn Revisited: Public Policy as Communicative Practice* (Durham and London: Duke University Press, 2012), p. 87.
2 As articulated in personal communications with former diplomats, bureaucrats and senior researchers at RIS and VIF in New Delhi in September and October 2015.
3 Personal communication with senior researcher at CPR, New Delhi on September 26, 2015.
4 Personal communication with former diplomat in New Delhi on October 13, 2015.
5 Personal communication with senior researcher at VIF, New Delhi on October 14, 2015.
6 Personal communication with former diplomat in New Delhi on October 13, 2015.
7 ibid.
8 Richard Higgott and Diane Stone, "The Limits of Influence: Foreign Policy Think Tanks in Britain and the USA", *Review of International Studies*, 20:1, January 1994, p. 28.
9 Daniel Drezner, "Ideas, Bureaucratic Politics and the Crafting of Foreign Policy", *American Journal of Political Science*, 44:4, October 2000, p. 734.
10 ibid., p. 746.

11 Jayati Srivastava, *Think Tanks in South Asia: Analysing the Knowledge-Power Interface* (London: Overseas Development Institute, December 2011), p. 19.
12 Contributing to this growth of "second wave institutes" was the "availability of a generation of Indians who had been involved in policy making by post-independence governments." Kuldeep Mathur, *Public Policy and Politics in India: How Institutions Matter* (New Delhi: Oxford University Press, 2013), p. 86.
13 Reliance Industries is an Indian conglomerate with businesses engaged in energy, petrochemicals, textiles, natural resources, retail, and telecommunications. www.ril.com/
14 Personal communication with senior researcher at ORF, New Delhi on September 9, 2015.
15 *Declaration of Domestic Contributions* (New Delhi: Observer Research Foundation, 2017), www.orfonline.org/declaration-of-contributions/
16 Prashant Jha, "India's Most Influential Think Tanks", *Hindustan Times*, August 16, 2015, www.hindustantimes.com/india/india-s-most-influential-think-tanks/story-emb0db2lmqltL8pKeYuZiL.html
17 More on VIF's official webpage: www.vifindia.org/AboutUs1
18 This back-channel is known to have been instrumental in working towards a resolution of the Kargil crises in 1999. While the Indian side remained tight-lipped about the details of the discussions, disclosures by the Pakistani negotiator Niaz Naik also indicated a possible deal towards resolving the Kashmir dispute, which could have included converting the LoC into an international border and the establishment of the two sides of Kashmir into an autonomous zone. For more, see Seema Mustafa, "Sharif-Vajpayee together in a Secret Deal", *The Asian Age*, September 15, 1999, www.jammu-kashmir.com/archives/archives1999/99september15a.html
19 For more, see "Back-Channel: The Promise and Peril", *Ministry of External Affairs*, May 20, 2003, www.mea.gov.in/articles-in-indian-media.htm?dtl/13817/Back+channel+the+promise+and+peril; "R K Mishra Passes Away", *The Hindu*, January 10, 2009, www.thehindu.com/todays-paper/R.K.-Mishra-passes-away/article16349286.ece
20 Arvind Gupta, "Brajesh Mishra's Legacy to National Security and Diplomacy", *IDSA Comment*, September 30, 2012, http://idsa.in/idsacomments/BrajeshMishrasLegacytoNationalSecurityandDiplomacy_agupta_300912
21 Some of these include the NSAB, India's National Knowledge Commission and a Supreme Court–appointed committee on elections in Indian universities.
22 *Annual Report: 2010–2011* (New Delhi: Centre for Policy Research, 2011).
23 Constantino Xavier and Stephen Cohen, "The Career and Ideas of K. Subrahmanyam", *Event Summary Brookings Institution*, February 2011, www.brookings.edu/events/2011/02/18-india-subrahmanyam
24 www.cprindia.org/people/bharat-karnad
25 Further in 2014, the Indian Ministry of Finance asked the ORF to draft strategy papers for India's position in the G20 on BRICS. In addition, the ORF hosted the fourth BRICS Academic Forum in New Delhi in March 2012. The recommendations that emerged from the deliberations were submitted to the Heads of States of BRICS nations, who met later that month in New Delhi. Puja Mehra, "G20: Finance Ministry Asks ORF for Stance on BRICS Bank", *The Hindu*, January 8, 2014, www.thehindu.com/business/Economy/g20-finance-ministry-asks-orf-for-stance-on-brics-bank/article5554469.ece
26 In September 2014, the ORF's Maritime Initiative with support from the MEA held the Indian Ocean Dialogue in Kochi with representatives from think tanks and civil society from 24 Member Nations and Dialogue Partners of the Indian Ocean Rim Association. *ORF Annual Report 2015* (New Delhi: Observer Research Foundation, 2016). It also organised the Indian Ocean dialogue with the MEA and in January 2015 hosted the first India Global Forum with the International Institute of Strategic Studies that allowed newly appointed Cabinet ministers to engage with global audiences. *ORF Annual Report 2015* (New Delhi: Observer Research Foundation, 2015).

27 *Raisina Dialogue: Conference Booklet* (New Delhi: Observer Research Foundation and Ministry of External Affairs, 2016).
28 Some of the topics that have been addressed by these dialogues have included: "Recent Developments in India-Pakistan Diplomatic Ties" by G. Parthasarathy in 2009; discussions on "Af-Pak issue" by Shyam Saran in 2010; discussions on Kashmir led by Amitabh Mattoo; "a look at the current Situation in Jammu and Kashmir". For more see, *Annual Report: 2009–2010* (New Delhi: Centre for Policy Research, 2009).
29 *Annual Report: 2011–2012* (New Delhi: Centre for Policy Research, 2012).
30 http://thesarcist.org/index.aspx
31 *Annual Report: 2011* (New Delhi: Vivekananda International Foundation, 2011).
32 Muzamil Jaleel, "A People's General", *The Indian Express*, April 17, 2011, http://archive.indianexpress.com/news/a-people-s-general/777108/
33 Praveen Swami, "Now, the Cover-Up", *Frontline*, 16:16, July 31–August 13, 1999, www.frontline.in/static/html/fl1616/16160220.htm
34 Viewpoints that emerged from personal communications with senior researchers at ORF, New Delhi in September 2015.
35 Sanjaya Baru, "Can Indian Think Tanks and Research Institutes Cope with the Rising Demand for Foreign and Security Policy Research", *ISAS Working Paper* (National University of Singapore), 67, June 16, 2009.
36 T. S. Papola, "Social Science Research in Globalising India: Historical Development and Recent Trends", *ISID Working Paper* (Institute for Studies in Industrial Development, Delhi), May 2010, p. 9.
37 Prashant Jha, "India's Most Influential Think Tanks", *Hindustan Times*, August 16, 2015, www.hindustantimes.com/india/india-s-most-influential-think-tanks/stoFry-emb0db2lmqltL8pKeYuZiL.html
38 Stella Ladi, "Think Tanks, Discursive Institutionalism and Policy Change", in Georgios Papanagnou (ed.) *Social Science and Policy Change: Democracy, Values and Capacities* (Paris: UNESCO, 2011), pp. 205–220.
39 Personal communication with senior member and former bureaucrat at RIS, New Delhi on September 4, 2015.
40 The association with the Task Force ended in mid-2004 as the new UPA Government decided to review the programme and pursue it departmentally. *Annual Report: 2003–2004* (New Delhi: Centre for Policy Research, 2004).
41 Personal communication with senior researcher and former defence personnel at IF, New Delhi on October 19, 2015.
42 The India Foundation conducts several events related to India's foreign policy concerns. Notable among them are the annual Counter-Terrorism conference and the Indian Ocean conference conducted in partnership with the MEA. For more on IF's events, see www.indiafoundation.in/
43 This argument was repeated again in his statement in April 2007 addressing the Third Roundtable Conference on J&K. This argument is also made in Ashutosh Misra's analysis of the dispute. For more, see Ashutosh Misra, *India-Pakistan: Coming to Terms* (New York: Palgrave MacMillan, 2010).
44 Avanti Bhati, "Kashmir: New Hope?", *ORF Commentaries*, October 23, 2003, www.orfonline.org/research/kashmir-new-hope/; "Pakistan's New Kashmir Offensive", *ORF Commentaries*, September 17, 2003, www.orfonline.org/research/pakistans-new-kashmir-offensive/; Sushant Sareen, "Running Faster to Maintain Status Quo?", *ORF Commentaries*, October 6, 2004, www.orfonline.org/research/running-faster-to-maintain-status-quo/
45 Personal communication with senior researcher at ORF, New Delhi on September 9, 2015.
46 Avanti Bhati, "Kashmir: New Hope?", *ORF Commentaries*, October 23, 2003, www.orfonline.org/research/kashmir-new-hope/
47 Gurmeet Kanwal, "Strategic Stalemate in Kashmir", *ORF Commentaries*, January 23, 2004, www.orfonline.org/research/strategic-stalemate-in-kashmir/

48 Wilson John, "The Jihadi Factor in India-Pakistan Peace Process", *ORF Issue Brief*, 6, May 2006, p. 3.
49 Nasim Zehra, "Musharraf's Kashmir Policy", *The News*, December 18, 2006, www.thenews.com.pk/archive/print/35741-musharrafs-kashmir-policy
50 Wilson John, "Checkmating Musharraf's Plan", *ORF Commentaries*, November 24, 2004, www.orfonline.org/research/checkmating-musharrafs-plan/
51 B. G. Verghese, "A Vision for J and K: Internal Settlement Unavoidable for India", *The Tribune*, April 14, 2005, www.tribuneindia.com/2005/20050414/edit.htm#4
52 B. G. Verghese, "A Bit of Musharraf-Speak", *The Tribune*, December 22, 2006, www.tribuneindia.com/2006/20061222/edit.htm
53 B. G. Verghese, "A Vision for J & K-2015: Local and National Consensus Will Help", *The Tribune*, April 15, 2005, www.tribuneindia.com/2005/20050415/edit.htm#4
54 ibid.
55 ibid.
56 ibid.
57 "General's Losing Battle", *ORF Commentaries*, December 7, 2005, www.orfonline.org/research/generals-losing-battle/
58 G. Parthasarathy, "India Can't Pull Out Troops", *The Tribune*, December 28, 2006, www.tribuneindia.com/2006/20061228/edit.htm
59 Gurmeet Kanwal, "Strategic Stalemate in Kashmir", *ORF Commentaries*, January 23, 2004, www.orfonline.org/research/strategic-stalemate-in-kashmir/
60 This cynicism was reflected in the PEW Research Center survey where terrorism and its linkages with Pakistan were perceived as major problems expressed by Indian respondents. For instance, 81% of Indians expressed a negative opinion of Pakistan. The survey, however, did reflect some hope for the process of dialogue (63%), stressing particularly on Indo-Pak trade to act as a peacemaker. "Indian See Threats from Pakistan, Extremist Groups", *Pew Research Center*, October 20, 2010, www.pewglobal.org/2010/10/20/indians-see-threat-from-pakistan-extremist-groups/
61 Satish Chandra, "Stop Appeasing Pakistan", *VIF Article*, February 4, 2013, www.vifindia.org/articles/2013/fedruary/04/stop-appeasing-pakistan
62 Satish Chandra, "Genuflecting before Pakistan", *VIF Article*, September 12, 2012, www.vifindia.org/article/2012/september/12/genuflecting-before-pakistan; Kanwal Sibal, "Nettlesome Neighbour", *VIF Article*, January 26, 2013, www.vifindia.org/article/2013/january/26/nettlesome-neighbour
63 For more, see "Pointers to Pakistan's Strategy", *ORF Commentaries*, September 14, 2004, www.orfonline.org/research/pointers-to-pakistans-strategy/; "The Process Is Unwinding", *ORF Commentaries*, July 12, 2005, www.orfonline.org/research/the-process-is-unwinding/; "Take It Along", *ORF Commentaries*, March 6, 2006, www.orfonline.org/research/take-it-along/
64 G. Parthasarathy, "Hurriyat Role in J & K", *The Tribune*, February 8, 2007, www.tribuneindia.com/2007/20070208/edit.htm
65 ibid.
66 Wilson John, "High Resolution Picture in Kashmir", *ORF Commentaries*, February 1, 2006, www.orfonline.org/research/high-resolution-picture-in-kashmir/
67 B. G. Verghese, "Gambols and Gambits in Kashmir", *The Tribune*, January 20, 2006, www.tribuneindia.com/2006/20060120/edit.htm
68 ibid.
69 Kanwal Sibal, "Soft State Style Won't Work in J & K", *VIF Article*, September 21, 2010, www.vifindia.org/article/2010/september/21/Soft-State-Style-Won-t-Work%20-In-J-K
70 ibid.
71 Amit Kumar, "Time for Dr. Singh to Step in", *ORF Commentaries*, August 9, 2010, www.orfonline.org/research/time-for-dr-singh-to-step-in/
72 "Kashmir, a Systemic Failure: Dialogue a Must", *ORF Event Report*, August 20, 2010, www.orfonline.org/research/kashmir-a-systemic-failure-dialogue-a-must/

73 G. Parthasarathy, "Separatism Needs Firmness", *The Tribune*, September 4, 2008, www.tribuneindia.com/2008/20080904/edit.htm; Pratap Bhanu Mehta, "The Question in Kashmir", *The Indian Express*, August 19, 2008, http://archive.indianexpress.com/news/the-question-in-kashmir/350345/
74 V. P. Malik, "Revisiting AFSPA: Don't Blame It for Kashmir Problems", *ORF Commentaries*, September 20, 2010, www.orfonline.org/research/revisiting-afspa-dont-blame-it-for-kashmir-problems/
75 "J&K: Need for a Bipartisan Consensus", *VIF Article*, February 7, 2011, www.vifindia.org/article/2011/february/7/J-K-Need-For-a-Bipartisan-Consensus
76 N. C. Vij, "Kashmir: Dilution Is No Answer", *VIF Article*, February 3, 2014, www.vifindia.org/article/2014/february/05/kashmir-dilution-is-no-answer
77 S. A. Hasnain, "The Current LoC Narrative and India's Response", *VIF Article*, August 19, 2015, www.vifindia.org/article/2015/august/19/the-current-loc-narrative-and-india-s-response; S. A. Hasnain, "The Ins & Outs of Infiltration: The Real Challenge in J&K: Part 2", *VIF Article*, June 16, 2016, www.vifindia.org/article/2016/june/16/the-ins-and-outs-of-infiltration-the-real-challenge-in-j-and-k-part-2
78 Gurmeet Kanwal, "Demilitarisation of Siachen", *ORF Event Report*, April 5, 2005, www.orfonline.org/research/demilitarisation-of-siachen/
79 Gurmeet Kanwal, "Siachen: National Consensus Needed", *ORF Commentaries*, May 30, 2006, www.orfonline.org/research/siachen-national-consensus-needed/
80 B. G. Verghese, "A Vision for J & K – 2015: Local and National Consensus Will Help", *The Tribune*, April 15, 2005, www.tribuneindia.com/2005/20050415/edit.htm#4
81 B. G. Verghese, "60 Years of Accession: It's Time to Fulfil Promises", *The Tribune*, October 1, 2007, www.tribuneindia.com/2007/20071001/edit.htm
82 B. G. Verghese, *Siachen Follies: Defining Facts and Objectives* (New Delhi: Centre for Policy Research, 2012), p. 17.
83 Vikram Sood, "Height of Folly", *ORF Commentaries*, May 15, 2006, www.orfonline.org/research/height-of-folly/; Vikram Sood, "Why India Cannot Afford to Give Up Siachen", *ORF Commentaries*, April 16, 2012, www.orfonline.org/research/why-india-cannot-afford-to-give-up-siachen/
84 Vikram Sood, "Story of Saltoro: From Ababeel to Meghdoot", *ORF Commentaries*, April 27, 2012, www.orfonline.org/research/story-of-saltoro-from-ababeel-to-meghdoot/
85 G. Parthasarathy, "The Saltoro Range: Pullout Will Be a Himalayan Blunder", *The Tribune*, May 4, 2006, www.tribuneindia.com/2006/20060504/edit.htm
86 Satish Chandra, "Why a Siachen Settlement Should Be a Non-Starter", *VIF Article*, May 14, 2012, www.vifindia.org/article/2012/may/14/why-a-siachen-agreement-should-be-a-non-starter
87 Kanwal Sibal, "No Ground to Vacate Siachen", *VIF Article*, May 8, 2012, www.vifindia.org/article/2012/may/08/no-ground-to-vacate-siachen
88 Sushant Sareen, "Steadfast in Siachen", *VIF Article*, February 22, 2016, www.vifindia.org/article/2016/february/22/steadfast-in-siachen
89 Gurmeet Kanwal, "Indo-Pak Nuclear CBMs: Time to Move Forward", *ORF Commentaries*, June 16, 2004, www.orfonline.org/research/indo-pak-nuclear-cbms-time-to-move-forward/
90 ibid.
91 *Ministry of External Affairs: Annual Report* (New Delhi: Ministry of External Affairs, GOI, 2004–2005).
92 Gurmeet Kanwal, "Tactical Nuclear Weapon's: Pakistan's Dangerous Game (or Quest)", *VIF Article*, October 8, 2012, www.vifindia.org/article/2012/october/08/tactical-nuclear-weapons-pakistan-s-dangerous-game-or-quest; Gurmeet Kanwal, "Tactical Nuclear Weapons: Lessons for India and Pakistan", *VIF Article*, June 4, 2013, www.vifindia.org/article/2013/june/04/tactical-nuclear-weapons-lessons-for-india-and-pakistan
93 Satish Chandra, "Prepare against Pakistan's Nukes", *VIF Article*, September 1, 2012, www.vifindia.org/article/2012/september/01/prepare-against-pakistan-nukes

94 Satish Chandra, "Stop Appeasing Pakistan", *VIF Article*, February 4, 2013, www.vifindia. org/articles/2013/fedruary/04/stop-appeasing-pakistan
95 Ramaswamy Iyer, "Water in India-Pakistan Talks", *The Hindu*, March 3, 2010, www. thehindu.com/todays-paper/tp-opinion/article721712.ece
96 B. G. Verghese, "It's Time for Indus II", *The Tribune*, May 26, 2005, www.tribuneindia. com/2005/20050526/edit.htm
97 ibid.
98 B. G. Verghese, "Indus Water Woes", *The Tribune*, April 27, 2006, www.tribuneindia. com/2006/20060427/edit.htm
99 B. G. Verghese, "Indus Valley Cooperation", *The Indian Express*, February 16, 2007, http://archive.indianexpress.com/news/indus-valley-cooperation/23430/0
100 Ramaswamy Iyer, "Writ in Water", *The Indian Express*, October 31, 2008, http://archive.indianexpress.com/news/writ-in-water/379421/0
101 Ramaswamy Iyer, "What Water Wars?", *The Indian Express*, April 1, 2010, http://archive.indianexpress.com/news/what-water-wars-/594319/0
102 B. Raman, "Unequal Accommodation: A National Stockholm Syndrome", *ORF Commentaries*, April 19, 2005, www.orfonline.org/research/unequal-accommodation-a-national-stockholm-syndrome/; Kanwal Sibal, "To Talk Now Is Wrong", *ORF Commentaries*, February 22, 2010, www.orfonline.org/research/to-talk-now-is-wrong/
103 P. V. Ramana and Wilson John, "Mumbai Blasts: Time to Act", *ORF Policy Brief*, July 20, 2006.
104 Pratap Bhanu Mehta, "State of Vacuum in Times of Terror", *The Indian Express*, July 12, 2006, http://archive.indianexpress.com/news/state-of-vacuum-in-times-of-terror/8369/0
105 G. Parthasarathy, "Dangerous Compromises", *The Tribune*, September 21, 2006, www. tribuneindia.com/2006/20060921/edit.htm
106 G. Parthasarathy, "Are We Fighting Terrorism? India's Approach Can Lead to Nowhere", *The Tribune*, November 30, 2006, www.tribuneindia.com/2006/20061130/edit.htm
107 G. Parthasarathy, "How Kandahar Hijacked Us", *The Indian Express*, February 6, 2008, http://archive.indianexpress.com/news/how-kandahar-hijacked-us/269673/
108 Wilson John, "The Jihadi Factor in India-Pakistan Peace Process", *ORF Issue Brief*, 6, May 2006, p. 3.
109 Vikram Sood, "Terror from across the Border: Why Isn't War an Option?", *ORF Commentaries*, January 6, 2016, www.orfonline.org/research/terror-from-across-the-border-why-isnt-war-an-option/
110 Wilson John, "Concerted International Action Needed to Rein in Pakistan Terror Groups", *ORF Policy Brief*, 9, February 2009, p. 5.
111 Brahma Chellaney, "Don't Compromise India", *India Today*, August 23, 2013, http://indiatoday.intoday.in/story/india-pakistan-relations-loc-ceasefire/1/300969.html
112 Wilson John and Kaustav Dhar Chakrabarti, "India-Pakistan Relations after Mumbai Attacks", *ORF Issue Brief*, 21, September 2009, p. 7.
113 Aijaz Ashraf Wani and Sajad Padder, "Understanding the Discredited Institution of Dialogue in Kashmir", *Greater Kashmir*, September 11, 2016, www.greaterkashmir. com/news/op-ed/understanding-the-discredited-institution-of-dialogue-in-kashmir/228223.html
114 "Kashmiri Leaders from Both Sides Should Sit together", *ORF Event Report*, April 28, 2007, www.orfonline.org/research/kashmiri-leaders-from-both-sides-should-sit-together/
115 Personal communication with senior retired defence personnel in New Delhi on 20 October, 2015.
116 B. G. Verghese, *A J &K Primer: From Myth to Reality* (New Delhi: Centre for Policy Research, 2007).
117 B. G. Verghese, "60 Years of Accession: It's Time to Fulfil Promises", *The Tribune*, October 1, 2007, www.tribuneindia.com/2007/20071001/edit.htm
118 B. G. Verghese, *Siachen Follies: Defining Facts and Objectives* (New Delhi: Centre for Policy Research, 2012).

119 Vivien A. Schmidt, "Discursive Institutionalism: The Explanatory Power of Ideas and Discourse", *Annual Review of Political Science*, 11, 2008, p. 305.
120 Personal communication with senior researcher and retired defence personnel at IF, New Delhi on October 19, 2015.
121 Personal communication with senior researcher at CAPS, New Delhi on October 21, 2015.
122 Personal communication with senior member and retired defence personnel at IPCS, New Delhi on September 29, 2015.
123 Personal communication with academic at JNU, New Delhi on September 7, 2015.
124 Personal communication with mid-level bureaucrat at the MEA in New Delhi on October 7, 2015.

6
PEACEBUILDING THINK TANKS

The previous chapters have examined think tanks that are embedded into the bureaucratic set-up in India and receive funding and patronage from key government departments. The linkages with the government have also provided direction to research agendas at these institutions, particularly with respect to foreign and security policy. In addition to government-funded entities, there also exist smaller non-government think tanks in India that have emerged in the post-liberalisation and the post-nuclear test era of Indian politics. While India's economic liberalisation paved the way for its rising economic credentials, the nuclear tests in 1998 created recognition for India as a significant strategic and military power. This has also impacted the policy research landscape in India, as has been highlighted in previous chapters. There was also an increase in interest from international donor agencies to invest in Indian think tanks and towards the conduct of independent policy research during this period. The emergence of new institutions at this time also coincided with the changing global definitions of security and an increasing interest in conflict resolution, peacebuilding and human security, reflected also in the context of India–Pakistan relations and specific aspects of the dialogue process.

In part two of the analysis on non-government think tanks, this chapter looks in detail at the Institute of Peace and Conflict Studies (IPCS), the Delhi Policy Group (DPG), the Centre for Dialogue and Reconciliation (CDR) and the Women in Security, Conflict Management and Peace (WISCOMP). With respect to the analysis covered in previous chapters, these think tanks are smaller in scale and membership, and there also exist noticeable differences in their membership patterns and engagement with the policy establishment in India. While highlighting these differences, the chapter also asks if the positions that these think tanks adopt on India's conflict with Pakistan have differed from government think tanks or other non-government think tanks discussed previously.

The following analysis looks at both discourse as well as interaction with policy-making institutions, and a few common elements stand out. While larger and more resourceful think tanks that were analysed in previous chapters lack what Parmar calls an "institutional line" and rather have a de facto institutional worldview, peacebuilding think tanks have displayed clear institutional positions and often distinctly defined narrow organisational goals.[1] This is partly due to the funding structures in operation which are project driven and partly due to the narrow constituency of knowledge elites. The focus at these non-government think tanks has also been on training and networking – through a focus on developing women's networks and encouraging youth trainings and simulations. Thus, while reaching out to policy elites and mobilising public opinion has been a goal, an emphasis on grassroots initiatives and expanding stakeholders towards peace with Pakistan has also been visible.

Nature of intellectual elite – patterns in institutional worldviews and collaborations with the state

Non-government think tanks in this category look visibly different from those addressed in the previous chapter. They are smaller in size and composition. More notably, they reflect significant differences in funding structures. These think tanks are not funded by the government, other than small project grants to IPCS. Established in post-liberalised India, research agendas therefore have been more independent of government direction, but this also indicates a lack of patronage and support from the government. Further, in terms of their research agendas, in addition to policy enquiry, the advocacy and training component is significant. Particular emphasis is on projects dedicated to conflict resolution, peacebuilding and training for peace, and in addition to this, there is a sustained attention to NTS issues. The emphasis of these research agendas is also a reflection of the nature of intellectuals that are involved in these think tanks, who focus on civil society activism and are also more actively involved in non-government multi-track processes.

Benefiting from the open economic environment of post-liberalised India, the Delhi Policy Group (DPG) was founded in 1994, under the leadership of Radha Kumar and founding director V.R. Raghavan. The institutional focus "was on strategic issues of critical national interest and research over the years expanded into special areas of peace and conflict studies and national security."[2] Through an emphasis on research and advocacy, the DPG's interactions have covered a wide canvas, including strategic and geo-political issues, geo-economics, defence and security. Research programmes supported primarily by the Ford Foundation began with the National Security Program that focused on regional security, internal security, emerging security challenges and nuclear policy and disarmament.[3] In 2003, the program was expanded, and a chair on NTS was instituted held by T.K. Oommen and B.G. Verghese.[4] Radha Kumar's expertise in peace and conflict studies led to the initiation of the Peace and

Conflict Studies program in 1998, with specific attention given to conflicts in Afghanistan, Jammu and Kashmir, Pakistan and India's northeast. While the Pakistan program focused on bilateral peacemaking between India and Pakistan, the program on J&K dealt with issues of internal reconciliation in the state. Key target groups for the DPG have been legislators, civil society and trade organisations, with a specific focus on women's dialogues and women's networks within South Asia.

Founder Radha Kumar's ideas were a crucial influence on the research design at the DPG. An academic by training, Kumar is a specialist in ethnic conflicts, peacemaking and peacebuilding, a focus that was visible in the DPG formulations at the time.[5] Kumar was also instrumental in setting up and running the Nelson Mandela Centre for Peace and Conflict Resolution at Jamia Millia Islamia as Director from 2005–2010 and, from October 2010 to October 2011, served as one of the government-appointed interlocutors for J&K.[6] Another key influence at the DPG in its early years was Gen. V.R. Raghavan, one of India's prominent strategic thinkers, with significant operational experience serving in Siachen and Kargil, where he retired as the DGMO in 1994. At the DPG he implemented projects on South Asian Comprehensive Security, focusing on the political, economic and environmental security issues; NTS premised on non-military security threats; and nuclear policy stewardship aimed at sharpening the nuclear debate in India for introducing restraint and responsibility in nuclear policy.[7] The current Director General, Hemant Krishan Singh, is also a former bureaucrat and a former career diplomat in the IFS. His expertise is essentially in India-Japan relations and India's policy in South East Asia manifested in the Look East Policy.[8] Other notable names associated with the DPG have been K. Shankar Bajpai, Arvind Virmani,[9] Aditya Singh,[10] Arun Sahgal[11] and Rana Banerji.[12]

India's liberalisation and the developing interest in independent policy research also prompted the establishment of the Institute of Peace and Conflict Studies (IPCS) in 1996. The brainchild of P.R. Chari and Dipankar Banerjee, while initially focused on non-military security issues and threats to the region, the research agenda was expanded following India's nuclear tests in 1998 and developments in the post-9/11 period.[13] Leadership at the IPCS has been a combination of academics and practitioners, knowledge elites composed of seasoned diplomats and former bureaucrats, including Salman Haidar, I.P. Khosla, Leela Ponappa and A.S. Dulat, armed forces veterans, namely A.S. Lamba, Uday Bhaskar and several academics. The IPCS also claims to have had "the youngest profile in terms of its faculty and also invites young scholars from other regions to host them as interns and visiting fellows."[14]

Much direction for its research agenda and specific programmes has come from the late P.R. Chari – a former bureaucrat and an early member of the think tank community in India. He was Director at the IDSA from 1975–1980 and Research Professor at the CPR from 1992–1996. Chari is known to have been an authority on issues of disarmament and nuclear proliferation. He was on the faculty at the South Asian Summer School conceived by George Perkovich aimed at creating a network of young researchers with expertise on arms control and conflict resolution strategies in South Asia.[15] While rhetoric in the years following the 1998 nuclear tests was in favour of hawkish national security positions, in academic circles, Chari was known for promoting a "consensual approach on the nuclear issue."[16] Serving as Research Professor at the IPCS until 2015, Chari was also closely involved in the training and development of young professionals.[17]

While Chari's strength was his academic background, co-founder Dipankar Banerjee was a retired Army officer. He was also Senior Fellow at the IDSA from 1987–1990 and Deputy Director from 1992–1996, after which he helped build the IPCS.[18] With a keen interest in disarmament issues, Banerjee has also remained interested in border security and security sector reforms. Other researchers have included Suba Chandran and Mallika Joseph, who have written prolifically on foreign policy issues such as security sector reforms, relations with Pakistan and the developing political dynamics in Kashmir.[19]

Since it was established, the IPCS has networked with international institutes including the Brookings Institution, the Sandia National Lab, the International Institute for Strategic Studies (IISS) (London), the China Research Forum and Konrad Adenauer Stiftung, among others. In South Asia, it is the founding member of the Consortium of South Asian Think Tanks (COSATT), a network of leading think tanks in the region, and the Strategic Studies Network led by the Near East South Asia Center involving think tanks and scholars from North Africa, West Asia, Central Asia and South Asia. It enjoys relative independence from government financial support, although some grants have been from the MEA and the government of J&K. Most funding for the IPCS programmes has come from the Nuclear Threat Initiative (NTI), Konrad Adenauer Stiftung, the MacArthur Foundation, the Korea Foundation, the Japan Foundation, the Ford Foundation and Ploughshares, among others. In addition to the research and training element, the IPCS has also organised Track II dialogues involving the strategic community from other countries on select issues such as nuclear security, India–Pakistan and Afghanistan, and water security.

Membership patterns at the DPG and the IPCS are different from the two smaller think tanks in this category. Intellectuals at the CDR and the WISCOMP have been primarily focused on civil society activism. The CDR was established in 2000 by Sushobha Barve, with a focus on research and advocacy through dialogue forums geared towards building networks. These included cross-LoC civil society dialogues (since 2005), cross-LoC women's dialogues (since 2009), youth leadership and inter-community dialogue in J&K, and India–Pakistan Track II dialogues (with Jinnah Institute since 2010). Listed as a not-for-profit company, funding comes from Friedrich Naumann Stiftung (FNS) and the European Union. Board members have included prominent names such as Rajmohan Gandhi, Wajahat Habibullah,[20] Syeda Hameed[21] and Teesta Setalvad.[22] However, the primary influence on the CDR's worldviews has been from founder Sushobha

Barve, who has worked in the area of peace and conflict resolution with firsthand experience of communal violence during the 1984 riots in Delhi. Barve has also worked in other conflict zones, including Gujarat, Maharashtra and J&K. In 1992, she set up the Mumbai Mohalla Committee Movement Trust and mobilised a citizens' police force.[23] In J&K, Barve has set up several innovative women's empowerment and peace initiatives, such as peace education training for teachers and interregional, intercommunity, and intracommunity dialogue between Hindus and Muslims, and Kashmiris and residents of Jammu. In addition to Barve, the CDR has been unable to hire other full-time research staff until it received bigger grants from the FNS and the EU.[24] Other researchers, less known, have been based in Kashmir and have worked primarily at the field level.

Similarly smaller in scale, the WISCOMP is an initiative of the Foundation for Universal Responsibility (FUR), which was established with funds from the Nobel Peace Prize awarded to the Dalai Lama in 1999.[25] A key focus at the WISCOMP has been to initiate a discourse on women, peace and security in South Asia, which is done through a combination of research, training and advocacy. A clear institutional position has emphasised the role of women as "peacebuilders" and "agents for nonviolent social change."[26] Further emphasis has been on "empowering a new generation of women and men with the expertise and skills to engage in peace activism through educational and training programs in Conflict Transformation."[27] The organisation's stated focus is on a "people-oriented discourse on issues of security" through advocating for peace, multi-track diplomacy and civil society dialogues.[28]

In addition to the trust fund from the FUR, the WISCOMP's programmes have been funded by the Ford Foundation, the Embassy of Finland and small project grants from the MacArthur Foundation and the International IDEA.[29] In terms of leadership, the primary influence has been founder Meenakshi Gopinath. An educationist, Gopinath was Principal of Lady Shri Ram (LSR) College in New Delhi (1988–2014) and also the first woman to serve on the NSAB (2004–2006). Mainstreaming gender and highlighting human security concerns have been her key focus, and she has been a member of several India–Pakistan peace initiatives including the Neemrana dialogue, the Pakistan India People's Forum for Peace and Democracy (PIPFPD) and the Chaophraya Dialogue. In addition, Manjri Sewak has led WISCOMP's Conflict Transformation (CT) programme. With training in the field of peacebuilding, she has significant expertise in CT and curriculum development. In addition to designing WISCOMP's Indo-Pak CT project, in 2004–2005, Sewak was part of a team that designed a Diploma Program in Conflict Transformation and Peacebuilding at the LSR, where she also served as Visiting Faculty.[30] In addition to research staff, the WISCOMP's advisory board includes prominent names such as Shyam Saran, Leila Seth, Varun Sahni, Amitabh Mattoo and Satish Kumar, among others. Most of these have been associated with a think tank or have held prominent policy-making positions, and are considered to be significant knowledge elites in each of their areas of expertise.

With significant focus on capacity building and creating long-term knowledge networks, the WISCOMP began its work with a public dialogue on *Reporting Conflict Through a Peace Lens*, focusing on the relationship between gender, conflict reportage and peacebuilding in South Asia. Other research programmes have included the CT project and projects on Gender Peace and Security and Educating for Peace. Within these broad themes, the focus has been on gender sensitivity training through the project on violence against women titled *Partners in Wellbeing*; "engendering security" through the South Asian collaborative research project titled *Transcending Conflict: Gender and Non-Traditional Security*;[31] and supporting women-led civil society initiatives in the Northeast and Kashmir (*Women Building Peace*). Of particular significance to this research is the *Athwaas* project situated in J&K, which will be detailed later. Between 2000 and 2008, the WISCOMP with support from the Ford Foundation funded research studies by mid-career researchers on South Asian political and social issues in the *Scholar of Peace* fellowship programme. In addition, collaborations with other international and regional organisations has been an active part of the research agenda.[32]

With differences in elite composition and research agendas, the approaches that shape peacebuilding think tank discourse on India's relations with Pakistan also differ. The next two sections examine the differences in their approach by first expanding on policy discourse on Pakistan and second, by considering the ability and efforts of these think tanks to introduce an alternative policy narrative based on an increased focus on civil society activism and NTS issues.

Policy discourse and mobilisation of dominant government narratives

Embracing the incremental nature of the CD formulation and its emphasis on civil society engagement, research programmes have focused on grassroots peacebuilding initiatives, particularly in Kashmir – with women's networks (WISCOMP, DPG, CDR), engaging with the youth through educational programmes (IPCS, DPG) or with traders and other economic actors as in the case of the CDR. While the agendas were project driven and were based on funding arrangements, there was also a very clear and sustained engagement with dialoguing with Pakistan and building networks beyond the borders. The role of the intellectual elite also comes into play, with the involvement of experts such as Radha Kumar, V.R. Raghavan, P.R. Chari and Meenakshi Gopinath in government advisory and research positions. There is also evidence of an interest in India–Pakistan dialogue that predated the CD. Thus, as early as May 1997, the DPG commissioned a study on Kashmir, one that led to significant academic and policy debates under the co-directorship of Kanti Bajpai, Dipankar Banerjee and Amitabh Mattoo.[33] The project was undertaken in four phases and comprised background papers on internal security, foreign policy, economic development and centre-state relations, as well as extensive fieldwork in J&K between June–October 1997 with briefings from the MEA and the DGMO. While conducted under the sponsorship of the DPG, the report was a result of an independent research effort by key specialists and provided significant policy recommendations both for internal reconciliation as well as relations with Pakistan. Some key suggestions included military cooperation with Pakistan to include CBMs, a cautious defence posture and a nuclear safety assistance and collaboration zone; settlement of smaller disputes including Siachen, Sir Creek and Wullar Barrage; economic cooperation through concessions to Pakistani exports, facilitating business visas and revisiting the pipeline proposals; and Track II diplomacy as well as engagement with third parties that could enhance cooperative deals with Pakistan.[34] The language of some of these recommendations was similar to the official formulations of the CD process initiated in 2004. However, the causal link between them is difficult to determine because of lack of information and transparency in the policy processes.

The initiation of the CD provided a further impetus, and think tanks began to engage more actively with its various debates. Their particular approach towards key issues is discussed further. In addition to policy research by both the DPG and the IPCS, publications from think tanks (particularly the IPCS) also tracked the official dialogue through comprehensive chronologies, creating significant scholarship on the process.[35] Also noteworthy was the research by junior academics or students that formed a part of the youth component at the IPCS, several of whom moved on to other think tanks or acquired academic positions after their experience at the institute.

Kashmir – In addition to the DPG's analysis of Kashmir before the CD, the IPCS policy briefs and commentaries also focused on the different elements of the conflict, concentrating on political leadership, both mainstream and separatist with attention to the alienation of the people of the region. The impact of the conflict on the disillusionment within the populace was a common thread within the IPCS research discourse, becoming more prominent after 2004.[36] Elections and issues regarding local governance were also considered, in addition to suggestions for an "institutionalised" dialogue with the Hurriyat party.[37] The DPG's early viewpoints on Kashmir also focused on internal reconciliation and redressal of Kashmiri grievances and the promised autonomy and the concept of "soft partition" – very similar to the concept of open borders envisioned by the PM in later years.[38] Kumar, however, at that stage was sceptical about the acceptance of an open border if "the rest of the border between India and Pakistan [was] closed."[39]

As in the previous analysis, here too, the dual focus on Kashmir – as both an internal and a bilateral conflict – remained. The need for an "institutionalised bilateral mechanism" between India and Pakistan, particularly with regards to their discussions on the Kashmir conflict, was emphasised.[40] The DPG also offered suggestions for cooperation in earthquake relief and key formulations on Kashmir by President Musharraf and Manmohan Singh were considered.[41] With G. Parthasarathy (CPR), Radha Kumar published the *Frameworks for a Kashmir Settlement* – to suggest ways in which complex factors related to a solution for J&K

could be addressed through discussions on key issues such as self-governance and conflict resolution strategies.[42] Early proposals towards the Srinagar-Muzaffarabad bus service, which became an important CBM in the following years, were also discussed in detail at the IPCS.[43] Additionally, the new initiatives for dialogue were understood to have stemmed from the realisation that "all parties to the Kashmir imbroglio have to make compromises and that maximalist rhetoric, addressed to domestic audiences is counter-productive."[44] There were also visible differences of opinion among intellectuals at the IPCS regarding the process. While the CBMs suggested in 2003 were welcomed by Chandran, Banerjee seemed sceptical about them owing to Pakistan's stubborn attitudes and suggestions to bring in UN monitoring for the Kashmir bus service and meetings between Pakistan and Kashmiri separatist leadership.[45]

The IPCS continued to engage with key decisions on Kashmir policy, including the initiation of the bus service and the Kashmir roundtables that led to the constitution of working groups, specifically on cross-LoC trade. Research scholarship at the time brought to light psychological perceptions of the Kashmiri people towards the government in New Delhi and argued that cross-LoC trade would marginalise extremist voices in the valley.[46] In addition to presenting political ideas, the IPCS's participation in the policy process also helped to fill in gaps in the government's knowledge of ground realities. Owing to its running projects in J&K and the empirical knowledge acquired, several recommendations on cross-LoC interactions emphasised more effective trade and introduced the idea of cross-LoC tourism, both religious and adventure – ideas that were new and underexplored. To facilitate cross-LoC interactions, it was suggested that the Jammu-Sialkot and the Kargil-Skardu routes should also be opened, and heritage routes for tourism and regional festivals including the Pir Panjal Festival and the Poonch festival should be revived.[47] It was also suggested that cross-LoC trade should be made an economic CBM rather than just a political tool – thus expanding the basket of goods and providing banking facilities instead of the barter system currently in place.[48]

There was significant engagement at these think tanks with the internal dialogue in Kashmir. Policy ideas went beyond a review of the army's presence and Kashmir's strategic value. The events and discussions since 2004 took on board key issues under consideration, and the IPCS became an important actor for mobilising public opinion and through its communicative discourse, became relevant to the presentation of political ideas to the public. These ideas included but were not limited to the potential demilitarisation of Siachen as a key to resolving the Kashmir dispute, while also addressing counter-insurgency operations in the region.[49] The impact of alienation of the Kashmiri people owing to the intense militarisation was also an idea that was discussed at length.[50] In May 2006, responding to the PM's Kashmir roundtables and the organisation of the different working groups, the DPG also organised simulations based on the working group on Centre-State relations, which it believed "touche[d] on the crux of the problem: Kashmir's political status."[51] This initiative was supported by the EU, particularly the European Cross-Cultural Programme (ECCP). The conference and many of the policy recommendations that emerged from these conferences drew on other comparative conflicts, such as in Northern Ireland and Israel and Palestine, often referencing the Oslo agreement. A noteworthy argument that emerged was the idea of a "Non-Retractable 370" that essentially proposed that the rights to self-rule that Article 370 of the Indian Constitution provided to J&K be extended to all of the former princely states and made non-retractable with regional and international guarantees towards its implementation.[52]

Unlike government think tanks, the role of the Hurriyat in the internal dialogue in Kashmir was seen differently at peacebuilding think tanks. It was argued that while not the sole representative, the Hurriyat party represented significant Kashmiri public opinion that must be taken on board within the dialogue.[53] The Hurriyat, it was argued, "provides the much-needed political space between militancy and the moderate demand for an independent Kashmir or maximum autonomy," and the union government should therefore attempt to engage with the moderate leadership within the Hurriyat, including Mirwaiz Umar Farooq and Sajad Lone.[54] Recommendations were also made in favour of allowing a Hurriyat delegation to Pakistan and PAK. This was significantly different from the position taken by think tanks examined earlier, who recommended limiting the Hurriyat's connection to PAK and relegated its relevance to only as an actor in the domestic dynamics.

Radha Kumar was also a member of the team of interlocutors appointed by Manmohan Singh in October 2010. With extensive interviews (700 delegations in the 22 districts of J&K) and three roundtable conferences, key suggestions from the team were the recommendations for CBMs related to human rights and rule of law reforms; a review of the AFSPA; improvements in police-community relations; providing better relief and rehabilitation for widows and orphans of violence in the state; and facilitating the return of Kashmiris stranded across the LoC, many of whom had crossed over for arms training.[55] The appointment of the interlocutors was also potentially an admission by the Government of India of the lack of adequate information from the region. Think tanks and intellectual elites within think tanks with expertise on Kashmir-specific issues were well placed to provide insight. The team of interlocutors also promoted the recommendations of the PM's Working Groups and endorsed the idea of "irrelevant borders." Radha Kumar further asserted that the report's impetus was on a "settlement of core political issues" rather than one focused on CBMs.[56] The report was submitted in October 2011 and was made public for an informed debate in May 2012. It did not, however, receive any serious official consideration.

Think tanks in this category also contributed to debates on the changed nature of India–Pakistan relations and the continuing radicalisation in the state of J&K that was visible in the Amarnath and Shopian incidents.[57] The IPCS, for instance, undertook a project titled *Jammu, Kashmir and Ladakh: Building Peace and Countering Radicalisation* (2009), that aimed to bring together younger generations from the different regions to gain an understanding of key issues and deliberate on preventive measures for further radicalisation. The project focused on three kinds of radicalisation – regional, religious and ethnic – and divided into three phases, concentrated on field surveys across the three regions. It commissioned research papers and conducted a workshop in collaboration with the University of Jammu in December 2009.[58] Key recommendations that emerged focused on the need to address regional and religious differences in the state with an emphasis on internal displacement, governance and decentralisation. Suggestions also reflected a need for better communication, easy travel, revival of tourism and other cross-regional cultural and educational activities.[59]

Peace and Security – In addition to the active discourse on Kashmir, peacebuilding think tanks also engaged with the debate on nuclear weapons. As early as 2001, the DPG in collaboration with the Islamabad Peace Research Institute (IPRI) facilitated a dialogue on nuclear risk reduction.[60] The talks involved briefing the foreign office and sought to develop "a shared and agreed lexicon" on key nuclear concepts such as "minimum nuclear deterrence."[61] The dialogue "facilitated an interaction between two sets of experts comprising former Foreign Secretaries, defence services officers, nuclear strategy analysts and academicians."[62] Commenting on this interaction, Raghavan noted the "differing interpretations placed on commonly used nuclear phraseology. It was also a revelation to note how adversely, immature political rhetoric in one country affects the mood in the other."[63]

Raghavan's influence and his support for nuclear disarmament and abolition could be clearly seen on the DPG's worldviews. In 2002 and 2003, he was a part of a Carnegie–NTI and Stimson Center enabled Track II workshop, as well as a part of a working group on an expanded non-proliferation system between November 2009 and June 2011. The impetus of these dialogues was to formulate Nuclear Risk Reduction Measures (NRRM) for the subcontinent.[64] At the IPCS, this expertise lay with Chari and Banerjee, and the issue of nuclear non-proliferation, particularly with regards to the nuclear relationship between India and Pakistan since 1998, was considered. Several dialogues were conducted by the IPCS under the India-Pakistan-China trilateral Nuclear Strategic Dialogue with support from the NTI.[65] With funding from the NTI, the IPCS also organised capacity-building workshops at a student level, for media and young professionals in 2008 and 2009 on Nuclear Weapons, Global Disarmament and Regional Security.[66] In addition, between 2007 and 2009, in collaboration with the IDSA, the IPCS organised workshops on disarmament and nuclear issues for government officials and armed forces personnel.

Chari was the most vocal proponent of nuclear disarmament at the institute, often highlighting the need for enlarging mutual understandings of security concepts and nuclear doctrines, more so since 2004.[67] In addition, he recommended that India should concede to Pakistan's request to include cruise missiles in the pre-notification of missile test agreement signed in 1999. Chari was sceptical about the recommendation to increase channels of communication between air forces and nuclear establishments and in several commentaries during the early phase of the dialogue process, emphasised the need for conventional CBMs to progress simultaneously with nuclear CBMs and called for the extension of the 1988 agreement to include population centres and major economic assets.[68] Dipankar Banerjee was also vocal about nuclear disarmament, insisting on "elimination through binding commitment" with a focus on transparency and verification.[69]

As part of the India-Pakistan-China trialogue organised by the IPCS since 2008, similar issues regarding nuclear power and threat perceptions; existing nuclear CBMs; fissile material stockpiles and control and production ban; particular emphasis on Asian nuclear stability and security; harmonising doctrines for cooperative security; and aspects of nuclear weapons and terrorism were taken up among key interlocutors from India, China and Pakistan.[70]

Siachen – By and large, viewpoints on Siachen have questioned the strategic significance of the area for both India and Pakistan. The potential demilitarisation of Siachen was also linked to resolving the Kashmir dispute.[71] The shift in Pakistan's position, reflected in Army Chief Kayani's proposal after the Gayari avalanche, was perceived as a "major departure" from Pakistan's previous position.[72] The proposal, it was argued, should result in a positive Indian response that would be helpful in asserting again that Siachen/Saltoro ridge is not of strategic significance and should be resolved. The IPCS thus adopted a more reconciliatory position, while many in the think tank community in India were suspicious of Pakistan's motivations.

Terrorism – Unlike other think tanks that focused on India–Pakistan relations, peacebuilding think tanks did not consider the issue of terrorism as extensively. The only organisation that addressed the issue in their policy discourse was the IPCS. The issues of terrorism and armed violence were, however, perceived at the IPCS through a South Asian perspective, and very often recommendations focused on a joint South Asian strategy to counter terrorism in the region.[73] This was in contrast to the steadfast focus on a Pakistan-centred policy on terrorism as reflected in government think tank discourse. The IPCS discourse before the Mumbai attacks also considered issues of internal conflicts and left-wing extremism. Thus, in August 2005, the IPCS collaborated with the Social Science Research Council and the Norwegian Institute of International Affairs to conduct an intensive study, incorporating two years of field research and analyses of protracted violent conflicts from around the world, focusing particularly on Kashmir, Sri Lanka and Indonesia.[74] Further in 2005, a research study analysed the Jaish-e-Mohammed (JeM) and its activities and operations in India.[75] In addition, as was popular practice at the IPCS, several publications highlighted terrorist attacks in India, particularly in J&K. The post-Mumbai focus was on strengthening internal security through improvements in intelligence and implementation agencies – ideas that were expressed by other research organisations as well.[76]

Introducing alternative policy narratives

With regard to the discourse on security, research agendas at peacebuilding think tanks were defined through a particular perception of security – with an emphasis on non-traditional security issues including a focus on gender and resource politics. This emphasis was also more clearly visible in their adopted approach towards the India–Pakistan dialogue process. There was a noticeable emphasis on building cross-border networks, particularly with like-minded constituencies and civil society in Pakistan and in training the youth, seen as future stakeholders in the conflict and hence relevant to the creation of resolution strategies. Even within India, the emphasis of these institutes was on civil society engagements seen more squarely in the programmes of the WISCOMP and the CDR, even though there was some attention to this aspect at the IPCS and the DPG. The training and professional backgrounds of intellectuals within these think tanks was also reflected in their focus on conflict resolution, peacebuilding and an alternate conceptualisation of security issues. Thus, while the IPCS and the DPG focused on the broader issues regarding Pakistan, the CDR and the WISCOMP emphasised engagements with civil society.

The CDR's approach encouraged leading civil society initiatives to facilitate cross-LoC dialogue in Kashmir. Not classifying itself as a "purely security oriented organisation," CDR dialogues took on board debate and discussion on India–Pakistan relations, but the approach was to consider seemingly non-political issues and frame them in such a way to avoid contention with state policy.[77] Thus, rather than a direct reference to the IWT, the CDR considered issues such as water security, public health and education. This strategy was used to retain the interest of policymakers and maintain viability as a research institute. The programmes at the WISCOMP also reflected an interest in conflict resolution, with particular emphasis on the role of women as peacebuilders and specifically the role of women's organisations in building peace between India and Pakistan. In 2000, it was part of the India–Pakistan women's bus for peace initiative launched by Nirmala Deshpande (in the backdrop of Vajpayee's Lahore bus).[78] This was perhaps the first group to initiate cross-border dialogue in the aftermath of the Kargil conflict.

The shaping of the formal dialogue gave fillip to the DPG programmes as well, and in 2005, the DPG launched its two-year program on *Developing Durable Peace Processes and Partners*, "built around India's renewed peacemaking engagements."[79] The project "combine[d] closed door policy conferences with student workshops, in an effort to expand policy-oriented research on peace and security between Indian and European think tanks and universities."[80] Significant focus was on training and simulation exercises on key aspects of the Kashmir dispute. The discourse at the WISCOMP also engaged with the academic and policy debate on Kashmir, both through its research and its more participant-driven forums. Its CT workshops, for instance, included drafting of joint statements on

Kashmir between Indian and Pakistani participants (2001) and conducted workshop simulations on conflict resolution strategies (2004).[81]

The creation of civil society networks was also a crucial agenda for peacebuilding think tanks. In addition to an emphasis on internal dialogue and reconciliation, the CDR maintained a collaborative partnership with the Jinnah Institute – a think tank based in Islamabad with which the CDR has jointly organised Track II dialogues since 2010.[82] In addition, a one-year education partnership was initiated with the Lahore University of Management Sciences. These cross-LoC interactions were expanded based on participant feedback and focused on participation from both sides of the border in Kashmir, in an attempt to bring to the table differing viewpoints and varying regional problems and perspectives.[83] Academic research studies on pertinent issues in J&K were also commissioned, including a comparative analysis of documents related to the autonomy question in Kashmir funded by the FNS and the EU; another on the issues of the Indus River Basin with support from the FNS – an outcome of deliberations during the CDR-Jinnah Institute dialogue on common concerns in the Indus Basin.[84] The DPG has also collaborated with other organisations, for instance, in November 2006, a conference titled *Pluralism and Democracy after 9/11: Europe and India* was organised in collaboration with the Nelson Mandela Centre and with the support of the ECCP. The conference particularly mobilised public opinion to consider and adapt conflict resolution strategies from Europe to the South Asian region.[85]

Further to mobilising opinion on cross-LoC dynamics, there was also a focus on intra-regional dynamics in Kashmir and the need to address the concerns of all three regions of the state, namely Kashmir, Jammu and Ladakh. Responding to the "MEA's admission that they lacked information on LoC areas in the Jammu region, or the divided families in the Jammu region," the CDR conducted *Intra-Region Dialogues*.[86] Based on participant recommendations, the dialogues were expanded across the LoC and since 2005, ten cross-LoC dialogue conferences have been conducted parallel to developments in the official dialogue that have focused specifically on cross-LoC Kashmir CBMs adopted since 2005. Conflict resolution ideas that have emerged from these dialogues have stressed the need to reduce violence, initiate a dialogue process that includes people of all regions and communities of the divided state and end human rights violations. There have also been suggestions for a calibrated reduction of security forces from civilian areas in the state.

The CDR has also commissioned several studies on specific problems faced by people in the border districts between India and Pakistan and by divided families and Kashmiri Pandits living in the valley, reports of which were circulated to relevant policy elites. It was the organisation's assertion that "the new suggestions for opening of routes for travel and trade in all three regions of the state" was owing to the recommendations made by the CDR dialogues, particularly the opening of the Poonch-Rawalakot route, which it claimed was a "direct result of suggestions made through the CDR initiated Track III civil society meetings."[87]

In addition, the organisation has claimed that fencing across the LoC was modified as a response to the CDR's suggestions.[88] The ideas emerging from the intra-region dialogues were also centred on the reduction of violence and the need to allow for easy trade and travel. A crucial aspect within these dialogues was the inclusion of participation from AJK, Gilgit and Baltistan, usually ignored actors in the political dynamics. These dialogue forums involved the participation of a wide selection of experts, both political and civil society actors from all regions in J&K, as well as significant participation from PAK, and bureaucrats and policymakers from Delhi and Islamabad. It was one of the rare dialogue forums that managed to organise a meeting in Islamabad, whereas many other organisations were unable to, owing to visa and funding restrictions. This was perceived as an indication that the government was receptive to such dialogue forums.[89]

In addition to the dialogue groups, there was also an emphasis on developing modules for peace education training to improve communication and enable an understanding of the conflict and the diversity of opinion in Kashmir. During the period from 2004–2007, the CDR conducted peace education programmes for 200 government secondary schools and teachers from 100 schools in Kashmir.[90] It also launched its water initiative in 2010 in recognition of "issues related to water, climate change, the environment, transboundary aquifers, changing demographics, cooperation for joint disaster management and possible joint studies on issues of common concerns in the Indus Basin."[91] This project also took the form of an India–Pakistan dialogue in collaboration with the Jinnah Institute. Further along this line, the IPCS's project titled *Jammu, Kashmir and Ladakh: Building Peace and Countering Radicalization* (2009) also aimed to bring together younger generations from the different regions to gain an understanding of key issues and deliberate on preventive measures for further radicalisation. As part of the project, a workshop with students focused on critical issues of concern to the three regions.[92] These included the role of the Amarnath land row agitation in polarising communities and its spill-over effect in other states, the gradual waning of Sufi influence in the Valley, the displacement of Kashmiri Pandits, the alienation of Rajouri and Poonch districts, the growing Gujjar-Pahari divide in these twin districts and the challenges that confront Ladakh since its division into Leh and Kargil districts, among other topical issues in the context of J&K.

A key goal of the CDR initiatives was also to create a "deeper understanding between stakeholders" by developing networks within Kashmir, primarily among the women who have suffered due to years of violence.[93] The impetus to civil society engagement was also undertaken in the WISCOMP programmes. Influenced by the ideas of John Paul Lederach, particularly the concept of conflict transformation and the "three tier pyramid" model, the WISCOMP also emphasised the engagement of stakeholders at different levels of social and political hierarchies.[94] Special attention was given to women's empowerment and gender-based violence, particularly in the context of armed conflict. In 2000, the WISCOMP organised a roundtable on *Breaking the Silence: Women in Kashmir*. A direct result of the roundtable was the creation of *Athwaas* – an all-Kashmiri women's network in 2001 that focused on income-generating activities in Kashmir, the rehabilitation of widows and orphans, trauma healing and peace education workshops, in addition to creating peace education programs for the youth in Kashmir. The *Athwaas* initiative also created *Samanbals* – a safe space in various locations in Kashmir to dialogue in conjunction with an income-generating activity.[95]

In response to Manmohan Singh's roundtable conferences in Kashmir, which lacked the participation and representation of women's voices, in August 2006, the WISCOMP also organised a convention titled *Women in Dialogue: Envisioning the road ahead in Jammu and Kashmir*. A primary goal of the convention was to "contribute proactively to the ongoing dialogue on the peace process in Jammu and Kashmir by placing womens' perspectives, and their visions of the road ahead squarely on the table."[96] In addition to advocacy and social development, the WISCOMP's work in Kashmir was also focused on prolific academic research on various aspects of Kashmir's political and socio-economic dynamics, both internally as well as in relation to Pakistan.

Peacebuilding think tanks were also more actively engaged with multi-track initiatives on conflict resolution and trust-building in general and with explicit focus on Kashmir. This role is particularly relevant in the light of the deteriorating status of the official dialogue since 2008. Think tanks therefore enabled a forum for interaction when official channels of dialogue were suspended. Through their grassroots initiatives, they were also able to highlight the political dynamics and changing public perceptions in Kashmir. During the Amarnath agitation, for instance, the CDR teams travelled extensively in the region and remained in communication with their existing networks in the state. Meetings were held in the towns of Poonch, Mendhar, Surankot and Mandi, which were most affected by the rioting, and reports were sent to the state administration. The DPG also organised a conference in March 2012, titled *Achieving Peace in Jammu and Kashmir: Options Today* that focused on the need for CBMs for conflict resolution, particularly the need to incorporate a dialogue process among legislators.[97] On similar lines, the IPCS initiated its Indo-Pak dialogue on Conflict Resolution and Peace Building in 2009, and as part of the project published a series of background papers that provided a detailed narrative of the history of India–Pakistan disputes with a specific focus on cross-LoC interactions, IWT, terrorism, trade and regional cooperation. The papers were uniquely designed to provide both an Indian and a Pakistani perspective on these issues. The Indo-Pak dialogue initiated by the IPCS also featured a Track II meeting in Bangkok in October 2009 with support from the Ploughshares Fund. Terrorism and associated issues formed a crucial part of this interaction, in addition to focused discussions on religious radicalism and the dangers of terrorism and violence and evolving better joint mechanisms to counter terrorism.[98] Other aspects included a need to review and expand CBMs and the possibility of third-party intervention in the absence of a successful bilateral dialogue process. The dialogue also considered a review of the IWT.

Subsequently, in March 2013, a Track II Indus water dialogue was conducted by the IPCS with support from the Ploughshares fund, and several issue briefs were commissioned that provided insight into multiple dimensions related to the Indus River Basin.[99] The papers dealt with a range of issues including climate change, cross-LoC CBMs and the status of the IWT. The dialogue titled *Towards Building an Indus Community* focused on contemporary issues related to the sharing of Indus waters based on the existing approaches and issues from the perspectives of India, Pakistan and the two parts of J&K. Besides comprehending the discourse on rivers of the global commons between both states in terms of sharing the Indus waters, the bilateral identified new approaches and recommendations on cross-LoC CBMs over the Indus. It schemed innovative methods and alternatives with respect to working together on issues related to the environment, climate change, supply-demand deficit gap, joint projects and making effective use of the IWT and, ultimately, garnering all efforts towards a policy orientation.[100]

Peacebuilding think tanks and India's Pakistan policy: a summary

Based on the bureaucratic politics literature, think tanks explored in this chapter are best described as "insulated agencies" as seemingly more insulated from formal bureaucratic positions and thus different from the "embedded institutions" categorisation that better describes government think tanks such as the IDSA or more resourceful non-government think tanks such as the ORF.[101] Yet, the insulation from bureaucracy restricted the ability of peacebuilding think tanks to have better inputs into policy making. The lack of government patronage and resources meant that research could not be sustained, and very often these think tanks moved towards adopting "more palatable" research agendas that were not in conflict with the formal bureaucracy. This is reflected in the CDR's framing of issues or the DPG's expansion of programmes to a focus on Afghanistan as the India–Pakistan dialogue lost momentum after 2008. With new leadership, the focus of other DPG programmes also appears to have changed with visibly reduced attention to peace and conflict studies. The power of the state in forging consensus is thus very visible here.

Further, aspects of bureaucratic bargaining and "research brokerage" are also evident as these think tanks were dependent on tacit government support to organise many of their cross-border initiatives (in the form of official approvals and visas) and to enable their continued funding from international agencies. The role of these think tanks, however, in building discourse and mobilising public opinion during 2004–2008 is visible, and the communicative discourse aspect expressed through publications, public outreach and networking programmes, aided also by new methods like social media groups and formal media engagements, was strong. The linkages with formal policy making, however, were weak and very often considered as "bleeding heart" organisations, so the narratives introduced by peacebuilding think tanks were not given considerable value. Yet, the work of these organisations in expanding narratives, in creating spaces for articulation of civil society's aspirations and their attention to train and empower younger generations makes them unique. The networks that these think tanks created – with Pakistan and within Kashmir – were sustained even when official dialogue was suspended, although only to a marginal degree.

Conclusion

Presenting the second part of the analysis on non-government think tanks, this chapter has conducted a critical examination of the research agendas focused specifically on peacebuilding and reconciliation. Taken together, peacebuilding think tanks are smaller in scale and membership, and they demonstrate noticeable differences in membership patterns when compared with government think tanks or more resourceful non-government think tanks including the CPR and the ORF. Also distinct is their engagement with the policy establishment, with visibly reduced ties to policy elites and an added emphasis on advocacy. The chapter also explored the policy positions on the conflict with Pakistan, highlighting programmes geared towards training and networking, creating women's networks and enabling forums for training of the youth. Thus, while reaching out to policy elites and mobilising public opinion is a goal, an emphasis on grassroots initiatives and expanding stakeholders towards peace with Pakistan is also visible. While these peacebuilding think tanks significantly expanded the discourse on Pakistan to include civil society and women's perspectives, their distance from official narratives and lack of proximity to policy elites curtailed their institutional relevance and provides evidence of the state's role and predominant place in forging policy consensus. The state's role in building consensus can also be seen through the control of funding and access to these think tanks, limiting their institutional potential in creating a changed discourse on India–Pakistan relations.

Notes

1 Inderjeet Parmar, *Think Tanks and Power in Foreign Policy* (New York: Palgrave MacMillan, 2004), p. 77.
2 More on DPG's official webpage: www.delhipolicygroup.org/about-us
3 With new leadership, DPG programmes also appear to have changed. The new website (www.delhipolicygroup.org) highlights a focus on strategic and geopolitical issues including regional security challenges; geo-economic issues like India's political economy, regional economic integration including regional connectivity initiatives; defence and security issues include, national security policy, defence technology and trade, maritime security and issues of non-traditional security. There is less emphasis on peace and conflict studies now.
4 A renowned sociologist and professor emeritus at JNU, Oommen was a member of the Sachar Committee set up by the PM to study the social, economic and educational status of the Muslims in India as well as a Chairman of the Advisory Committee of the Gujarat Harmony Project constituted after the 2002 Gujarat communal riots. Known

to be an expert on water security issues, Verghese had a long-term association with CPR, and his viewpoints have been discussed in the previous chapter.
5 Kumar was Executive Director of the Helsinki Citizen's Assembly in Prague (1992–1994) and Associate Fellow at the Institute for War and Peace Studies at Columbia University (1994–1996). She has also been a senior fellow in peace and conflict studies at the CFR in New York (1999–2003). She currently is on the board of the Stockholm International Peace Research Institute and the Council of the United Nations University, where she was appointed as Chair in 2016.
6 The Nelson Mandela Centre for Peace and Conflict Resolution was launched in 2004 and was one of the first of its kind in an Indian university. Its chief focus is comparative and contemporary studies, and it aims to address the lack of serious and purposeful analysis of types and sources of conflict in our country and neighbourhood, and the methods of dealing with them that India has adopted. For more, see http://jmi.ac.in/cpcr
7 After DPG he moved to the Centre for Security Analysis, Chennai, as President, where he has led programmes on peninsular India's security perspectives, relations with South East Asia and on Civil Society–Governance interface. http://disarmament.nrpa.no/wp-content/uploads/2008/02/Bio_Raghavan.pdf
8 A seasoned diplomat, before joining DPG, Singh was Professor for Strategic Studies at ICRIER (2011–2016) and has been associated with several public policy initiatives and Track II / Track 1.5 strategic dialogues involving major think tanks of India, Japan, Asia and the US. He has written and worked extensively on the ongoing transformation of India's relations with the United States and Japan and their growing convergences in shaping Asia's emerging economic and security architecture.
9 Virmani has been an advisor to the GOI at the highest levels for 25 years, including as Chief Economic Advisor, Ministry of Finance and Principle Advisor, Planning Commission. His affiliation with think tanks extends to his membership in the Governing Board of the Forum for Strategic Initiatives (FSI) and CPR.
10 A former member of the NSAB, General Singh retired in September 2007 as GOC of the Southern Command
11 A retired Brigadier in the Indian Army, in addition to being a research fellow at DPG, Sahgal is the Executive Director of the Forum for Strategic Initiatives, a policy think tank focusing on national security, diplomacy and Track II Dialogues. He was previously the founding Director of the Office of Net Assessment, Indian Integrated Defense Staff, Head of the Center for Strategic Studies and Simulation, USI, and Senior Fellow at the IDSA. His research comprises scenario planning workshops, geopolitical and strategic assessments related to Asian security, and issues concerning nuclear doctrine and strategic stability in South Asia. He has been a member of the Task Force on Net Assessment and Simulation, under the NSC, and a consultant with DRDO. He is a member of many Track 1.5 and Track II initiatives.
12 A former bureaucrat, Banerji has held important positions in the state of Assam as well as in Indian missions abroad, dealing particularly with security and intelligence-related issues impinging on National Security Policy formulation, with focused expertise on the South Asian region.
13 www.ipcs.org/about-us
14 More about the IPCS Internship programme can be viewed at: www.ipcs.org/internship-program
15 The South Asian Summer School in Arms Control was an annual summer school for young South Asian (and Chinese) journalists, officials and scholars (about 25–30 participants, 6–8 international faculty). The first and second sessions were held in 1993 and 1994 in Pakistan, while the third took place in India in August 1995. The goals were to transfer knowledge about arms control, verification, and conflict resolution, and to create a network of younger scholars that transcends regional borders. For more, see Sundeep Waslekar, "Track Two Diplomacy in South Asia", *ACDIS Occasional Paper* (Urbana-Champaign: University of Illinois, October 1995). Chari was also involved in

a study on the Brasstacks Crisis of 1987 – a study co-organised by Kanti Bajpai, Pervaiz Cheema, Sumit Ganguly and Stephen Cohen, that culminated in a detailed book, *Brasstacks and Beyond: Perception and Management of Crisis in South Asia* (New Delhi: Manohar Press, 1995).
16 According to C. Uday Bhaskar, Former Director at IDSA, www.thehindu.com/news/national/nuclear-disarmament-advocate-pr-chari-passes-away/article7466792.ece
17 Chari's particular interest in nurturing young minds is fondly recalled by his colleague. Dipankar Banerjee's comment in, "Tribute: P R Chari", *Mainstream*, 53:34, August 15, 2015, www.mainstreamweekly.net/article5879.html
18 Banerjee was also briefly Executive Director at the Regional Centre for Strategic Studies (RCSS) from 1999–2002, a prominent Sri Lankan think tank. In addition, he was associated with the US Institute of Peace and was on a UN Panel of Governmental Experts on Conventional Arms.
19 Chandran edited *Armed Conflicts in South Asia* – an annual publication from IPCS to map and analyse the nature of armed conflicts in the region. With significant experience in the field of conflict resolution and peace studies, Chandran's specific focus has been on issues within the Kashmir conflict. He is currently affiliated with the National Institute of Advanced Studies in Bangalore, http://nias.res.in/professor/d-suba-chandran. Mallika Joseph specialises in security sector reforms and has been Director of IPCS since 2015, prior to which she was Executive Director at the RCSS in Sri Lanka from 2012–2014.
20 Former chairperson of the National Commission for Minorities and former Chief Information Commissioner of India.
21 A prominent social and women's rights activist, Hameed is a former member of the Planning Commission. She has previously chaired the Steering Committee of the Commission on Health, which reviewed the National Health Policy of 2002, which was later replaced by the NITI Aayog. Hameed is also founding trustee of the Women's Initiative for Peace in South Asia and a former member of the National Commission for Women (1997–2000).
22 Setalvad is an Indian civil rights activist, journalist and secretary of Citizens for Justice and Peace, an organisation formed to fight for justice for the victims of communal violence in the state of Gujarat in 2002.
23 http://india.ashoka.org/fellow/sushobha-barve
24 Personal communication with senior member at CDR, New Delhi, on October 7, 2015.
25 www.furhhdl.org
26 Mission of the organisation provided on their website that can be accessed at http://wiscomp.org/our-mission
27 ibid.
28 In a personal communication with a senior member at WISCOMP, New Delhi, on September 7, 2015, it was argued that the think tank's and NGO's conceptions of security changed from a hard-core state security focus in the early 2000s to one where both people's security and state security began to be considered. This was also the time when the MEA and at a larger level the UN started giving more credibility to NGOs.
29 Institute for Democracy and Electoral Assistance (IDEA), www.idea.int
30 The center has now been renamed the Aung San Suu Kyi Center for Peace and courses offered include Conflict Analysis and Conflict Transformation; Dialogue; Mediation; Gandhi; Justice, and Reconciliation. http://lsr.edu.in/ASSK-Centre-for-Peace.asp
31 Initiated in 2002, this research project was the first systematic attempt to foreground, through case studies from the South Asian region, the need to develop methodologies that situate gender concerns squarely within the security discourse. It facilitated cross-border research, published as monographs, by scholars from Pakistan, Bangladesh, Nepal, Sri Lanka, Bhutan, and India on areas of conflict within the country of their residence. http://wiscomp.org/programs/gender-and-nts-south-asia
32 WISCOMP has partnered with the Peace Research Institute Oslo in its multi-year project on "Making Women Count for Peace" and organised a roundtable on Women

and Peace Building in 2015; association with PAIMAN Trust in Pakistan to strengthen people-to-people contact between India and Pakistan. Mossarat Qadeem, Founder and CEO, PAIMAN Trust has been a WISCOMP Scholar of Peace Fellow in 2002 and a regular at WISCOMP's annual CT workshops. It is also one of the 14 founding members of the NTS Consortium based at the Rajaratnam School of International Studies, Nanyang Technological University, Singapore. Further, WISCOMP is a member of the Global Partnership for the Prevention of Armed Conflict. The Women Peacemakers Program, an initiative of the International Fellowship of Reconciliation set up in 1997 in the Netherlands, has also given financial support to WISCOMP to bring together women from regions of armed conflict in South Asia for dialogues on peacebuilding.

33 The draft report written in November 1997 was presented to the DPG trustees and directors and subsequently presented in New Delhi in 1998.
34 Kanti Bajpai, Dipankar Banerjee, Amitabh Mattoo, et al., *Jammu and Kashmir: An Agenda for the Future* (New Delhi: Delhi Policy Group, 1999), pp. vi, vii.
35 Detailed chronological information on the progress of the different baskets of issues in the CD were catalogued at IPCS over the years. These include K.S. Manjunath, "Indo-Pak Peace Process: Chronology of Events 2004–2005", *IPCS Special Report*, 6, January 2006; K.S. Manjunath, Seema Sridhar and Beryl Anand, "Indo-Pak Composite Dialogue 2004–2005: A Profile", *IPCS Special Report*, 12, February 2006; Priyashree Andley, "Third Composite Dialogue: An Overview of Indo-Pak Relations in 2006", *IPCS Special Report*, 36, March 2007; Sameer Suryakant Patil, "Indo-Pak Composite Dialogue: An Update", *IPCS Special Report*, 53, June 2008 and Samarjit Ghosh, "Indo-Pak Composite Dialogue-2008: A Review", *IPCS Special Report*, 65, February 2009.
36 In 2000, commenting on the rise of the Hizbul Mujahideen (HM), Chandran brought to light this alienation coupled with the disillusioned youth as a key factor in the rise of the HM. D. Suba Chandran, "The Hizbul Mujahideen", *IPCS Articles*, 405, August 14, 2000, www.ipcs.org/article/terrorism-in-jammu-kashmir/the-hizbul-mujahideen-405.html
37 In August 2002, IPCS conducted a field survey in the Kashmir valley on the forthcoming elections, highlighting Kashmiri reluctance to participate in elections attributed primarily to bad governance and rigging. D. Suba Chandran, "Recent Developments in Kashmir II-Hizbul Cease-Fire: Implications", *IPCS Articles*, 402, August 7, 2000, www.ipcs.org/article/terrorism-in-jammu-kashmir/recent-developments-in-kashmir-ii-hizbul-cease-fire-implications-402.html. See also: Suba Chandran, "Kashmir: Need for an Internal Dialogue", *IPCS Articles*, 354, May 11, 2000, www.ipcs.org/article/jammu-kashmir/kashmir-need-for-an-internal-dialogue-354.html
38 Radha Kumar, "Untying the Kashmir Knot", *World Policy Journal*, 19:1, Spring 2002, p. 21.
39 ibid.
40 D. Suba Chandran, "The Indo-Pak Riddle: Neither Forward Nor Backward Nor Stationary", *IPCS Articles*, 1036, May 18, 2003, www.ipcs.org/article/indo-pak/the-indo-pak-riddle-neither-forward-nor-backward-nor-stationary-1036.html
41 In 2005, after the Kashmir earthquake, DPG put together a collection of articles by legislators in J&K and academics and policy experts on specific areas of concern detailing priorities for relief and rehabilitation jointly between India and Pakistan. *Kashmir: After the Quake: Prospects for Peace* (New Delhi: Delhi Policy Group, 2005).
42 G. Parthasarathy and Radha Kumar, *Frameworks for a Kashmir Settlement* (New Delhi: Delhi Policy Group, 2006).
43 D. Suba Chandran, "New Indian Initiatives in Kashmir", *IPCS Issue Brief*, 13, November 2003.
44 P. R. Chari, Pervaiz Iqbal Cheema and Stephen P. Cohen, *Four Crises and a Peace Process: American Engagement in South Asia* (Washington, DC: Brookings Institution, 2007), p. 214.
45 D. Suba Chandran, "New Indian Initiatives in Kashmir", *IPCS Issue Brief*, 13, November 2003; Dipankar Banerjee, "India-Pakistan Imbroglio over CBMs", *IPCS Articles*,

1200, November 6, 2003, www.ipcs.org/article/indo-pak/india-pakistan-imbroglio-over-cbms-1200.html
46 It was highlighted that the fruit industry in Sopore region, an area that Geelani belonged to, if allowed to trade its apples across the LoC, would help counter the adverse propaganda by Geelani and his militant supporters in PoK. D. Suba Chandran, "Cross LoC Trade: Challenges and Opportunities in J & K", *IPCS Issue Brief*, 66, May 2008.
47 D. Suba Chandran, "Poonch Festival: A Strategy to Integrate Border Regions in J & K", *IPCS Special Report*, 64, January 2009; D. Suba Chandran, "Pir Panjal Regional Festival", *IPCS Issue Brief*, 142, April 2010.
48 D. Suba Chandran, "Expanding Cross LoC Interactions: Perspectives from India", *IPCS Issue Brief*, 131, September 2009.
49 "Kashmir: Looking Further", *IPCS Article*, 1382, May 5, 2004, www.ipcs.org/article/indo-pak/kashmir-looking-further-1382.html
50 Radha Kumar, Anjali Puri and Saurabh Naithani (eds.), *What Makes a Peace Process Irreversible: A Conference Report* (New Delhi: Delhi Policy Group, 2005).
51 "Simulation Exercise: Frameworks for a Kashmir Settlement", in *DPG Programme on Developing Peace Processes and Partners* (New Delhi: Delhi Policy Group, 2006).
52 ibid., p. 9.
53 D. Suba Chandran, "New Indian Initiatives in Kashmir", *IPCS Issue Brief*, 13, November 2003, p. 1.
54 ibid.
55 Radha Kumar, M. M. Ansari and Dileep Padgaonkar, *A New Compact with the People of Jammu and Kashmir*, Final Report of the Group of Interlocutors for J & K, October 2011.
56 Radha Kumar, "To a Battery of Ever-Ready Denunciators", *Outlook*, June 11, 2012, www.outlookindia.com/magazine/story/to-a-battery-of-ever-ready-denunciators/281116
57 Mass protests broke out in Kashmir in May 2009 after the bodies of two women, who were believed to be raped and murdered by Indian troops, were discovered in the Shopian district of the Kashmir valley. For more, see Altaf Hussain, "Deaths Provoke Kashmir Protests", *BBC News*, June 1, 2009, http://news.bbc.co.uk/2/hi/south_asia/8076666.stm
58 The focus was specifically on ten towns: Jammu, Rajouri, Doda, Kishtwar, Anantnag, Srinagar, Baramulla, Sopore, Kargil, and Leh.
59 *Jammu, Kashmir and Ladakh: Building Peace and Countering Radicalisation* (New Delhi: IPCS, March 2010).
60 Islamabad Peace Research Institute (IPRI) is a prominent think tank in Pakistan operational since 1999. www.ipripak.org
61 Manjrika Sewak, "Multi-Track Diplomacy between India and Pakistan: A Conceptual Framework for Sustainable Security", in *RCSS Policy Studies*, Vol. 30 (New Delhi: Manohar Press, 2005), p. 45.
62 V. R. Raghavan, "South Asian Nuclear Dialogue", *The Hindu*, September 1, 2000, www.thehindu.com/2000/09/01/stories/05012523.htm
63 ibid.
64 In addition, among the participants were future national security advisers M.K. Narayanan and Mahmud Durrani, as well as Salman Haidar, V.P. Malik, S.K. Mehra, V.R. Raghavan, Rahul Roy-Chaudhury, Raja Menon, Jehangir Karamat, Najmuddin Shaikh, Shaharyar Khan, and Feroz Khan. For more detailed information about these workshops, see Michael Krepon, "Nuclear Risk Reduction Redux in South Asia", *Stimson Center Issue Brief*, June 14, 2012, www.stimson.org/content/nuclear-risk-reduction-redux-south-asia
65 For more information on the trialogue interactions, see *Debriefing the India-China-Pakistan Strategic Dialogue: Towards a Stable Nuclear Order in Asia* held at the Fudan University, Shanghai on August 8–9, 2009 (New Delhi: IPCS, September 2009); *Review of the Shanghai Meeting and the Future Agenda* (New Delhi: IPCS, October 2009).
66 For more on the youth programmes, see D. Suba Chandran and Rekha Chakravarthi, "Nuclear Disarmament & Regional Security: Reintroducing the Disarmament Debate

among Young Scholars", *IPCS Workshop Report*, August 2008; *Second Annual Workshop on Nuclear Disarmament and Regional Security* (New Delhi: IPCS, September 2009).
67 P. R. Chari, "Nuclear CBMs: What Is Possible?", *IPCS Issue Brief*, 22, June 2004. The need for a common "nuclear lexicon" and "military terminology" between India and Pakistan was also emphasised in a personal communication in New Delhi on 20 October, 2015.
68 P. R. Chari, "Nuclear CBMs between India and Pakistan", *IPCS Issue Brief*, 24, July 2004.
69 Banerjee's comments as part of joint workshop organised by IPCS and Department of Political Science, Madras Christian College (MCC) in September 2008. For more, see R. Sridhar (ed.), "Nuclear Disarmament and South Asian Security: A Regional Dialogue", *IPCS-MCC Workshop Report* (New Delhi: IPCS, 2008).
70 Five rounds of dialogue were conducted starting from December 2008–September 2011. The trialogues where conducted with support from the NTI and were held in neutral locations like Thailand, Singapore and China.
71 "Kashmir: Looking Further", *IPCS Article*, 1382, May 5, 2004, www.ipcs.org/article/indo-pak/kashmir-looking-further-1382.html
72 Dipankar Banerjee, "Special Commentary: Resolving the Siachen Dispute", *IPCS Article*, 3613, April 2012, www.ipcs.org/article/indo-pak/special-commentary-resolving-the-siachen-dispute-3613.html
73 Devyani Srivastava, "Terrorism, Religious Radicalism and Violence: Perspectives from India", *IPCS Issue Brief*, 120, September 2009.
74 Rohit Honawar, Seema Sridhar and Priyanka Singh, "Terrorism and Political Violence: Kashmir, Sri Lanka and Aceh", *IPCS Special Report*, 1, August 2005.
75 Rohit Honawar, "Jaish-e-Mohammed", *IPCS Special Report*, 4, November 2005.
76 D. Suba Chandran, "Fighting Terrorism: Strengthen and Modernise the State Police", *IPCS Issue Brief*, 88, December 2008.
77 Personal communication with senior member at CDR, New Delhi, on October 7, 2015.
78 Sewak has argued that the 'bus for peace' represented the "most public cross-border collaboration between women from the two countries" and "brought into greater focus the need to open the channels of communication between the people." Manjrika Sewak, "Multi-Track Diplomacy between India and Pakistan: A Conceptual Framework for Sustainable Security", in *RCSS Policy Studies*, Vol. 30 (New Delhi: Manohar Press, 2005).
79 Radha Kumar, Anjali Puri and Saurabh Naithani (eds.), *What Makes a Peace Process Irreversible?: A Conference Report* (New Delhi: Delhi Policy Group, 2005).
80 ibid.
81 For further details on these simulations, see Meenakshi Gopinath and Manjrika Sewak, *Transcending Conflict* (New Delhi: WISCOMP, 2004). More details on this are available in the workshop report: Manjrika Sewak, *Rehumanizing the Other* (New Delhi: WISCOMP, 2002).
82 The Jinnah Institute is a think tank in Pakistan focusing on policy research. It has collaborated with several Indian think tanks including the DPG and the CDR in addition to spearheading the Chaophraya dialogue in collaboration with the Australia India Institute (AII).
83 The first Intra-Kashmir Women's conference was held in Delhi in 2007 with support from the IDRC. Subsequent conferences were held in Srinagar (2009) and Gulmarg (2011). For more details, see *Bridging Divides: A Report on Intra-Kashmir Women's Conference* (New Delhi: Centre for Dialogue and Reconciliation, 2007).
84 The documents that this study focused on were Naya Kashmir produced by J&K National Conference under Sheikh Abdullah in 1977; the self-rule framework of resolution produced by the J&K People's Democratic Party in October 2008; Achievable Nationhood produced by J&K People's Conference under Sajad Gani Lone in December 2006; Report on J&K Regional Autonomy by Balraj Puri in 1999; and the Report of the State Autonomy Committee adopted by the state legislative assembly in June

2000. For more, see Arif Aayaz Parrey, *Anatomy of the Autonomy* (New Delhi: Centre for Dialogue and Reconciliation); Shakil A. Romshoo, *Indus River Basin: Common Concerns and the Roadmap to Resolution* (New Delhi: Center for Dialogue and Reconciliation, 2012).
85 Radha Kumar and Ellora Puri (eds.), *Peace-Building: Indian and European Perspectives* (New Delhi: Delhi Policy Group, 2006).
86 Personal communication with senior member of CDR, New Delhi, on October y, 2015.
87 *Beyond Borders: In Search of a Solution for Kashmir* (New Delhi: Centre for Dialogue and Reconciliation, 2009), p. 16.
88 ibid.
89 Personal communication with senior member of CDR, New Delhi, on October 7, 2015.
90 *Beyond Borders: In Search of a Solution for Kashmir* (New Delhi: Centre for Dialogue and Reconciliation, 2009), p. 11.
91 *India-Pakistan Water Roundtable: Joint Statement* (Bangalore: CDR and Jinnah Institute, 2014).
92 Resource persons at the workshop included academics Varun Sahni (VC –University of Jammu), Siddiq Wahid (VC – Islamic University, Srinagar), Dipankar Sengupta (University of Jammu), and former bureaucrats S.S. Bloeria (former Chief Secretary, J&K), Mohd. Ashraf (former Director, J&K Tourism) and Ved Marwah (former Governor).
93 *Beyond Borders: In Search of a Solution for Kashmir* (New Delhi: Centre for Dialogue and Reconciliation, 2009), p. 8.
94 John Paul Lederach, *Building Peace: Sustainable Reconciliation in Divided Societies* (Washington, DC: United States Institute of Peace Press, 1997), p. 39.
95 The *Samanbals* created were Psychosocial Counseling Center – Zohama, Budgam district, Helpline Samanbal, Bijbehara, Anantnag District, Purkho Migrant Camp Samanbal in Jammu, Widows' Support Center, Dardpora, Kupwara. For more on WISCOMP's *Athwaas* initiative, see http://wiscomp.org/programs/women-building-peace/; Sumona DasGupta, *Breaking the Silence: Women in Kashmir* (New Delhi: WISCOMP, 2001); Soumita Basu, *Building Constituencies of Peace: A Women's Initiative in Kashmir, Documenting the Process* (New Delhi: WISCOMP, 2004).
96 *Envisioning Futures: Women in Dialogue in Jammu and Kashmir: A National Consultation* (New Delhi: WISCOMP, 2007), p. 3.
97 A Conference Report, *Achieving Peace in Jammu and Kashmir: Options Today* (New Delhi: Delhi Policy Group, 2012).
98 *Conflict Resolution and Peace Building: India-Pakistan Dialogue* (New Delhi: IPCS, 2009).
99 The following issue briefs formed a part of this project – P.R. Chari, *Indus Waters Treaty II: Optimizing the Potential*; M. Ismail Khan, *Gilgit-Baltistan: Melting Water Towers of the Indus*; Shafqat Kakakhel, *Climate Change and the Indus Basin*; Shaheen Akhtar, *Cross-LoC CBMs on the Indus*; Sardar Muhammad Tariq, *Managing the Indus Waters: Alternative Strategies*; Mushtaq Hussain Awan, *Kishenganga and AJK: Views from Muzaffarabad*; B.G. Verghese, *The Inconvenient Truth: Responding to Pakistan's Water Concerns and Challenges*; D. Suba Chandran, *Towards an Indus Basin Community*; Kavita Suri, *Indus and J & K.*
100 The high-level panel included a long list of participants that varied from the governmental sector, civil society, media, conservation NGOs, think tanks, academia, as well as international agencies from India, Pakistan and Azad Kashmir.
101 Daniel W. Drezner, "Ideas, Bureaucratic Politics and the Crafting of Foreign Policy", *American Journal of Political Science*, 44:4, October 2000, p. 734.

7
FOREIGN POLICY THINK TANKS
Challenging or building consensus on India's Pakistan policy?

The starting point of enquiry for this research project was to examine think tanks and situate them within India's policy-making arena. The book has interrogated the placement and understanding of think tanks as policy actors/ agents/ idea brokers and information filters. In doing so, it has problematised the role of these non-state actors and their specific engagement with India's relationship with Pakistan. This research has built upon literature on think tanks worldwide and contributes particularly to the study of Indian think tanks. It is the first of its kind to explore the activities of Indian think tanks through an examination of their policy discourse on Pakistan at a given time and their specific role in promoting and mobilising public opinion on the Indian government's policies. To be able to account for think tank role in policy, I have used the discursive institutionalist approach in conjunction with a Gramscian understanding of state-society relations. The DI-Gramscian model developed in this research has helped to trace think tank interactive processes – their coordinative and communicative discourse on Pakistan – as well as enabled a critical analysis of Indian think tanks' role and relevance to policy making, together with an examination of their relative position in the policy structure. It has also brought to light significant challenges faced by think tanks in India to both retain their institutional independence and maintain their policy relevance.

The international literature and theoretical formulations on think tanks have gradually accepted their role as policy actors, but each approach has differed on the specific position of think tanks vis-à-vis policy establishments. In this book I argue that how think tanks are defined should take into account the context in which they operate and develop. Thus, scholarship on American think tanks and the application of that to the Indian political scenario is problematic. As relatively new actors, the understanding of think tank involvement in the policy process must consider the structural environment, i.e. India's specific political context and the various institutional structures and material realities that have had a direct impact on the growth of think tanks in India. The use of DI enabled an understanding of the various processes through which Indian think tanks seek to have an impact on policy. DI's emphasis on the right timing, the right audience and the various levels at which interactions between think tanks and policy-making bodies occur was found particularly useful.[1] Further, Ladi's phenomenon of a "critical juncture" was able to explain how the Composite Dialogue period was particularly significant to think tank engagement with India's Pakistan policy.[2] The development of the DI-Gramscian approach has further allowed for an examination of the material and structural constraints that think tanks in India face. It provided a better understanding of the nature of relationships between think tank intellectuals and policy-making elite in India – a relationship that is particularly relevant for the adoption of think tank ideas and their continued institutional importance. The use of distinct categories further highlighted differences in think tank affiliations: membership patterns and their subsequent policy ideas and policy interactions. This, in turn, allowed for an examination of specific constraints – structural and ideological – that transformed the way a particular think tank was situated in the Indian policy-making scene. The following sections revisit some of the main arguments that have emerged from this analysis.

Nature of intellectual elite – patterns in institutional worldviews and collaborations with the state

The examination of think tanks in India involved a closer look at their composition and institutional positions. The ability of a think tank to influence policy particularly in India was directly related to their relationship and proximity to the policy-making apparatus. Literature on Indian think tanks, however, was found inadequate to explain these dynamics. The application of Gramsci's attention to the differences between civil society and political society and the symbiotic relationship that exists provided a good framework.[3] Think tanks in India are notable for their knowledge elites, and the ability to relay their ideas to policymakers was found directly connected to their institutional policy relevance. The established positions and proximity to leadership of K. Subrahmanyam and Jasjit Singh, for instance, as intellectual elites added to the credibility of the IDSA and the CAPS, respectively. R. K. Mishra's close proximity to Vajpayee and the Reliance group was also able to secure the initial funding and institutional impetus for the ORF, as was the case with the VIF's close connections with NSA Ajit Doval. Proximity to policymakers, however, also had a reverse effect visible in the declining influence of the IDSA and the ICWA under new leadership. The relationship and ability of think tank intellectuals to establish their networks and maintain proximity to policymakers was therefore beneficial for a think tank and greatly enhanced the possibility of acceptance of its policy ideas.

Through the DI-Gramscian framework, this aspect of state–think tank cooperation was expanded to the examination of think tank linkages with the foreign policy establishment in India. The manifestation of a "knowledge/power nexus" among think tanks and policy elites in India indicated that the government used the resources of think tanks to privilege a particular understanding of a foreign policy issue, and think tanks behaved more substantially than merely a bridge between civil society and policy.[4] Think tanks adjusted their discourse to suit government policy directions in order to balance government patronage and policy relevance.

Institutional structures at think tanks were also found to closely resemble the government. Membership patterns displayed a similarity in professional and socio-economic backgrounds and political positions. There was also visible an over-reliance on senior researchers and high-profile leadership, together with considerable personal linkages that benefited think tanks. Though capacity building for younger researchers was encouraged in a few think tanks – namely, the CPR, the ORF and the IPCS – the presence of former bureaucrats and diplomats and their vast experience was largely preferred. Also visible was a gendered dynamic, with a small sample of women-led think tanks or women researchers focused on research on issues of security and foreign policy. Representative of Gramsci's power bloc, membership patterns have also impacted the way ideas were represented in think tank discourse, with only limited attention to foreign policy ideas that focused on the varying impact that the India–Pakistan conflict had on men and women.

Intellectual elite at government think tanks (IDSA, ICWA, CAPS, CLAWS and NMF) came from similar professional backgrounds and have experienced common training methods. The government, particularly the MEA and MoD, played an important role in the creation and support to this body of elites and this power bloc – both through financial support and involvement in policy initiatives – indicative of the growing need for policy expertise on defence and strategic issues. The physical office spaces occupied by government think tanks were also often provided by government grants of land.[5] These similarities in membership and government funding (though for specific projects) were also noticeable in non-government think tanks. There was, however, an added attention to academic research at the ORF, the CPR, the VIF and the IF, in addition to noticeable linkages with business interests in India and affiliations with political parties (namely, the BJP). While funding structures were more diverse in non-government think tanks, there was some project-based funding from the MEA. There was also implicit government control and regulation of foreign funding through legislations such as the FCRA (1976).[6] In addition to enabling foreign contributions, the GOI has also involved these think tanks for specific policy initiatives. Thus, intellectual elites including K. Subrahmanyan, B.G. Verghese and Ramaswamy Iyer were invited to participate in government committees owing to their academic expertise, while the operational experience of former military service professionals enabled a better insight into defence policy directions.

The analysis in previous chapters has also indicated that in the absence of funding opportunities from the government, the level of interaction and proximity of think tank intellectuals to policy elites was also reduced. Thus, smaller and less resourceful peacebuilding think tanks – namely, the DPG, the IPCS, the WISCOMP and the CDR – lacked government patronage and support. They were funded instead through philanthropic organisations including the Ford Foundation and have had noticeably different membership patterns. Established in post-liberalised India, in addition to academics trained in conflict resolution and peacebuilding strategies (WISCOMP, DPG, IPCS), civil society activism was a dominant characteristic at these think tanks. The different training and worldviews of elites and funding bodies has had a direct impact on the nature of research agendas. Thus, these smaller non-government think tanks reflected a particular emphasis on projects that were focused on conflict resolution, peacebuilding and training for peace. Further, the advocacy (CDR, WISCOMP) and training component (DPG, IPCS, WISCOMP) was significant, in addition to active participation in multi-track processes. Although independent research agendas enabled them to articulate alternate policy narratives, it has curtailed the ability of these think tanks to have an impact on policy.

The proximity and similarities between policy elites and think tank intellectuals give rise to arguments that government think tanks offered nothing more than an "an extension of government thinking."[7] Their role has often been criticised for providing a narrow and limited engagement and a perpetuation of government narratives. The distance from policy making, however, as prevalent in the case of non-government peacebuilding think tanks discussed in Chapter 6, has challenged their ability to communicate their new policy ideas to the relevant policymakers.

Think tank contribution to policy discourse

With respect to policy research agendas, think tanks in India are found to concentrate on a variety of issues including social and political policy, political and military strategy, socio-economic development, political participation, and non-traditional security issues related to drug and human trafficking and terrorism. There has been considerable policy emphasis on India's strategy regarding Pakistan, with most think tanks in India adopting an active research and advocacy component centred on the dispute with Pakistan. The beginning of the formal dialogue and the debates initiated by the CD created further interest, and think tanks played a consultative role and provided advisory policy ideas. Yet, these ideas were restricted to specific policies rather than a paradigmatic shift in India's position on Pakistan. Unlike Zimmerman's assertion that think tanks created "discursive spaces" to inform foreign policy agendas and change dominant narratives by framing and setting agendas, policy agendas on Pakistan have remained the domain of the Indian state.[8]

In institutionalising and funding think tanks, the GOI has therefore also engaged in a consensus-building role on policy directions on Pakistan. However, this "constant restatement of policy message via different formats and products" enabled government think tanks to have a place in the process.[9] Working closely with government ministries on particular issues and owing to their direct relationship with government patrons provided government think tanks the opportunity to interact with actors at the centre of policy formation. This significantly broadened the scope of their "coordinative discourse." Yet, while proximity provided an opportunity for the transfer of policy ideas, it restricted the adoption of alternative narratives, as the evidence shows. Government patronage and funding and the similarities in elite composition have also indicated that these think tanks have taken their cues from the funding agencies – in this case, the MoD and the MEA. Dominant discourse on Pakistan, reflected in research projects at the IDSA, the CLAWS, the CAPS and the NMF, have therefore led to policy recommendations that centred on national security with a focus on threats from a failing Pakistani state with basic irreconcilable ideological differences with India. Think tank discourse perpetuated government narratives on Pakistan, Kashmir, Siachen and nuclear doctrines and side-lined alternative conceptualisations on resolution of key conflicts. Government think tanks also did not engage adequately with issues of trade, people-to-people contact or the Sir Creek dispute. The similarity in viewpoints with the defence and foreign policy community in India has therefore emphasised the Indian government position on Kashmir, argued for a continued military presence in the region and continued to stress opposing differences in nuclear doctrines and strategies.

Even though non-government think tanks were funded externally, there continued to be a certain dependence on government accounts on Pakistan and investment in the dialogue process owing to project funding. However, differences in the nature of intellectual elites and institutional agendas that focused on academic research did expand the academic understanding of India–Pakistan issues. As proximity became distant, the ability of think tanks to suggest policy alternatives was more visible, for instance, in the CDR, the WISCOMP and the IPCS with an increased emphasis on gender-based violence and conflict over resources. In their approach towards the India–Pakistan dialogue process, there was therefore a noticeable emphasis on building cross-border networks, particularly with likeminded constituencies and civil society in Pakistan and in involving the youth as future stakeholders in the conflict and relevant to new designs on resolution strategies. Even within India, the emphasis of peacebuilding institutes, particularly the WISCOMP and the CDR, was on civil society engagements and reconciliation, which also highlighted their proactive involvement in non-governmental multitrack processes. As "insulated agencies," however, these think tanks were unable to have better inputs into policy making.[10] Their lack of government patronage and resources meant that research could not be sustained, and these think tanks often moved towards adopting "more palatable" agendas that were not in conflict with formal bureaucracy.[11] Research issues at peacebuilding think tanks were also framed strategically to avoid conflict with the government position. The CDR, for instance, stayed away from political issues, and the DPG changed its emphasis on peacebuilding to incorporate the government's developing interests in Afghanistan, particularly after 2008 and the collapse of the CD.

Think tank contribution as communicative actors

Operating within a top-down policy-making structure, while think tanks did not introduce policy agendas, they did inform public opinion on the ongoing policy initiatives of government.[12] As carriers of communicative discourse, think tank research on government policies, disseminated through meetings, conferences, research publications and writings in the media, completed the cycle – bringing government policy to the wider public arena. With their influence in shaping/gauging public opinion, Indian think tanks became repositories of knowledge and offered an academic understanding of policy changes.[13] On relations with Pakistan, as this book has highlighted, policy standards were created by the state, yet think tanks participated in refining and promoting these ideas through their research and analysis.

Think tanks in India have promoted key government initiatives – such as the Kashmir dialogue (both internal and bilateral) as well as the CBMs introduced as part of the dialogue process. Through specific research projects on PAK and cross-LoC interactions (IDSA), AFSPA (IDSA), and IWT (CPR, IDSA, IPCS), think tanks have introduced these debates into the popular discourse. This role is particularly useful as there are limited avenues for insights into government policy, particularly on issues of defence policy. The public discussion around key debates therefore helped to popularise the Indian government's position on Kashmir and its emphasis on PAK as occupied Indian territory. The defence policy think tanks have also provided a review of the continued army presence in Kashmir, their humanitarian activities in the state of J&K and have distinguished these with human rights violations and the lack of democratic and political rights in PAK. Non-government think tanks enabled an academic understanding of water conflicts, particularly with respect to river water disputes (both Verghese and Iyer played a crucial role here), the impact of armed conflict on civilian populations (IPCS, WISCOMP, CDR) and the gendered nature of conflict in J&K (WISCOMP, DPG). The prolific writing by former diplomats and public intellectuals such as M.K. Rasgotra, G. Parthasarathy, Pratap Bhanu Mehta, Brahma Chellaney, C. Raja Mohan, Manoj Joshi and others have also provided a better understanding of complex government policy on Pakistan.

New think tanks and contemporary India–Pakistan relations – continuity or change?

The November 2008 attacks on Mumbai by the Pakistan-linked militant group Lashkar-e-Taiba, in addition to the ousting of Musharraf from power in Pakistan, contributed to the slowing pace of the CD process after 2008. While it significantly impacted public opinion on dialogue with Pakistan, the UPA government led by Manmohan Singh took a restrained approach in the wake of the Mumbai attacks. It refrained from a military response, attempted to continue the CD and did not publicly acknowledge the Indian army's covert cross-border operations across the LoC to prevent infiltrations by militants and cease-fire violations.[14] In 2009, following the re-election of his government, Manmohan Singh also met with the new Pakistani Prime Minister, Yousaf Raza Gilani, on the sidelines of the Nonaligned Movement (NAM) Summit, and issued a joint statement agreeing to resume the dialogue. Subsequently, however, the third round of the CD in 2013 was aborted. The joint statement was criticised for delinking action against terrorism by Pakistan with the resumption of dialogue and mentioning Pakistan's concerns about separatism in Balochistan, which it has long alleged is fanned by Indian intelligence officers. The statement was condemned by senior members of the Congress Party, the Indian media and the opposition BJP, which staged a walk-out of parliament.[15] In his memoir, Shivshankar Menon has attributed the negative public reaction to the statement at the NAM Summit, and domestic politics in general, for scuppering the government's attempts to resume the peace process.[16]

In addition to being an indication of the UPA government's inability to achieve its aim of creating strong and resilient constituencies for peace within the Indian state, the demise of the dialogue also reflected crucial structural constraints of policy making. While there was some progress on the issues under consideration in the CD, policy initiatives largely suffered from an over-dependence on top-down leadership, a lack of bureaucratic support and the reluctance of the defence establishment to think beyond law and order in Kashmir. At the broader level of dialogue with Pakistan, there remained an over-dependence on top-down political will and leadership to sustain the process. Thus, even though the Kashmir proposals set forth by Musharraf and Singh represented a shift in posture, the UPA could not ease bureaucratic processes with regard to trade and has been criticised for its inability to take timely decisions on crucial aspects such as the demilitarisation of Siachen or to build sustainable linkages with actors within Pakistan. Multi-track efforts, including the back-channel, remained tied to the political fortunes of individual politicians and lost momentum when Musharraf lost power and when political agendas shifted in India with the rise of the BJP. Further, due to the absence of coordination and collaboration between foreign policy bureaucracies, ideas remained unimplemented. Thus, while specific policy initiatives including cross-LoC trade and travel were aimed at economic growth as an incentive for peace, the implementation of these programmes lacked bureaucratic support and failed to enable the expansion of Kashmiri economy outside the valley region.[17]

At the level of civil society, though economic links between India and Pakistan and the two parts of Kashmir expanded, they continued to be limited, and the civil society linkages established by the CD process were not deep enough to constitute a tangible peace constituency with Pakistan, particularly after the 2008 Mumbai attacks. The attacks re-empowered a national security elite within government think tanks, the MoD and the armed forces, who insisted on using a military strategy to resolve the Kashmir conflict and control Pakistan. Arguments in favour of precision military strikes against terrorist strongholds gained momentum, as did criticisms of the UPA's lack of cohesive decision making to attack Pakistan and the need for building better counter-terrorism capabilities. Such arguments were particularly visible in the post-Mumbai discourse at government and defence think tanks in India and the new think tanks, including the VIF led by former Intelligence Bureau chief Ajit Doval and the IF, largely supported by the BJP-RSS elites.[18] Think tanks also developed outside the national capital region around this time. Thus, the Takshashila Institution was established in Bangalore in 2009 and the Gateway House was set up in Mumbai.

As the evidence in this book suggests, think tanks in India depend to a great degree on the government for financial and institutional support. They found a strong voice for policy research and articulation when government interests reflected the desire for dialogue with Pakistan. However, as public opinion and political motivations shifted in the post-Mumbai policy landscape, structural constraints both external and internal restricted the autonomy and ability of think tanks to effectively interject in the policy process. While external funding provided non-government and peacebuilding think tanks the opportunity to conduct independent research and develop alternative ideas, the same process also significantly restricted their influence. The strict legal framework that exists for the regulation of think tanks in receipt of foreign donations limited the autonomy of foreign-funded think tanks. Non-government think tanks were also dependent on information produced by government agencies for their program development and required sustainable state support for institutional relevance and to organise cross-border initiatives (in the form of official approvals and visas), to retain their networks and to enable their continued funding from international agencies. Thus, when government attention shifted from a dialogue with Pakistan, so did think tank interest.

Contemporary India–Pakistan relations and the Modi government's relationship with think tanks

While India–Pakistan relations began to deteriorate after the 2008 Mumbai attacks, the Manmohan Singh government continued with its efforts towards dialogue, receiving significant criticism from the opposition parties, particularly the BJP. While the BJP under Vajpayee had been instrumental in initiating the CD with Pakistan, as an opposition party, it was severely critical of the UPA government's "soft stance" on Pakistan, particularly after 2008. The BJP's criticism was reflected in the election manifesto of 2014 that referred to the need to deal with cross-border terrorism with a firm hand even while affirming friendly relations with the neighbourhood was reiterated.[19]

The BJP-led government elected in 2014 and then subsequently reelected in 2019 has been unable to initiate a dialogue with Pakistan, despite several attempts to restart a formal process of negotiations. The government's policy is guided significantly by the NSA Ajit Doval, who through his close relationship with the Prime Minister, Narendra Modi, has made ideas that emphasise a militaristic strategy to combat terrorism emanating from Pakistan central to India's approach to both Pakistan and the Kashmir conflict. In recent years, there has been increase in cross-border ceasefire violations along the border in Kashmir as well as an increase in violence in Indian-administered Kashmir. India's current Kashmir policy under Modi also places emphasis on a militaristic strategy and encourages an active use of force towards civil unrest. As evidence of this change in strategy, in the first such publicised incident in September 2016, India claimed to have conducted a "surgical strike" in Pakistan-controlled Kashmir across the LoC. While Pakistan denied this move, it represents a significant shift in India's military strategy in Kashmir.[20] The escalation of the conflict with Pakistan reached a new level in February 2019, following an attack on a convoy of paramilitary forces in Indian-administered Kashmir. The attack on a convoy of the Central Reserve Police Force (CRPF) on February 14 is perhaps one of the most serious single attacks against security forces in the troubled region of Kashmir. Traveling from Jammu to Srinagar, the convoy was attacked by a vehicle laden with 350 kilograms of explosives, leaving behind nothing but death and destruction of lives, infrastructure and most importantly, the already fragile state of security in the state. The attack was claimed by the Pakistan-based Jaish-e-Mohammad and was carried out by a radicalised 20-year-old Kashmiri youth from the South Kashmir Pulwama district. Further esclating the conflict, on February 26, 2019, India allegedly carried out an air-strike into Pakistani territory in Balakot to destroy terror camps. While Islamabad denied any casualties from the Indian operation, it retaliated with its own air force operation across the LoC, which resulted in the downing of an Indian plane and the capture of an Indian pilot, who was subsequently released. While the crisis was defused somewhat, there has been a rise in ceasefire violations on the LoC amid significant diplomatic tensions between the two nations.

Tensions have also been on the rise in Kashmir. On August 5, 2019, the ruling BJP government reversed the constitutional autonomy provided to Indian Kashmir since its accession in 1947. In an unexpected move, the Modi government through two presidential orders revoked Article 370 of the Indian constitution, withdrawing the "special rights" and autonomy for the state of Kashmir, and announced the bifurcation of the state into two union territories of Jammu and Kashmir and Ladakh. The decision was announced amidst an increased military deployment and an extensive and prolonged communications blockade of the Kashmir valley that included detention of local Kashmiri leadership. With respect to the focus of this book, political circumstances in Kashmir today and the relationship with Pakistan appear in stark contrast to the critical juncture and the dialogic opportunities opened up by the CD process.

Modi and think tanks

The nature of the relationship between think tanks and policymakers has also undergone a change since the election of Narendra Modi as Prime Minister. The

Modi government has a stated intention to draw on think tank expertise and, indeed, "build rigorous and competitive think-tanks" as "a natural corollary of a globalised society" as India transitions into a "leading power."[21] The government has prioritised engagement with corporate-funded think tanks such as the ORF, the Brookings Institution India and the Carnegie Endowment India, and especially think tanks linked to the Hindu nationalist movement, including the IF and the VIF. The IF has partnered with the MEA to carry out the government's public diplomacy initiatives while the ORF's research programmes and its Raisina Dialogue in particular has attracted significant government attention. Besides the Raisina Dialogue, the MEA has also been holding the Gateway of India Dialogue, in partnership with the Gateway House, to conduct multilateral talks on geoeconomic issues, along with partnerships with the Institute of Chinese Studies, the Indian Council of World Affairs.[22] Thus, while think tanks that emerged after the Composite Dialogue period had a limited engagement with India–Pakistan issues, they remain relevant for the new government. Intellectual composition at these new think tanks, both within and outside the national capital, is also similar to other older think tanks, with a concentration of retired diplomats, bureaucrats and academic professionals.

On India's relations with Pakistan, while official dialogue remains suspended, unofficial interest and discourse on India–Pakistan relations has also changed. Research institutions in Delhi – including the IDSA, the ORF and the VIF, to name a few – have welcomed the Modi government's robust foreign policy towards Pakistan and largely believe that the "firm hand" towards ceasefire violations were what was missing in India's foreign policy overtures previously.

So-called government-approved think tanks, particularly the VIF, the ORF and the IF, can now be seen propagating the government discourse while institutions outside of the government have become weaker.[23] Members of the civil society, both peacebuilding organisations and several people's initiatives for peace, have been marginalised and rendered weaker by stringent funding structures. Those that remain have changed their dominant agendas and are more comfortable adopting programs and positions that do not contradict the government's agendas.[24] The lack of alternative voices has also transformed the public opinion on peace with Pakistan, thus the popular consensus that Vajpayee claimed was influential in a rethinking of positions has been lost, as has the "critical juncture" achieved by the CD formulations. This is evident in the lack of people-to-people contact, strict measures on inter-cultural interactions and an increase in militarised responses and a charged political rhetoric. While this book has made a case that government think tanks perpetuated dominant government narratives even under the UPA, there was some tolerance for alternative narratives from think tanks. These were manifested in the ability to get foreign grants, hold events and consultations with Pakistani participants and the easy grant of visas to conduct training and networking programmes.[25] Think tanks embraced the depoliticisation strategy of the UPA while the government provided intellectual space for the generation of an alternative discourse, even if the discourse was not uniformly adopted.

Since 2014, think tanks funded by international donors have been targeted by government legislation including the FCRA.[26] Owing to this, for instance, while IPCS funding from the Ford Foundation has been affected, other think tanks such as the DPG appear to have shifted their research focus from peace and conflict studies to the new and emerging India-Afghanistan relationship. A former Director at IPCS highlighted that "the BJP is not open to intellectual discussions and it is very difficult to have an objective dialogue between India and Pakistan."[27] Other analysts have also pointed out that there was more role for think tanks in the UPA government and that in the Modi government, institutes close to the government dispensation, namely the VIF, have more traction.[28]

Though the role of peacebuilding think tanks in official foreign policy processes has diminished after 2008 and has ceased completely under the new BJP government, think tanks, in general, remain important actors in foreign policy. Think tanks in India are flourishing, and research agendas are constantly evolving to provide expertise on new issues of foreign policy. New think tanks including the Gateway House: Indian Council on Global Relations, Brookings Institution India and Carnegie Endowment India, which are funded primarily by corporate interests in India, have emphasised the evolving relationship with the United States, lacking a sustained interest in India–Pakistan relations. In addition, older think tanks particularly the ICWA have been given a new lease on life even though they appear to function primarily as a MEA platform for visits by foreign delegations.

Despite an evolving relationship, think tanks in India remain crucial actors. Although policy directions and foreign policy agendas are decided by the government and top leadership in India, Indian think tanks have been critical for the promotion of ideas, the generation of public debate in support of a certain set of ideas and fulfilling the capacity for new policy areas. Think tanks have created what Medvetz has described as an "institutional subspace" for IR professionals in India.[29] Within the backdrop of India's policy on Pakistan, think tanks have reacted, engaged, elaborated and promoted the dialogue agenda in their own institutional styles, reflective of their particular funding structures and their predominant elite influence. To summarise, think tanks are neither neutral bridges between academia and politics nor have they always functioned for the public good. They have acted as carriers of coordinative and communicative discourse, a role that is at the heart of the political debate.

Notes

1 Vivien Schmidt, "Reconciling Ideas and Institutions through Discursive Institutionalism", in Daniel Beland and Robert Cox (eds.) *Ideas and Politics in Social Science Research* (New York: Oxford University Press, 2011), p. 57.
2 Stella Ladi, "Think Tanks, Discursive Institutionalism and Policy Change", in Georgios Papanagnou (ed.) *Social Science and Policy Challenges: Democracy, Values and Capacities* (Paris: UNESCO, 2011), p. 208.

3 Thomas R. Bates, "Gramsci and the Theory of Hegemony", *Journal of the History of Ideas*, 36:2, 1975, p. 353.
4 Diane Stone, "Recycling Bins, Garbage Cans or Think Tanks? Three Myths Regarding Policy Analysis Institutes", *Public Administration*, 85:2, June 2007, p. 276.
5 Jayati Srivastava, *Think Tanks in South Asia: Analysing the Knowledge-Power Interface* (London: Overseas Development Institute, December 2011), p. 19.
6 ibid.
7 Personal communication with senior member and retired defence personnel at IPCS, New Delhi, on September 29, 2015.
8 Zimmerman highlights that "to enhance their discursive ability, think tanks have created unique discursive spaces where they can control the discursive process. These spaces are often located alongside formal governing processes but are free from the strict political limitations imposed on governmental venues." For more, see Erin Zimmerman, *Think Tanks and Non-Traditional Security: Governance Entrepreneurs in Asia* (Basingstoke: Palgrave MacMillan, 2016).
9 Diane Stone, "Recycling Bins, Garbage Cans or Think Tanks? Three Myths Regarding Policy Analysis Institutes", *Public Administration*, 85:2, 2007, p. 274.
10 Daniel W. Drezner, "Ideas, Bureaucratic Politics and the Crafting of Foreign Policy", *American Journal of Political Science*, 44:4, October 2000, p. 734.
11 Richard Higgott and Diane Stone, "The Limits of Influence: Foreign Policy Think Tanks in Britain and the USA", *Review of International Studies*, 20:1, January 1994, p. 28.
12 Vivien A. Schmidt, "Discursive Institutionalism: Scope, Dynamics and Philosophical Underpinnings", in Frank Fischer and Herbert Gottweis (eds.) *The Argumentative Turn Revisited: Public Policy as Communicative Practice* (Durham and London: Duke University Press, 2012), p. 86.
13 Personal communication with senior researcher at VIF, New Delhi, on October 14, 2015.
14 Shivshankar Menon, "Earlier Cross-LoC Strikes Had Different Goals: Former NSA", *The Hindu*, www.thehindu.com/news/national/former-national-security-ad...on-on-crossloc-strikes/article9208838.ece?homepage=true&css=print
15 Pranay Sharma, "Quills and Spills", *Outlook*, August 3, 2009; Coomi Kapoor, "Joint Statement: After the Blooper, a Bizarre Assumption", *Indian Express*, 22, July 2009.
16 Shivshankar Menon, *Choices: Inside the Making of India's Foreign Policy* (Washington, DC: Brookings Institution, 2015).
17 Moeed Yusuf, "Promoting Cross LoC Trade in Kashmir: An Analysis of the Joint Chamber", *USIP Special Report*, 230.
18 Harish Khare, "Hold the Vajpayee Manmohan Line", *The Hindu*, August 4, 2013, www.thehindu.com/opinion/lead/hold-the-vajpayeemanmohan-line/article5019657.ece; Vivekenanda International Foundation (VIF), "Press Statement on India-Pakistan Relations by Members of India's Strategic Community", August 9, 2013, www.vifindia.org/event/report/2013/august/09/press-statement-on-India-Pakistan-relations-by-members-of-india-s-strategiccommunity
19 Bhartiya Janata Party (BJP), *Election Manifesto 2014*, p. 40.
20 For more, see Shawn Snow, "Is Pakistan Capable of a Surgical Strike in Pakistan Controlled Kashmir?", *The Diplomat*, September 30, 2016, http://thediplomat.com/2016/09/is-india-capable-of-a-surgical-strike-in-pakistan-controlled-kashmir/
21 Subrahmanyam Jaishankar, "Indian Foreign Secretary Subrahmanyam Jaishankar's Remarks", *Carnegie India*, http://carnegieindia.org/2016/04/06/indian-foreign-secretary-subrahmanyamjaishankar-s-remarks/iwq8
22 S. Gogna, "The Rise of India's Think Tank Diplomacy", *South Asian Voices*, February 16, 2018, https://southasianvoices.org/rise-indias-think-tank-diplomacy/
23 Jyoti Malhotra, "The Growing Role of Government-Approved Think Tanks", *NDTV*, March 1, 2017, www.ndtv.com/opinion/think-tanks-controlled-by-foreign-ministry-are-supplanting-the-media-1664683

24 As mentioned during personal communication with a senior member of CDR, New Delhi, on October 7, 2015.
25 It is reported that the Indian missions in Pakistan processed only 30 visas in June 2003, which went up to over 30,000, during the high noon of the Composite Dialogue. In early 2007, an average of 12,000 visas had been issued for Pakistani visits to India. Meenakshi Gopinath, "Processing Peace: To Speak in a Different Voice", *Peace Prints: South Asian Journal of Peacebuilding*, 4:2, Winter 2012, p. 4.
26 The Ford Foundation was one of the few organisations that were targeted by the new Indian Government, citing violations of the FCRA. For more, see "From Greenpeace to Ford Foundation: Modi Govt's Controversial Crackdown on NGOs", *Firstpost*, June 2, 2016, www.firstpost.com/india/from-greenpeace-to-ford-foundation-modi-govts-controversial-crackdown-on-ngos-2812196.html
27 Personal communication with senior member and retired defence personnel at IPCS, New Delhi, on September 29, 2015.
28 Personal communication with an International Relations academic at JNU, New Delhi, on September 7, 2015.
29 Thomas Medvetz, *Think Tanks in America* (Chicago: University of Chicago Press, 2012), p. 7.

BIBLIOGRAPHY

Abelson, Donald E., "Old World, New World: The Evolution and Influence of Foreign Affairs Think-Tanks" *International Affairs*, 90:1, 2014, pp. 125–142.

Acharya, Amitav, "How Ideas Spread: Whose Norms Matter? Norm Localization and Institutional Change in Asian Regionalism" *International Organisation*, 58, 2004, pp. 239–275.

Achieving Peace in Jammu and Kashmir: Options Today (New Delhi: Delhi Policy Group, 2012).

Ahmed, Ali, "Reviewing India's Nuclear Doctrine" *IDSA Policy Brief*, April 24, 2009.

———, "Pakistani Nuclear Use and Implications for India" *Strategic Analysis*, 34:4, 2010, pp. 531–544.

———, "Reconciling Doctrines: Prerequisite for Peace in South Asia" *IDSA Monograph Series*, 3, September 2010.

Alagappa, Muthiah, "Galvanising International Studies" *Pragati: The Indian National Interest Review*, 30, September 2009, pp. 11–16.

Anant, Arpita, "Counter-Insurgency and 'Op Sadhbhavana' in Jammu and Kashmir" *IDSA Occasional Paper*, 19, October 2011.

——— and Smruti Pattanaik, "Cross-LoC Confidence Building Measures between India and Pakistan: A Giant Leap or a Small Step towards Peace?" *IDSA Issue Brief*, February 12, 2010.

Andley, Priyashree, "Third Composite Dialogue: An Overview of Indo-Pak Relations in 2006" *IPCS Special Report*, 36, March 2007.

Annual Report: 2003–2004 (New Delhi: Centre for Policy Research, 2004).

Annual Report: 2009–2010 (New Delhi: Centre for Policy Research, 2009).

Annual Report: 2010–2011 (New Delhi: Centre for Policy Research, 2011).

Annual Report: 2011–2012 (New Delhi: Centre for Policy Research, 2012).

Appadorai, A., "International and Area Studies in India" *International Studies (JNU)*, 24:2, 1987.

ASEAN-India Eminent Persons' Report to the Leaders (Indonesia: ASEAN Secretariat, 2012).

Babu, D. Shyam, "India's National Security Council: Stuck in the Cradle?" *Security Dialogue*, 34:2, 2003, pp. 215–230.

"Back Channel: The Promise and Peril" *Ministry of External Affairs*, May 20, 2003, www.mea.gov.in/articles-in-indian-media.htm?dtl/13817/Back+channel+the+promise+and+peril

Bajpai, Kanti, Dipankar Banerjee, Amitabh Mattoo, et al., *Jammu and Kashmir: An Agenda for the Future* (New Delhi: Delhi Policy Group, 1999).

Bajpai, Kanti, Pervaiz Cheema, Sumit Ganguly and Stephen Cohen, *Brasstacks and Beyond: Perception and Management of Crisis in South Asia* (New Delhi: Manohar Press, 1995).

Bajpai, Kanti and Byron Chong, "India's Foreign Policy Capacity" *Policy Design and Practice*, 2019, DOI: 10.1080/25741292.2019.1615164

Bandyopadhyaya, J., *The Making of India's Foreign Policy: Determinants, Institutions, Processes, and Personalities* (Bombay: Allied Publishers, 1970).

Banerjee, Dipankar, "India-Pakistan Imbroglio over CBMs" *IPCS Articles*, 1200, November 6, 2003, www.ipcs.org/article/indo-pak/india-pakistan-imbroglio-over-cbms-1200.html

———, "Special Commentary: Resolving the Siachen Dispute" *IPCS Article*, 3613, April 2012, www.ipcs.org/article/indo-pak/special-commentary-resolving-the-siachen-dispute-3613.html

———, "Tribute: P R Chari" *Mainstream*, 53:34, August 15, 2015, www.mainstreamweekly.net/article5879.html

Bansal, Alok, "The Growing Alienation in Gilgit-Baltistan: The Future Portents" in Virendra Gupta and Alok Bansal (eds.) *Pakistan Occupied Kashmir: An Untold Story* (New Delhi: IDSA, 2007).

———, "Maritime Threat Perceptions: Non-State Actors in the Indian Ocean Region" *Maritime Affairs: Journal of the National Maritime Foundation of India*, 6:1, Summer 2010, pp. 10–27.

Baru, Sanjaya, "The Growing Influence of Business and Media on Indian Foreign Policy" *ISAS Working Paper*, (National University of Singapore) 49, February 5, 2009.

———, "Can Indian Think Tanks and Research Institutes Cope with the Rising Demand for Foreign and Security Policy Research" *ISAS Working Paper*, (National University of Singapore) 67, June 16, 2009.

———, *The Accidental Prime Minister: The Making and Unmaking of Manmohan Singh* (London: Penguin, Kindle Edition, 2014).

Basu, Soumita, *Building Constituencies of Peace: A Women's Initiative in Kashmir, Documenting the Process* (New Delhi: WISCOMP, 2004).

Bates, Thomas R., "Gramsci and the Theory of Hegemony" *Journal of the History of Ideas*, 36:2, 1975, pp. 351–366.

Behuria, Ashok, "Deciphering Kayani-Speak: One Avalanche Leads to Another?" *IDSA Comment*, April 20, 2012.

Beland, Daniel and Robert Henry Cox (eds.), *Ideas and Politics in Social Science Research* (New York: Oxford University Press, 2011).

Bell, Stephen, "The Power of Ideas: The Ideational Shaping of the Structural Power of Business" *International Studies Quarterly*, 56:4, December 2012, pp. 661–673.

Besussi, Elena, "Policy Networks: Conceptual Developments and Their European Applications" *UCL Working Paper Series*, Paper 102, March 2006.

Beyond Borders: In Search of a Solution for Kashmir (New Delhi: Centre for Dialogue and Reconciliation, 2009).

Bhaskar, C. Uday, "KS: Vamana of Indian Nuclear Theology?" in C. Uday Bhaskar (ed.) *Subbu at 75: A Bouquet of Tributes* (New Delhi: Shri Avtar Printing Press, 2004).

———, "No Snakes in the Backyard: Clinton to Kayani" original article in Hindi in *Dainik Jagran*, October 22, 2011, http://post.jagran.com/no-snakes-in-the-backyard-1320489442

Bhati, Avanti, "Kashmir: New Hope?" *ORF Commentaries*, October 23, 2003, www.orfonline.org/research/kashmir-new-hope/

Bhatnagar, Stuti, Deepti Mahajan and Manjrika Sewak, *Collaborative Explorations: Fifth Annual Conflict Transformation Workshop Report* (New Delhi: WISCOMP, 2007).

Bhonsle, Rahul K, "Winning Hearts and Minds: Lessons from Jammu and Kashmir" *Manekshaw Papers*, 14 (New Delhi: Centre for Land Warfare Studies, 2009).

Bieler, Andreas, "Questioning Cognitivism and Constructivism in IR Theory: Reflections on the Material Structure of Ideas" *Politics*, 21:2, 2001, pp. 93–100.

Bindra, Sukhwant S., "Domestic Milieu of India and Foreign Policy Making Process: A Theoretical Perspective" *The Indian Journal of Political Science*, 65:2, April–June 2004, pp. 245–258.

Blyth, Mark, "Ideas, Uncertainty and Evolution" in Daniel Beland and Robert Henry Cox (eds.) *Ideas and Politics in Social Science Research* (New York: Oxford University Press, 2011), pp. 83–101.

Branka, Andjelkovic, "A Limited Dialogue: Think Tanks and the Policy Making Process in Serbia" in UNDP (ed.) *Thinking the Unthinkable* (Bratislava: UNDP Regional Bureau for Europe and the Commonwealth of Independent States, 2003).

Bridging Divides: A Report on Intra-Kashmir Women's Conference (New Delhi: Centre for Dialogue and Reconciliation, 2007).

"Brief on India's Neighbourhood" *IDSA Policy Brief*, May 28, 2009.

Campbell, John L., "Ideas, Politics and Public Policy" *Annual Review of Sociology*, 28, 2002, pp. 21–38.

Chacko, Priya, *Indian Foreign Policy: The Politics of Postcolonial Identity* (London: Routledge, 2012).

———, "The Right Turn in India: Authoritarianism, Populism and Neoliberalisation" *Journal of Contemporary Asia*, 48:4, 2018, pp. 541–565.

Chadha, Vivek (ed.), "Heart as a Weapon': A Fresh Approach to the Concept of Hearts and Minds" *IDSA Policy Brief*, November 16, 2011.

———, "Armed Forces Special Powers Act: The Debate" *IDSA Monograph Series*, 7, November 2012.

———, "Security Situation in J & K: A Reality Check" *IDSA Comment*, June 28, 2013, www.idsa.in/idsacomments/SecuritySituationinJandK_vchadha_280613

———, "Kashmir: Finding Lasting Peace" *IDSA Policy Brief*, June 26, 2014, www.idsa.in/policybrief/KashmirFindingLastingPeace_vchadha_260614

Chandra, Satish, "Why a Siachen Settlement Should Be a Non-Starter" *VIF Article*, May 14, 2012, www.vifindia.org/article/2012/may/14/why-a-siachen-agreement-should-be-a-non-starter

———, "Prepare against Pakistan's Nukes" *VIF Article*, September 1, 2012, www.vifindia.org/article/2012/september/01/prepare-against-pakistan-nukes

———, "Genuflecting before Pakistan" *VIF Article*, September 12, 2012, www.vifindia.org/article/2012/september/12/genuflecting-before-pakistan

———, "Stop Appeasing Pakistan" *VIF Article*, February 4, 2013, www.vifindia.org/articles/2013/fedruary/04/stop-appeasing-pakistan

Chandran, Suba D., "Kashmir: Need for an Internal Dialogue" *IPCS Articles*, 354, May 11, 2000, www.ipcs.org/article/jammu-kashmir/kashmir-need-for-an-internal-dialogue-354.html

——, "Recent Developments in Kashmir II-Hizbul Cease-Fire: Implications" *IPCS Article*, 402, August 7, 2000, www.ipcs.org/article/terrorism-in-jammu-kashmir/recent-developments-in-kashmir-ii-hizbul-cease-fire-implications-402.html

——, "The Hizbul Mujahideen" *IPCS Article*, 405, August 14, 2000, www.ipcs.org/article/terrorism-in-jammu-kashmir/the-hizbul-mujahideen-405.html

——, "The Indo-Pak Riddle: Neither Forward Nor Backward Nor Stationary" *IPCS Article*, 1036, May 18, 2003, www.ipcs.org/article/indo-pak/the-indo-pak-riddle-neither-forward-nor-backward-nor-stationary-1036.html

——, "New Indian Initiatives in Kashmir" *IPCS Issue Brief*, 13, November 2003.

——, "Cross LoC Trade: Challenges and Opportunities in J & K" *IPCS Issue Brief*, 66, May 2008.

——, "Fighting Terrorism: Strengthen and Modernise the State Police" *IPCS Issue Brief*, 88, December 2008.

——, "Poonch Festival: A Strategy to Integrate Border Regions in J & K" *IPCS Special Report*, 64, January 2009.

——, "Expanding Cross LoC Interactions: Perspectives from India" *IPCS Issue Brief*, 131, September 2009.

——, "Pir Panjal Regional Festival" *IPCS Issue Brief*, 142, April 2010.

Chandran, D. Suba and Rekha Chakravarthi, "Nuclear Disarmament & Regional Security: Reintroducing the Disarmament Debate among Young Scholars" *IPCS Workshop Report*, August 2008.

Chari, P. R., "Nuclear CBMs: What Is Possible?" *IPCS Issue Brief*, 22, June 2004.

——, "Nuclear CBMs between India and Pakistan" *IPCS Issue Brief*, 24, July 2004.

——, Pervaiz Iqbal Cheema and Stephen P. Cohen, *Four Crises and a Peace Process: American Engagement in South Asia* (Washington, DC: Brookings Institution, 2007).

Chawla, Shalini, "How Do We Deal with Pakistan?" *CAPS Issue Brief*, 93:13, August 13, 2013.

Chellaney, Brahma, "Don't Compromise India" *India Today*, August 23, 2013, http://indiatoday.intoday.in/story/india-pakistan-relations-loc-ceasefire/1/300969.html

Conflict Resolution and Peace Building: India-Pakistan Dialogue (New Delhi: IPCS, 2009).

Das, Pushpita, "Securing the Northern Coast of Gujarat: Challenges and Responses" *IDSA Fellows Seminar*, November 28, 2008, www.idsa.in/event/indiancoastline_pushpitadas_281108

DasGupta, Sumona, *Breaking the Silence: Women in Kashmir* (New Delhi: WISCOMP, 2001).

——, "Kashmir and the India-Pakistan Composite Dialogue Process" *RSIS Working Paper*, 291, May 21, 2015.

Debriefing the India-China-Pakistan Strategic Dialogue: Towards a Stable Nuclear Order in Asia held at the Fudan University, Shanghai on August 8–9, 2009 (New Delhi: IPCS, September 2009).

Donthi, Praveen, "Undercover: Ajit Doval in Theory and Practice" *The Caravan*, September 1, 2017, www.caravanmagazine.in/reportage/ajit-doval-theory-practice

Drezner, Daniel, "Ideas, Bureaucratic Politics and the Crafting of Foreign Policy" *American Journal of Political Science*, 44:4, October 2000, pp. 733–749.

Dryzek, John S., *Discursive Democracy: Politics, Policy and Political Science* (Cambridge: Cambridge University Press, 1995).

Dulat, A. S., *Kashmir: The Vajpayee Years* (Noida: Harper Collins, 2015).

Dye, Thomas R., *Top Down Policymaking* (New York and London: Chatham House, 2001).

Envisioning Futures: Women in Dialogue in Jammu and Kashmir: A National Consultation (New Delhi: WISCOMP, 2007).

"From Greenpeace to Ford Foundation: Modi Govt's Controversial Crackdown on NGOs" *Firstpost*, June 2, 2016, www.firstpost.com/india/from-greenpeace-to-ford-foundation-modi-govts-controversial-crackdown-on-ngos-2812196.html

"From Vivekananda to PMO Stars: Meet Modi's Favourite Think Tank" *Firstpost*, June 17, 2014, www.firstpost.com/politics/from-vivekananda-to-pmo-stars-meet-modis-favourite-think-tank-1574369.html

Gandhi, Jatin, "Govt. Forms Panel to Review Official Secrets Act" *The Hindu*, April 15, 2015, www.thehindu.com/news/national/govt-forms-panel-to-review-official-secrets-act/article7105495.ece

Ganguly, Sumit (ed.), *India's Foreign Policy: Retrospect and Prospect* (New Delhi: Oxford University Press, 2010).

———, "Has Modi Truly Changed India's Foreign Policy?" *The Washington Quarterly*, 40:2, 2017, pp. 131–143.

Ganguly, Sumit and Manjeet Pardesi, "Sixty Years of India's Foreign Policy" *India Review*, 8:1, 2009, pp. 4–19.

Gautam, P. K., "Issues of National, Ecological and Human Security in the Siachen Glacier Region" *IDSA Comment*, April 25, 2012, www.idsa.in/idsacomments/IssuesofNational EcologicalandHumanSecurityintheSiachenGlacierRegion_pkgautam_250412

"General's Losing Battle" *ORF Commentaries*, December 7, 2005, www.orfonline.org/research/generals-losing-battle/

George, Alexander L. and Andrew Bennett, *Case Studies and Theory Development in the Social Sciences* (Cambridge, MA: Belfer Center for Science and International Affairs, 2005).

Ghosh, Samarjit, "Indo-Pak Composite Dialogue-2008: A Review" *IPCS Special Report*, 65, February 2009.

Glaser, Bonnie S. and Phillip C. Saunders, "Chinese Civilian Foreign Policy Research Institutes: Evolving Roles and Increasing Influence" *The China Quarterly*, 171, September 2002, pp. 597–616.

Gofas, Andreas and Colin Hay (eds.), *The Role of Ideas in Political Analysis* (London and New York: Routledge, 2010).

Gogna, S. "The Rise of India's Think Tank Diplomacy" *South Asian Voices*, February 16, 2018, https://southasianvoices.org/rise-indias-think-tank-diplomacy/

Gopinath, Meenakshi, "Processing Peace: To Speak in a Different Voice" *Peace Prints: South Asian Journal of Peacebuilding* (New Delhi: WISCOMP), 4:2, Winter 2012.

Gopinath, Meenakshi and Manjrika Sewak, *Transcending Conflict* (New Delhi: WISCOMP, 2004).

Gupta, Arvind, "Brajesh Mishra's Legacy to National Security and Diplomacy" *IDSA Comment*, September 30, 2012, http://idsa.in/idsacomments/BrajeshMishrasLegacytoNationalSecurityandDiplomacy_agupta_300912

———, "R.I.P. Air Commodore Jasjit Singh AVSM, VrC, VM, IAF (Retd) (1934–2013)" *Strategic Analysis*, 37:6, 2013, pp. 764–765.

Gupta, Arvind, S. Kalyanaraman and Ashok K. Behuria, "India-Pakistan Relations after the Mumbai Terror Attacks: What Should India Do?" *Strategic Analysis*, 33:3, May 2009, pp. 319–323.

Gupta, Ashwani, "Ballot Bites the Bullet: Pakistan's Desperate Tactics in Kashmir" *CLAWS Article*, 1300, December 9, 2014, www.claws.in/1300/ballot-bites-the-bullet-pakistans-desperate-tactics-in-kashmir-ashwani-gupta.html

Gupta, Shekhar, "Modi Is Wise to Return to Vajpayee's Pakistan Policy" *Indian Defense News*, December 9, 2015, www.indiandefensenews.in/2015/12/modi-is-wise-to-return-to-vajpayees.html

Gurjar, Sankalp, "Time to Resurrect the Asian Relations Conference" *The Diplomat*, April 18, 2017, https://thediplomat.com/2017/04/time-to-resurrect-the-asian-relations-conference/

Haas, Peter M., "Introduction: Epistemic Communities and International Policy Coordination" *International Organisation*, 46:1, Winter 1992, pp. 1–35.

Haider, Suhasini, "Foreign Policy Making in India: An Institutional Perspective" in Amitabh Mattoo and Happymon Jacob (eds.) *India and the Contemporary International System* (New Delhi: Manohar Press, 2014), pp. 97–124.

———, "MEA Opens Doors to IR Experts as Consultants" *The Hindu*, June 29, 2015, www.thehindu.com/news/external-affairs-ministry-opens-doors-to-international-relations-experts-as-consultants/article7367713.ece

———, "South Block in the Shade" *The Hindu*, May 13, 2016, www.thehindu.com/opinion/op-ed/south-block-in-the-shade/article8591271.ece

Hall, Ian, "Is a 'Modi Doctrine' Emerging in Indian Foreign Policy?" *Australian Journal of International Affairs*, 69:3, 2015, pp. 247–252.

Hamre, John J., "The Constructive Role of Think Tanks in the Twenty-First Century" *Asia-Pacific Review*, 15:2, 2008, pp. 2–5.

Hasnain, S. A., "The Current LoC Narrative and India's Response" *VIF Article*, August 19, 2015, www.vifindia.org/article/2015/august/19/the-current-loc-narrative-and-india-s-response

———, "The Ins & Outs of Infiltration: The Real Challenge in J&K: Part 2" *VIF Article*, June 16, 2016, www.vifindia.org/article/2016/june/16/the-ins-and-outs-of-infiltration-the-real-challenge-in-j-and-k-part-2

Higgott, Richard and Diane Stone, "The Limits of Influence: Foreign Policy Think Tanks in Britain and the USA" *Review of International Studies*, 20:1, January 1994, pp. 15–34.

Hobden, Stephen and Richard Wyn Jones, "Marxist Theories of International Relations" in John Baylis and Steve Smith (eds.) *The Globalization of World Politics* (Oxford: Oxford University Press, 2005), pp. 225–250.

Honawar, Rohit, "Jaish-e-Mohammed" *IPCS Special Report*, 4, November 2005.

Honawar, Rohit, Seema Sridhar and Priyanka Singh, "Terrorism and Political Violence: Kashmir, Sri Lanka and Aceh" *IPCS Special Report*, 1, August 2005.

Hope, Mat and Ringa Raudla, "Discursive Institutionalism and Policy Stasis in Simple and Compound Polities: The Cases of Estonian Fiscal Policy and United States Climate Change Policy" *Policy Studies*, 33:5, September 2012, pp. 399–418.

Husain, Ishrat, "Managing India-Pakistan Trade Relations" in Michael Kugelman and Robert M. Hathaway (eds.) *Pakistan-India Trade: What Needs to Be Done? What Does It Matter?* (Washington: Wilson Center, 2013), pp. 59–74.

Hussain, Altaf, "Deaths Provoke Kashmir Protests" *BBC News*, June 1, 2009, http://news.bbc.co.uk/2/hi/south_asia/8076666.stm

"Indian See Threats from Pakistan, Extremist Groups" *Pew Research Center*, October 20, 2010, www.pewglobal.org/2010/10/20/indians-see-threat-from-pakistan-extremist-groups/

India-Pakistan Water Roundtable: Joint Statement (Bangalore: CDR and Jinnah Institute, 2014).

"Internal Security" *IDSA Policy Brief*, June 2009.

Iyer, Ramaswamy, "Writ in Water" *The Indian Express*, October 31, 2008, http://archive.indianexpress.com/news/writ-in-water/379421/0

———, "Water in India-Pakistan Talks" *The Hindu*, March 3, 2010, www.thehindu.com/todays-paper/tp-opinion/article721712.ece

———, "What Water Wars?" *The Indian Express*, April 1, 2010, http://archive.indianexpress.com/news/what-water-wars-/594319/0

Jacob, Happymon, *Does India Think Strategically?* (New Delhi: Manohar Press, 2014).

Jaishankar, Dhruv, "Can India's Think Tanks Be Truly Effective?" *The Huffington Post India*, April 15, 2016, www.huffingtonpost.in/dhruva-jaishankar/can-indias-think-tanks-be_b_9688434.html

Jaishankar, Subrahmanyam, "Indian Foreign Secretary Subrahmanyam Jaishankar's Remarks" *Carnegie India*, http://carnegieindia.org/2016/04/06/indian-foreign-secretary-subrahmanyamjaishankar-s-remarks/iwq8

Jaleel, Muzamil, "A People's General" *The Indian Express*, April 17, 2011, http://archive.indianexpress.com/news/a-people-s-general/777108/

Jammu, Kashmir and Ladakh: Building Peace and Countering Radicalisation (New Delhi: IPCS, March 2010).

Jha, Prashant, "India's Most-Influential Think Tanks" *Hindustan Times*, August 16, 2015, www.hindustantimes.com/india/india-s-most-influential-think-tanks/story-emb0db2lmqltL8pKeYuZiL.html

"J & K: Need for a Bipartisan Consensus" *VIF Article*, February 7, 2011, www.vifindia.org/article/2011/february/7/J-K-Need-For-a-Bipartisan-Consensus

John, Wilson, "Checkmating Musharraf's Plan" *ORF Commentaries*, November 24, 2004, www.orfonline.org/research/checkmating-musharrafs-plan/

———, "High Resolution Picture in Kashmir" *ORF Commentaries*, February 1, 2006, www.orfonline.org/research/high-resolution-picture-in-kashmir/

———, "The Jihadi Factor in India-Pakistan Peace Process" *ORF Issue Brief*, No. 6, May 2006.

———, "Concerted International Action Needed to Rein in Pakistan Terror Groups" *ORF Policy Brief*, 9, February 2009.

———, "Pakistan Occupied Kashmir: An Emerging Epicentre of Global Jihad" in K. Warikoo (ed.) *The Other Kashmir: Society, Culture and Politics in the Karakoram Himalayas* (New Delhi: IDSA, 2014), pp. 307–323.

John, Wilson and Kaustav Dhar Chakrabarti, "India-Pakistan Relations after Mumbai Attacks" *Issue Brief*, 21, September 2009.

Kanwal, Gurmeet, "Strategic Stalemate in Kashmir" *ORF Commentaries*, January 23, 2004, www.orfonline.org/research/strategic-stalemate-in-kashmir/

———, "Indo-Pak Nuclear CBMs: Time to Move Forward" *ORF Commentaries*, June 16, 2004, www.orfonline.org/research/indo-pak-nuclear-cbms-time-to-move-forward/

———, "Demilitarisation of Siachen" *Event Report*, April 5, 2005, www.orfonline.org/research/demilitarisation-of-siachen/

———, "Siachen: National Consensus Needed" *ORF Commentaries*, May 30, 2006, www.orfonline.org/research/siachen-national-consensus-needed/

———, "Demilitarisation of the Siachen Conflict Zone: An Idea Whose Time Has Come" *CLAWS Journal*, Winter 2012, pp. 83–87.

———, "Tactical Nuclear Weapons: Pakistan's Dangerous Game (or Quest)" *VIF Article*, October 8, 2012, www.vifindia.org/article/2012/october/08/tactical-nuclear-weapons-pakistan-s-dangerous-game-or-quest

———, "Tactical Nuclear Weapons: Lessons for India and Pakistan" *VIF Article*, June 4, 2013, www.vifindia.org/article/2013/june/04/tactical-nuclear-weapons-lessons-for-india-and-pakistan

———, "Pakistani Army Firing across LoC: Raising the Ante in Kashmir" *CLAWS Article*, 1271, October 18, 2014, www.claws.in/1271/pakistan-army-firing-across-loc-raising-the-ante-in-kashmir-brig-gurmeet-kanwal.html

Bibliography

———, "Role of Think Tanks in National Security" *Forum for Strategic Initiatives*, January 12, 2015, www.fsidelhi.org

———, "Pakistan's 'Deep State' Continues to Sponsor Terrorism" *CLAWS Article*, 1417, August 9, 2015, www.claws.in/1417/pakistans-deep-state-continues-to-sponsor-terrorism-brig-gurmeet-kanwal.html

———, "Pakistan Atrocities in PoK and Gilgit-Baltistan" *CLAWS Article*, 1449, October 9, 2015, www.claws.in/1449/pakistan-atrocities-in-pok-and-gilgit-baltistan-brig-gurmeet-kanwal.html

Kapoor, Coomi, "Joint Statement: After the Blooper, a Bizarre Assumption" *Indian Express*, 22, July 2009.

Kapur, Paul S., "Ten Year of Instability in a Nuclear South Asia" *International Security*, 33:2, 2008, pp. 71–94, DOI: 10.1162/isec.2008.33.2.71

Karnad, Bharat, "Dedicated Nuclear Cadre" *Security Wise*, August 16, 2012, https://bharatkarnad.com/2012/08/16/dedicated-nuclear-cadre/

Kashmir: After the Quake: Prospects for Peace (New Delhi: Delhi Policy Group, 2005).

"Kashmir, a Systemic Failure: Dialogue a Must" *ORF Event Report*, August 20, 2010, www.orfonline.org/research/kashmir-a-systemic-failure-dialogue-a-must/

"Kashmiri Leaders from Both Sides Should Sit Together" *ORF Event Report*, April 28, 2007, www.orfonline.org/research/kashmiri-leaders-from-both-sides-should-sit-together/

"Kashmir: Looking Further" *IPCS Article*, 1382, May 5, 2004, www.ipcs.org/article/indo-pak/kashmir-looking-further-1382.html

Khare, Harish, "Hold the Vajpayee Manmohan Line" *The Hindu*, August 4, 2013, www.thehindu.com/opinion/lead/hold-the-vajpayeemanmohan-line/article5019657.ece

Khilnani, Sunil, Rajiv Kumar, et al., *Non Alignment 2.0: A Foreign and Strategic Policy for India in the Twenty First Century* (New Delhi: Penguin, 2014).

Khurana, Gurpreet, "India Needs Sea-Based 'Active' Deterrence against State-Sponsored Terrorism" *NMF Commentary*, March 25, 2015, www.maritimeindia.org/Commentry View.aspx?NMFCID=8397

Kothari, Smitu Kothari and Zia Mian (eds.), *Bridging Partition: Peoples' Initiatives for Peace between India and Pakistan* (Hyderabad: Orient Blackswan, 2010).

Krepon, Michael, "Nuclear Risk Reduction Redux in South Asia" *Stimson Center Issue Brief*, June 14, 2012, www.stimson.org/content/nuclear-risk-reduction-redux-south-asia

———, "Jasjit Singh" *Arms Control Wonk*, August 12, 2013, www.armscontrolwonk.com/archive/403863/jasjit-singh/

Kumar, Amit, "Time for Dr. Singh to Step in" *ORF Commentaries*, August 9, 2010, www.orfonline.org/research/time-for-dr-singh-to-step-in/

Kumar, Radha, "Untying the Kashmir Knot" *World Policy Journal*, 19:1, Spring 2002, pp. 11–24.

———, "India as a Foreign Policy Actor: Normative Redux" *CEPS Working Document*, 285, February 2008.

———, "To a Battery of Ever-Ready Denunciators" *Outlook*, June 11, 2012, www.outlookindia.com/magazine/story/to-a-battery-of-ever-ready-denunciators/281116

Kumar, Radha, M. M. Ansari and Dileep Padgaonkar, A *New Compact with the People of Jammu and Kashmir*, Final Report of the group of Interlocutors for J & K, October 2011.

Kumar, Radha and Ellora Puri (eds.), *Peace-Building: Indian and European Perspectives* (New Delhi: Delhi Policy Group, 2006).

Kumar, Radha, Anjali Puri and Saurabh Naithani (eds.), *What Makes a Peace Process Irreversible: A Conference Report* (New Delhi: Delhi Policy Group, 2005).

Kundu, Apurba, *Militarism in India: The Army and Civil Society in Consensus* (London: I.B. Tauris, 1998), pp. 100–121.

Ladi, Stella, *International Encyclopedia of Political Science* (Thousand Oaks: Sage, 2011).

———, "Think Tanks, Discursive Institutionalism and Policy Change" in Georgios Papanagnou (ed.) *Social Science and Policy Challenges: Democracy, Values and Capacities* (Paris: UNESCO, 2011), pp. 205–220.

Landman, Todd and Neil Robinson, *The SAGE Handbook of Comparative Politics* (London: Sage, 2009).

Lederach, John Paul, *Building Peace: Sustainable Reconciliation in Divided Societies* (Washington, DC: United States Institute of Peace Press, 1997).

Malhotra, Jyoti, "The Growing Role of Government-Approved Think Tanks" *NDTV*, March 1, 2017, www.ndtv.com/opinion/think-tanks-controlled-by-foreign-ministry-are-supplanting-the-media-1664683

Malik, V. P., "Revisiting AFSPA: Don't Blame It for Kashmir Problems" *ORF Commentaries*, September 20, 2010, www.orfonline.org/research/revisiting-afspa-dont-blame-it-for-kashmir-problems/

Malone, David M., *Does the Elephant Dance? Contemporary Indian Foreign Policy* (Oxford: Oxford University Press, 2011).

Manjunath, K. S., "Indo-Pak Peace Process: Chronology of Events 2004–2005" *IPCS Special Report*, 6, January 2006.

Manjunath, K. S., Seema Sridhar and Beryl Anand, "Indo-Pak Composite Dialogue 2004–2005: A Profile" *IPCS Special Report*, 12, February 2006.

Markey, Daniel, "Developing India's Foreign Policy 'Software'" *Asia Policy*, 8, July 2009, pp. 73–96.

Mathur, Kuldeep, *Public Policy and Politics in India: How Institutions Matter* (New Delhi: Oxford University Press, 2013).

———, "Policy Research Organisations in South Asia" *Working Paper Series: Centre for the Study of Law and Governance*, New Delhi, April 2009.

Mattoo, Amitabh, "A New Foreign Policy Agenda" *The Hindu*, April 8, 2014, www.thehindu.com/opinion/lead/a-new-foreign-policy-agenda/article5883940.ece

Mattoo, Amitabh and Happymon Jacob (eds.), *India and the Contemporary International System* (New Delhi: Manohar Press, 2014).

McGann, James G., *2012 Global Go to Think Tanks Report and Policy Advice* (Philadelphia: University of Pennsylvania, 2013).

———, "2018 Global Go to Think Tank Index Report" *TTCSP Global Go to Think Tank Index Reports*, 16, 2019, https://repository.upenn.edu/cgi/viewcontent.cgi?article=1017&context=think_tanks

McGann, James G. and Richard Sabatini, *Global Think Tanks: Policy Networks and Governance Global Institutions* (New York: Routledge, 2011).

McGann, James G. and R. Kent Weaver (eds.), *Think Tanks and Civil Societies: Catalysts for Ideas and Actions* (New Brunswick: Transaction Publishers, 2005).

Medvetz, Tom, *Think Tanks as an Emergent Field* (New York: Social Science Research Council, October 2008).

Medvetz, Thomas, *Think Tanks in America* (Chicago: University of Chicago Press, 2012).

Mehra, Puja, "G20: Finance Ministry Asks ORF for Stance on BRICS Bank" *The Hindu*, January 8, 2014, www.thehindu.com/business/Economy/g20-finance-ministry-asks-orf-for-stance-on-brics-bank/article5554469.ece

Mehta, Jal, "The Varied Roles of Ideas in Politics: From 'Whether' to 'How'" in Daniel Beland and Robert Henry Cox (eds.) *Ideas and Politics in Social Science Research* (New York: Oxford University Press, 2011), pp. 23–46.

Mehta, Pratap Bhanu, "State of Vacuum in Times of Terror" *The Indian Express*, July 12, 2006, http://archive.indianexpress.com/news/state-of-vacuum-in-times-of-terror/8369/0

———, "The Question in Kashmir" *The Indian Express*, August 19, 2008, http://archive.indianexpress.com/news/the-question-in-kashmir/350345/

———, "Still under Nehru's Shadow? The Absence of Foreign Policy Frameworks in India" *India Review*, 8:3, July–September 2009, pp. 209–233.

Menon, Shivshankar, *India and the Global Scene: Prem Bhatia Memorial Lecture*, August 11, 2011, National Maritime Foundation, http://maritimeindia.org/article/india-and-global-scene

———, *Choices: Inside the Making of India's Foreign Policy* (Washington, DC: Brookings Institution, 2015).

———, "Earlier Cross-LoC Strikes Had Different Goals: Former NSA" *The Hindu*, October 12, 2016, www.thehindu.com/news/national/former-national-security-ad...on-on-crossloc-strikes/article9208838.ece?homepage=true&css=print

Miller, Manjari Chatterjee, "India's Feeble Foreign Policy" *Foreign Affairs*, May/June 2013, pp. 14–19.

Ministry of External Affairs: Annual Report (New Delhi: Ministry of External Affairs, GOI, 2004–2005).

Misra, Ashutosh, "Unfazed New Delhi Continues the Dialogue Despite Hurriyat's Absence" *IDSA Comment*, March 3, 2006, www.idsa.in/idsastrategiccomments/UnfazedNewDelhiContinuestheDialogueProcessDespiteHurriyatsAbsence_AMisra_030306

———, *India-Pakistan: Coming to Terms* (New York: Palgrave MacMillan, 2010).

Mitra, Abhijit Iyer, "Long-Term Gain Must Be the Aim" *Nuclear Newsletter*, (CAPS) 7:17, July 2013.

Mohan, C. Raja, *Crossing the Rubicon: The Shaping of India's New Foreign Policy* (New Delhi: Penguin Viking, 2003).

———, "The Making of Indian Foreign Policy: The Role of Scholarship and Public Opinion" *ISAS Working Paper*, (National University of Singapore) 73, July 13, 2009.

———, "The Re-Making of Indian Foreign Policy: Ending the Marginalization of the International Relations Community" *International Studies*, 46:1 & 2, 2009, pp. 147–163.

Mohan, C. Raja and Ajai Sahni, *India's Security Challenges at Home and Abroad* (Washington: The National Bureau of Asian Research, 2012).

Mukherjee, Anit, "K Subrahmanyam and Indian Strategic Thought" *Strategic Analysis*, 35:4, 2011, pp. 710–713.

Munshi, Vikram, *Wars by Pakistan* (New Delhi: CAPS, 2014).

Munson, Marc, "Indian Maritime Security after Mumbai" *Capability Analysis*, (Center for International Maritime Security), July 2, 2012, http://cimsec.org/indian-maritime-security-after-mumbai/1634

Mustafa, Seema, "Sharif-Vajpayee together in a Secret Deal" *The Asian Age*, September 15, 1999, www.jammu-kashmir.com/archives/archives1999/99september15a.html

Nanda, Prakash, "Indian Foreign Policy under Modi" *Fearless Nadia Occasional Papers* (Australia-India Institute), 3, Winter 2014.

Narang, Vipin and Paul Staniland, "Institutions and Worldviews in Indian Foreign Security Policy" *India Review*, 11:2, 2012, pp. 76–94.

Narlikar, Amrita, "Peculiar Chauvinism or Strategic Calculation? Explaining the Negotiating Strategy of a Rising India" *International Affairs*, 82:1, 2006, pp. 59–76.

"National Security Advisory Board Reconstituted, But with Fewer Members" *The Wire*, October 10, 2016, https://thewire.in/72258/national-security-advisory-board-reconstituted/

Nayar, Lola, "Those Hard Thinking Caps Realigned" *Outlook*, June 9, 2014, www.outlookindia.com/magazine/story/those-hard-thinking-caps-realigned/290876

"NSAB Reconstituted with Ex-Envoy P S Raghavan as Head" *Indian Express*, October 9, 2016, http://indianexpress.com/article/india/india-news-india/nsab-national-security-advisory-board-p-s-raghavan-3073906/

ORF Annual Report 2015 (New Delhi: Observer Research Foundation, 2016).

The ORF BRICS Compilation (New Delhi: Observer Research Foundation, 2013), www.orfonline.org

Pai, Sudha and Pradeep Sharma, "New Institutionalism and Legislative Governance in the Indian States: A Comparative Study of West Bengal and Uttar Pradesh" *Working Paper Series* (Centre for the study of Law and Governance, JNU, New Delhi) March, 2005.

"Pakistan Occupied Kashmir: Changing the Discourse" *PoK Project Report* (New Delhi: IDSA, May 2011).

"Pakistan's New Kashmir Offensive" *ORF Commentaries*, September 17, 2003, www.orfonline.org/research/pakistans-new-kashmir-offensive/

Pant, Harsh, "India's Nuclear Doctrine and Command Structure: Implications for Civil-Military Relations in India" *Armed Forces & Society*, 33:2, January 2007, pp. 238–264.

———, "A Rising India's Search for a Foreign Policy" *Orbis*, 53:2 (2009), pp. 250–254.

Papola, T. S., "Social Science Research in Globalising India: Historical Development and Recent Trends" *ISID Working Paper*, (Institute for Studies in Industrial Development, Delhi), May 2010.

Parmar, Inderjeet, "Institutes of International Affairs: Their Roles in Foreign Policy-Making, Opinion Mobilization and Unofficial Diplomacy" in Diane Stone and Andrew Denham (eds.) *Think Tank Traditions: Policy Research and the Politics of Ideas* (Manchester: Manchester University Press, 2004), pp. 19–33.

———, *Think Tanks and Power in Foreign Policy* (New York: Palgrave MacMillan, 2004).

Parrey, Arif Aayaz, *Anatomy of the Autonomy* (New Delhi: Centre for Dialogue and Reconciliation).

Parthasarathy, G., "The Saltoro Range: Pullout Will Be a Himalayan Blunder" *The Tribune*, May 4, 2006, www.tribuneindia.com/2006/20060504/edit.htm

———, "Dangerous Compromises" *The Tribune*, September 21, 2006, www.tribuneindia.com/2006/20060921/edit.htm

———, "Are We Fighting Terrorism? India's Approach Can Lead to Nowhere" *The Tribune*, November 30, 2006, www.tribuneindia.com/2006/20061130/edit.htm

———, "India Can't Pull Out Troops" *The Tribune*, December 28, 2006, www.tribuneindia.com/2006/20061228/edit.htm

———, "Hurriyat Role in J & K" *The Tribune*, February 8, 2007, www.tribuneindia.com/2007/20070208/edit.htm

———, "How Kandahar Hijacked Us" *The Indian Express*, February 6, 2008, http://archive.indianexpress.com/news/how-kandahar-hijacked-us/269673/

———, "Separatism Needs Firmness" *The Tribune*, September 4, 2008, www.tribuneindia.com/2008/20080904/edit.htm

Parthasarathy, G. and Radha Kumar, *Frameworks for a Kashmir Settlement* (New Delhi: Delhi Policy Group, 2006).

Patil, Sameer Suryakant, "Indo-Pak Composite Dialogue: An Update" *IPCS Special Report*, 53, June 2008.

Pautz, Hartwig, "Revisiting the Think Tank Phenomenon" *Public Policy and Administration*, 26:4, 2011, pp. 419–435.

———, *Think Tanks, Social Democracy and Social Policy* (London: Palgrave MacMillan, 2012).

Pearson, Natalie Obiko, "India's 007, Former Super Spy, Is Shaping Modi's Foreign Policy" *Bloomberg*, September 19, 2016, www.bloomberg.com/news/articles/2016-09-18/india-s-007-former-super-spy-is-shaping-modi-s-foreign-policy

Peters, B. Guy, *Institutional Theory in Political Science* (London and New York: Bloomsbury Publishing, 2011).

Phadke, Ramesh, "A Siachen Resolution: Why Now?" *IDSA Comment*, November 8, 2012, www.idsa.in/idsacomments/ASiachenResolutionWhyNow_rphadke_081112

"Pointers to Pakistan's Strategy" *ORF Commentaries*, September 14, 2004, www.orfonline.org/research/pointers-to-pakistans-strategy/

"The Process Is Unwinding" *ORF Commentaries*, July 12, 2005, www.orfonline.org/research/the-process-is-unwinding/

Raghavan, Srinath, "Civil-Military Relations in India: The China Crisis and after" *Journal of Strategic Studies*, 32:1, 2009, pp. 149–175.

Raghavan, V. R., "South Asian Nuclear Dialogue" *The Hindu*, September 1, 2000, www.thehindu.com/2000/09/01/stories/05012523.htm

Raisina Dialogue: Conference Booklet (New Delhi: Observer Research Foundation and Ministry of External Affairs, 2016).

Raman, B., "Unequal Accommodation: A National Stockholm Syndrome" *ORF Commentaries*, April 19, 2005, www.orfonline.org/research/unequal-accommodation-a-national-stockholm-syndrome/

Ramana, P. V. and Wilson John, "Mumbai Blasts: Time to Act" *ORF Policy Brief*, July 20, 2006.

Rasgotra, Maharaja Krishan, *A Life in Diplomacy* (New Delhi: Penguin, 2016).

Rathbun, Brian C., "Interviewing and Qualitative Field Methods: Pragmatism and Practicalities" in Janet M. Box-Steffensmeier, Henry E. Brady and David Collier (eds.) *The Oxford Handbook of Political Methodology* (Oxford: Oxford University Press, 2008), pp. 685–701.

Review of the Shanghai Meeting and the Future Agenda (New Delhi: IPCS, October 2009).

Rich, Andrew, "Ideas, Expertise and Think Tanks" in Daniel Beland and Robert Henry Cox (eds.) *Ideas and Politics in Social Science Research* (New York: Oxford University Press, 2011), pp. 191–208.

"R K Mishra Passes Away" *The Hindu*, January 10, 2009, www.thehindu.com/todays-paper/R.K.-Mishra-passes-away/article16349286.ece

Romshoo, Shakil A., *Indus River Basin: Common Concerns and the Roadmap to Resolution* (New Delhi: Center for Dialogue and Reconciliation, 2012).

Roundtable on "Current Developments in J & K" organised by IDSA, New Delhi, August 28, 2008.

Saksena, K. P., "India's Foreign Policy: The Decisionmaking Process" *International Studies*, 33:4, 1996, pp. 391–405.

Saran, Shyam, *How India Sees the World: From Kautilya to the 21st Century* (New Delhi: Juggernaut, 2017).

Sareen, Sushant, "Running Faster to Maintain Status Quo?" *ORF Commentaries*, October 6, 2004, www.orfonline.org/research/running-faster-to-maintain-status-quo/

———, "Need for a Composite Back Channel with Pakistan Army" *IDSA Comment*, January 7, 2011, www.idsa.in/idsacomments/NeedforacompositebackchannelwithPakistanarmy_ssareen_070111

———, "Steadfast in Siachen" *VIF Article*, February 22, 2016, www.vifindia.org/article/2016/february/22/steadfast-in-siachen

Sasikumar, Karthika, "Learning to Play the Game: Strategic Culture and Nuclear Learning" in Happymon Jacob (ed.) *Does India Think Strategically?* (New Delhi: Manohar Press, 2014), pp. 25–51.

Schaffer, Teresita C. and Howard Schaffer, "When India's Foreign Policy Is Domestic" *The Brookings Institution*, April 2, 2013, www.brookings.edu/blog/up-front/2013/04/02/when-indias-foreign-policy-is-domestic/

Schmidt, Vivien, "Discursive Institutionalism: The Explanatory Power of Ideas and Discourse" *Annual Review of Political Science*, 11, 2008, pp. 303–326.

———, "Taking Ideas and Discourse Seriously: Explaining Change through Discursive Institutionalism as the Fourth 'New Institutionalism'" *European Political Science Review*, 2:1, 2010, pp. 1–25.

———, "Give Peace a Chance: Reconciling Four (Not Three) New Institutionalisms" an earlier chapter draft in Daniel Beland and Robert Cox (eds.) *Ideas and Politics in Social Science Research* (New York: Oxford University Press, 2011), pp. 47–64.

———, "Discursive Institutionalism: Scope, Dynamics and Philosophical Underpinnings" in Frank Fischer and Herbert Gottweis (eds.) *The Argumentative Turn Revisited: Public Policy as Communicative Practice* (Durham and London: Duke University Press, 2012), pp. 85–113.

Second Annual Workshop on Nuclear Disarmament and Regional Security (New Delhi: IPCS, September 2009).

Seminar on *Situation in Jammu and Kashmir and Contours of Future Strategy* organised by the Centre for Land Warfare Studies (CLAWS), January 2, 2008, www.claws.in/event-detail.php?eID=177

Seminar on *Terrorism in the India-Pakistan-Afghanistan Region: Linkages and Responses* organised by the Centre for Land Warfare Studies (CLAWS), February 17, 2009, www.claws.in/event-detail.php?eID=220

Sewak, Manjrika, *Rehumanizing the Other* (New Delhi: WISCOMP, 2002).

———, "Multi-Track Diplomacy between India and Pakistan: A Conceptual Framework for Sustainable Security" in *RCSS Policy Studies*, Vol. 30 (New Delhi: Manohar Press, 2005).

Shambaugh, David, "China's International Relations Think Tanks: Evolving Structure and Process" *The China Quarterly*, 171, September 2002, pp. 575–596.

Sharma, Pranay, "Quills and Spills" *Outlook*, August 3, 2009.

Sharma, Sheel Kant, "Strategic Situation: India Pakistan" *CAPS Issue Brief*, 86:13, February 28, 2013.

Sibal, Kanwal, "To Talk Now Is Wrong" *ORF Commentaries*, February 22, 2010, www.orfonline.org/research/to-talk-now-is-wrong/

———, "Soft State Style Won't Work in J & K" *VIF Article*, September 21, 2010, www.vifindia.org/article/2010/september/21/Soft-State-Style-Won-t-Work%20-In-J-K

———, "No Ground to Vacate Siachen" *VIF Article*, May 8, 2012, www.vifindia.org/article/2012/may/08/no-ground-to-vacate-siachen

———, "Nettlesome Neighbour" *VIF Article*, January 26, 2013, www.vifindia.org/article/2013/january/26/nettlesome-neighbour

Sikri, Rajiv, *Challenge and Strategy: Rethinking India's Foreign Policy* (New Delhi: Sage Publications, 2009).

"Simulation Exercise: Frameworks for a Kashmir Settlement" in *DPG Programme on Developing Peace Processes and Partners* (New Delhi: Delhi Policy Group, 2006).

Singh, Abhijit, "Pakistan Navy's 'Nuclear' Aspirations" *IDSA Comment*, June 29, 2012, www.idsa.in/idsacomments/PakistanNavysNuclearAspirations_AbhijitSingh_290612

Singh, Jasjit (ed.), *Pakistan Occupied Kashmir: Under the Jackboot* (New Delhi: Siddhi Books, 1995).

———, "War through Terror under the Nuclear Umbrella" *CAPS Issue Brief*, 1:2, December 5, 2008.

Singh, Rahul, "Action Please Not Words" *CLAWS*, June 21, 2012, www.claws.in/855/action-please-not-words-rohit-singh.html

Sinha, Aseema, "The Changing Political Economy of Federalism in India: A Historical Institutionalist Approach" *India Review*, 3:1, 2004, pp. 25–63.

Sinha, Uttam Kumar, "India and Pakistan: Introspecting the Indus Treaty" *Strategic Analysis*, 32:6, November 2008, pp. 961–967.

———, "Water a Pre-Eminent Political Issue between India and Pakistan" *Strategic Analysis*, 34:4, July 2010, pp. 482–485.

Snow, Shawn, "Is Pakistan Capable of a Surgical Strike in Pakistan Controlled Kashmir?" *The Diplomat*, September 30, 2016, http://thediplomat.com/2016/09/is-india-capable-of-a-surgical-strike-in-pakistan-controlled-kashmir/

Sood, Vikram, "Height of Folly" *ORF Commentaries*, May 15, 2006, www.orfonline.org/research/height-of-folly/

———, "Why India Cannot Afford to Give Up Siachen" *ORF Commentaries*, April 16, 2012, www.orfonline.org/research/why-india-cannot-afford-to-give-up-siachen/

———, "Story of Saltoro: From Ababeel to Meghdoot" *ORF Commentaries*, April 27, 2012, www.orfonline.org/research/story-of-saltoro-from-ababeel-to-meghdoot/

———, "Terror from across the Border: Why Isn't War an Option?" *ORF Commentaries*, January 6, 2016, www.orfonline.org/research/terror-from-across-the-border-why-isnt-war-an-option/

Sridhar, R. (ed.), "Nuclear Disarmament and South Asian Security: A Regional Dialogue" *IPCS-MCC Workshop Report* (New Delhi: IPCS, 2008).

Sridharan, E., "Improving Indo-Pakistan Relations: International Relations Theory, Nuclear Deterrence and Possibilities for Economic Cooperation" *Contemporary South Asia*, 14:3, 2005, pp. 321–339.

Srivastava, Devyani, "Terrorism, Religious Radicalism and Violence: Perspectives from India" *IPCS Issue Brief*, 120, September 2009.

Srivastava, Jayati, *Think Tanks in South Asia: Analysing the Knowledge-Power Interface* (London: Overseas Development Institute, 2011).

Stone, Diane, *Capturing the Political Imagination: Think Tanks and the Policy Process* (London: Frank Cass, 1996).

———, "Recycling Bins, Garbage Cans or Think Tanks? Three Myths Regarding Policy Analysis Institutes" *Public Administration*, 85:2, 2007, pp. 259–278.

———, "The ASEAN-ISIS Network: Interpretive Communities, Informal Diplomacy and Discourses of Region" *Minerva*, 49, 2011, pp. 241–262.

Subrahmanyam, K., "The Birth of the IDSA and Early Years" in N. S. Sisodia and Sujit Datta (eds.) *India and the World*, Vol. 1 (New Delhi: IDSA, 2005), pp. 1–38.

Subramaniam, Arjun, "Warrior, Pilot, Strategist, Scholar" *The Hindu*, August 7, 2013, www.thehindu.com/opinion/op-ed/warrior-pilot-strategist-scholar/article4996360.ece

Swami, Praveen, "Now, the Cover-Up" *Frontline*, 16:16, July 31–August 13, 1999, www.frontline.in/static/html/fl1616/16160220.htm

"Take It Along" *ORF Commentaries*, March 6, 2006, www.orfonline.org/research/take-it-along/

Tandon, Aakriti, "India's Foreign Policy Priorities and the Emergence of a Modi Doctrine" *Strategic Analysis*, 40:5, 2016, pp. 349–356.

Tanham, George, *Indian Strategic Thought: An Interpretive Essay* (Santa Monica, CA: Rand Corporation, 1992).

Taylor, Matthew, "Think Tanks, Public Policy and Academia" *Public Money & Management*, 31:1, 2011, pp. 10–11.

Tharoor, Shashi, "Our Diplomatic Deficit" *Indian Express*, August 24, 2012, http://archive.indianexpress.com/news/our-diplomatic-deficit/992257/

———, *Pax Indica: India and the World of the 21st Century* (New Delhi: Penguin, 2012).

Verghese, B. G., "A Vision for J and K: Internal Settlement Unavoidable for India" *The Tribune*, April 14, 2005, www.tribuneindia.com/2005/20050414/edit.htm#4

———, "A Vision for J & K-2015: Local and National Consensus Will Help" *The Tribune*, April 15, 2005, www.tribuneindia.com/2005/20050415/edit.htm#4

———, "It's Time for Indus II" *The Tribune*, May 26, 2005, www.tribuneindia.com/2005/20050526/edit.htm

———, "Gambols and Gambits in Kashmir" *The Tribune*, January 20, 2006, www.tribuneindia.com/2006/20060120/edit.htm

———, "Indus Water Woes" *The Tribune*, April 27, 2006, www.tribuneindia.com/2006/20060427/edit.htm

———, "A Bit of Musharraf-Speak" *The Tribune*, December 22, 2006, www.tribuneindia.com/2006/20061222/edit.htm

———, *A J & K Primer: From Myth to Reality* (New Delhi: Centre for Policy Research, 2007).

———, "Indus Valley Cooperation" *The Indian Express*, February 16, 2007, http://archive.indianexpress.com/news/indus-valley-cooperation/23430/0

———, "60 Years of Accession: It's Time to Fulfil Promises" *The Tribune*, October 1, 2007, www.tribuneindia.com/2007/20071001/edit.htm

———, *Siachen Follies: Defining Facts and Objectives* (New Delhi: Centre for Policy Research, 2012).

Varghese, K. George, "Domestic Politics of India's Foreign Policy Decision-Making" in Amitabh Mattoo and Happymon Jacob (eds.) *India and the Contemporary International System* (New Delhi: Manohar Press, 2014), pp. 125–156.

Vij, N. C., "Kashmir: Dilution Is No Answer" *VIF Article*, February 5, 2014, www.vifindia.org/article/2014/february/05/kashmir-dilution-is-no-answer

Vivekenanda International Foundation (VIF), "Press Statement on India-Pakistan Relations by Members of India's Strategic Community" August 9, 2013, www.vifindia.org/event/report/2013/august/09/press-statement-on-India-Pakistan-relations-by-members-of-india-s-strategiccommunity

Vivekanandan, B., "A Tribute to Life and Work of Professor M S Rajan" *International Studies*, 47:2–4, 2010, pp. 99–111.

Wani, Aijaz Ashraf and Sajad Padder, "Understanding the Discredited Institution of Dialogue in Kashmir" *Greater Kashmir*, September 11, 2016, www.greaterkashmir.com/news/op-ed/understanding-the-discredited-institution-of-dialogue-in-kashmir/228223.html

Waslekar, Sundeep, "Track Two Diplomacy in South Asia" *ACDIS Occasional Paper* (Urbana-Champaign: University of Illinois, October 1995).

Weaver, R. Kent and Paul B. Stares, *Guidance for Governance: An Overview* (Tokyo: Japan Center for International Exchange, 2001), pp. 71–88.

Weiner, Myron, "Social Science Research and Public Policy in India" *Economic and Political Weekly*, 14:37, September 1979, pp. 1579–1587.

Xavier, Constantino and Stephen Cohen, "The Career and Ideas of K. Subrahmanyam" *Event Summary Brookings Institution*, February 2011, www.brookings.edu/events/2011/02/18-india-subrahmanyam

Yadav, Yatish, "Modi Government to Mould National Security Advisory Board in New Avatar" *The New Indian Express*, February 8, 2015, www.newindianexpress.com/

thesundaystandard/2015/feb/08/Modi-Government-to-Mould-National-Security-Advisory-Board-in-New-Avatar-714663.html

Yusuf, Moeed, "Promoting Cross LoC Trade in Kashmir: An Analysis of the Joint Chamber" *USIP Special Report*, 230, 2009.

Zehra, Nasim, "Musharraf's Kashmir Policy" *The News*, December 18, 2006, www.thenews.com.pk/archive/print/35741-musharrafs-kashmir-policy

Zimmerman, Erin, *Think Tanks and Non-Traditional Security: Governance Entrepreneurs in Asia* (Basingstoke: Palgrave MacMillan, 2016).

INDEX

Actual Ground Position Line 98
AFSPA (Armed Forces Special Powers Act) 69, 97, 140
Agra summit 50, 88
AJK 75, 94, 125
All Parties Hurriyat Conference *see* APHC; Hurriyat
Amarnath agitation 70, 96–97, 103, 120, 125–126
APAOs (Alternative Policy Advisory Organisations) 18
APHC 70, 96, 118, 120
ASEAN (Association of South East Asian Nations) 19, 47
Azaadi 69

back-channel 52, 73, 88, 106
Baglihar Dam 100
Balochistan 73, 95, 141
Banerjee, Dipankar 114–115, 117, 119, 121–122
Barve, Sushobha 115–116
Bill and Melinda Gates Foundation 87
BJP (Bharatiya Janata Party) 90–91, 102, 105, 142–143, 145
BRICS 45, 59, 89, 106
Brookings India 42, 144

CAPS (Centre for Air Power Studies) 9, 42–43, 66, 136
Carnegie India 42, 144
CBMs (Confidence Building Measures) 51, 119
CD (Composite Dialogue) 4, 49–53, 68, 73, 141
CDR (Centre for Dialogue and Reconciliation) 42, 52, 115, 123–126
ceasefire violations 101, 143
Chaophraya dialogue 65, 92, 116
Chari, P.R. 65, 114–115, 121
Chatham House 18, 28, 29, 49
Chellaney, Brahma 41, 44, 89, 92, 101
China: China-Pakistan nexus/alliance 68, 76, 99, 121; think tanks 21, 26, 45, 48; trialogue 45, 122; *see also* BRICS
civil society 24, 27, 38, 42, 51–54, 93, 102, 113, 115
CLAWS (Centre for Land Warfare Studies) 42–43, 63, 66, 69–70, 72, 75, 137
coastal security 76; active deterrence 76; Gurpreet Khurana 66
communicative discourse 22–23, 44–46, 119, 127, 140
Consortium of South Asian Think Tanks 115
coordinative discourse 22–23, 44, 46, 90, 135
Council on Foreign Relations 15, 18, 42
CPR (Centre for Policy Research) 41, 45, 47, 87, 89–90, 92, 94–97, 99–100
critical juncture 8, 24, 53, 92, 95
cross-border terrorism 142
CRPF (Central Reserve Police Force) 96, 143
CT (conflict transformation) 116–117, 123

Index

deep state 69, 72, 101
DGMO (Director General of Military Operations) 49, 117
DI (discursive institutionalism) 7, 8, 21–29, 46, 136
DI-Gramscian 5, 17, 27–29, 74, 136
discursive spaces 12, 23, 138 *see also* DI (discursive institutionalism); think tanks; think tank interactive processes
discursive sphere 23, 85 *see also* DI (discursive institutionalism); think tanks; think tank interactive processes
divided families 53, 70, 103, 124 *see also* soft borders; CDR (Centre for Dialogue and Reconciliation)
DND (Draft Nuclear Doctrine) 47
Doval, Ajit 38, 47, 90–91, 142
DPG (Delhi Policy Group) 41, 52, 113–114, 117–119, 123–124, 126–127, 139

ECCP (Economic Cross-Cultural Programme) 120–124

FCRA (Foreign Contribution Regulation Act) 43, 87, 137, 145
Ford Foundation 87, 113, 115, 117, 145
four-point proposal 52, 94

Gateway House: Gateway of India dialogue 144; Indian Council on Global Relations 42, 142
Gayari avalanche 72, 103, 122; *see also* Pakistan, army
Gilgit and Baltistan 75, 125 *see also* PAK (Pakistan Administered Kashmir); PoK (Pakistan Occupied Kashmir)
Gopinath, Meenakshi 50, 116–117
Gramsci, Antonio 5, 27, 28, 54, 62–63, 77, 136–137
Gujral, Inder Kumar 4, 36, 42, 49–50
Gupta, Arvind 47, 65, 74, 90

Hasnain, Ata 90, 103
horizontal linkages 21, 48
human rights violations 70, 75, 95, 97, 124
human security 10, 44, 116
Hurriyat *see* APHC

ICRIER (Indian Council for Research on International Economic Relations) 41–42

ICWA (Indian Council of World Affairs) 39–40, 64, 136, 145
IDSA (Institute for Defence Studies and Analyses) 40–41, 43, 64–66, 69–75
IFS (Indian Foreign Service) 36–37
India Foundation 42, 87, 91, 93
Indus Waters Treaty 3, 71, 81, 99–100, 123, 126–127, 140; Indus II 100
institutional embeddedness 6, 21, 25, 27
interlocutors 114, 120
International Development Research Centre (IDRC) 87
interpretive communities 19, 47
IPCS (Institute of Peace and Conflict Studies) 42, 114–115, 118–119, 121–122, 125–127
Iyer, Ramaswamy 92, 99, 100

Jammu and Kashmir/Kashmir Article 370 69, 120, 143; cross LoC CBMs 69, 115, 119, 123, 127; Kashmiri pandits 96–97, 124–125; reconciliation 102, 114, 118, 124; Srinagar-Muzaffarabad bus service 119; *see also* AFSPA (Armed Forces Special Powers Act); ceasefire violations; LoC (Line of Control); soft borders
Jamaat-ud Dawa (JuD) 95
JATM (Joint Anti-Terror Mechanism) 100–101
JEM (Jaish-e-Mohammed) 122
Jinnah Institute 115, 124–125

Kanwal, Gurmeet 66, 72, 97, 103
Kargil-Skardu route 75, 119
Kargil War 49, 78, 88, 91, 106; KRC (Kargil Review Committee) 47, 78; *see also* back-channel
Kashmir roundtable 75, 103, 119; working groups 95
Khan, Sardar Abdul Qayyum 103
knowledge/power nexus 5, 17, 44, 137
Kumar, Radha 113–114, 118, 120

Ladi, Stella *see* critical juncture
Lahore Declaration 50
LeT (Lashkar-e-Taiba) 72, 95, 140
LoC (Line of Control) 52, 75, 94–95, 101–102, 115, 119, 124, 127

MEA (Ministry of External Affairs) 36, 40–41, 47, 64, 74, 77, 99
Medvetz, Thomas 24–25, 145

Mehta, Pratap Bhanu 47, 89, 90, 100
Menon, Shiv Shankar 90, 141
Mishra, Brajesh 88, 93, 102
Mishra, R. K 88, 93, 102, 136
MoD (Ministry of Defence) 40, 43, 47, 64, 66, 69
Modi, Narendra 38, 90–91, 105, 143; surgical strike 143; *see also* Jammu and Kashmir/Kashmir Article 370
multi-track diplomacy 3, 73, 116, 126; track II 129; *see also* back-channel
Mumbai attacks 76, 95, 140–141
Musharraf, Parvez 50, 52, 88, 94, 141; *see also* four-point proposal

NDA (National Democratic Alliance) 37, 50, 100
NMF (National Maritime Foundation) 42–43, 66, 68, 76
NSA (National Security Advisor) 36–38, 47, 65, 88, 90, 142
NSAB (National Security Advisory Board) 36–37, 57, 65, 89–90, 116
NSC (National Security Council) 36, 38, 89
Neemrana dialogue 92, 95, 116
Nehru, Jawaharlal 36, 39–40, 64, 94
non-traditional security 8, 26, 113, 123
NTI (Nuclear Threat Initiative) 115, 121
nuclear weapons 41, 68, 74, 101, 122; minimum credible deterrence 68; NRRM (Nuclear Risk Reduction Measures) 121; nuclear deterrence 99, 121

Official Secrets Act 37
Operation *Sadhbhavana* 70
ORF (Observer Research Foundation) 41–42, 45, 87–89, 92, 99, 103, 144

PAK (Pakistan Administered Kashmir) 95, 103, 120, 125
Pakistan: army 67, 94, 101; navy 68; *see also* deep state
Pakistan army chief Kayani 72, 98, 103, 122; *see also* Gayari avalanche; Siachen
Pakistan project (IDSA) 74
Parmar, Inderjeet 7, 17–19, 28–29, 54, 113
Parthasarathy, G. 89, 92, 100–101
peace education 116, 125
PoK (Pakistan Occupied Kashmir) 14, 71, 73–5; *see also* PAK (Pakistan Administered Kashmir)
proxy war 68, 71–72, 75, 94

Raisina Dialogue 89, 144
Raja Mohan, C. 28, 37, 41, 88
Rasgotra, M. 88, 95, 103
RAW (Research and Analysis Wing) 88, 90, 98, 101
research brokerage 27, 86, 127
RIS (Research and Information System for Developing Countries) 41, 47, 89
river water disputes *see* Indus Waters Treaty

Saltoro Ridge 71
Saran, Samir 88, 92
Saran, Shyam 47, 89, 90, 116
Schmidt, Vivien 22–23
Sharif, Nawaz. 4, 50
Siachen 3–4, 50, 103, 118; demilitarisation 71–72, 75, 97–98, 119, 122, 141; peace park 97–98; *see also* Actual Ground Position Line, Saltoro ridge; Gayari avalanche
Singh, Jasjit 65–66, 68
Singh, Manmohan 75, 93, 95–96, 99, 103, 120
Sir Creek 4, 49–50, 118, 139
soft borders 94, 102–103
Stone, Diane 17, 27, 29
Subrahmanyam, K. 40–41, 44–45, 47, 65, 68, 136

Terrorism - LeT (Lashkar-e-Taiba) 72, 95, 101; JeM (Jaish-e-Mohammed) 72, 122, 143; precision military strikes 75, 141; covert action 101, 140; surgical strike 143
think tank interactive processes *see* communicative discourse; coordinative discourse
Think tanks – definition 17, 38; ideational actors 5, 12, 19, 28, 34; bridging role 4, 5, 17, 54, 62; consultative role 85, 91, 138; policy relevance 5, 62–63, 86, 104, 137; *see also* knowledge/power nexus; think tank interactive processes; research brokerage
TNW (Tactical Nuclear Weapons) 99 *see also* nuclear weapons

UPA (United Progressive Alliance) UPA (United Progressive Alliance) 38, 70, 95–96, 100, 140–141, 144–145; inclusive growth 51; *see also* soft borders; Manmohan Singh; Kashmir roundtable

Vajpayee, Atal Bihari 37, 50, 70, 87–88, 93, 142; Lahore Bus 133; *see also* Lahore Declaration; Agra Summit
Verghese, B.G. 92, 95, 97–99, 102–103
VIF (Vivekananda International Foundation) 42, 58, 87, 90, 93, 95–97, 102

Winning Hearts and Minds 70, 80
WISCOMP (Women in Security, Conflict Management and Peace) 42, 116–117, 123, 126
World Bank 87
Wullar Barrage/Tulbul Navigation channel *see* Indus Waters Treaty

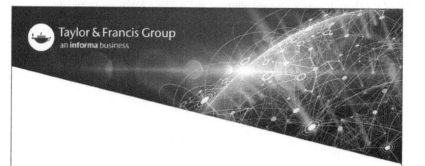